SOUL-CENTERED HEALING

A Psychologist's Extraordinary Journey into the Realms of Sub-Personalities, Spirits, and Past Lives

Thomas Zinser, Ed.D.

Paperback, ISBN 978-0-9834294-0-1

Published by
Union Street Press
2701 Union SE
Grand Rapids MI 49507

For Jane

Contents

Foreword

There are books that are a little ahead of their time and others that are far ahead of their time. The former are easier to assess because while they push the envelope of conventional wisdom, they usually leave enough of that wisdom intact to allow us to evaluate the success or failure of their innovations. Books that are far ahead of their time are considerably harder to assess because they often challenge the very foundations on which we stand. For that reason they tend to make us profoundly uncomfortable, even angry. They don't continue the conversation we were having but begin a new conversation in new territory, importing new assumptions that challenge conventional wisdom. *Soul-Centered Healing* by Thomas Zinser is such a book. It is an important book that is far ahead of its time.

Zinser is not interested in having the conversation that most psychologists are having today, enraptured as they are with mapping the various neurological correlates of human experience. Instead, in *Soul-Centered Healing* Zinser invites the reader into a dramatically expanded experiential landscape, a landscape so foreign to the modern mind that some readers will simply refuse to enter, regardless of the evidence, regardless of his positive clinical results. What a shame if this happens, because Zinser, in concert with other spiritually oriented therapists, is showing us a new continent.

The modern mind says that human beings live on Earth only once, but in *Soul-Centered Healing* Zinser's clients demonstrate that reincarnation is the rule. The modern mind says that unless psychopathology shatters it, the self speaks with one voice, but *Soul-Centered Healing* shows that the self is typically a chorus of many voices and integrated wholeness is one of life's great accomplishments. The modern mind says that the spiritual world is an illusion or compensation or a dubious hypothesis at best, while *Soul-Centered Healing* offers communion with luminous spiritual reality as the balm that heals the deeper wounds of life.

What is most jarring and innovative about *Soul-Centered Healing*, however, is the fundamental dialogue that set it in motion and that lies behind every page—a fifteen year dialogue between a university trained, secularly inclined therapist and a discarnate presence named Gerod, channeled by a co-worker. Out of this unusual dialogue emerged a clinical collaboration that shaped the contours of Zinser's entire professional life. In almost weekly sessions, Zinser brought his most difficult cases to Gerod, and Gerod advised him, acting as a kind of spiritual supervisor. In the interest of healing, Gerod shared what he was seeing from his non-physical perspective and offered Zinser suggestions and strategies he could use to circumvent the various blocks he was encountering with specific clients. Along the way, Gerod initiated Zinser into a vastly different psychological and spiritual landscape than he had absorbed in graduate school. Piece by piece, Gerod gave him a detailed map of the workings of the unconscious and invited him to test this map in his clinical practice, which is exactly what Zinser did.

Week after week, year after year, Zinser shuttled back and forth between his patients and his conversations with Gerod, systematically extending his knowledge of the deep psyche. Under Gerod's tutelage he learned to navigate its shoreline, identify its citizens, negotiate with its gatekeepers, and finesse its troublemakers. He tested Gerod's suggestions for bringing forward living memories of past trauma, for releasing soul-fragments, and for returning that which had been lost, or in some cases stolen. For years he battled with the forces that keep human experience fragmented, locked away in pockets of hidden pain and frozen time, living in shadows far removed from the Light. Make no mistake about it, Zinser was doing battle, for darkness does not give up its ground without a fight. This is not a book for the faint of heart or for those with a rose-tinted view of how one achieves spiritual wholeness. This is a book that follows human suffering to its source and asks deep questions about why life is the way it is. Its answers are profound, coherent, and deeply moving.

Those familiar with hypnosis will recognize Zinser's considerable clinical skill as a hypnotherapist, and those familiar with the literature on past-life therapy will recognize the courage of a clinician willing to follow his patients into territory he might not otherwise have explored. What sets Zinser's study apart, however, is the depth of the spiritual perspective that emerges in his work and the subtlety of his cartography of the soul. In order to heal his clients, Zinser had to understand the roots of the disorder that had overtaken their lives and the push-pull of forces that forge the human will. At this deep level, the line between physician and metaphysician becomes transparent. One cannot heal without crossing into spiritual reality and personally engaging the powerful forces of both Darkness and Light.

In *Soul-Centered Healing* Zinser takes his readers on a spiritual journey that stretched over many years as he peeled back layer after layer of the soul. In pithy chapters punctuated with rich case histories drawn from his client notes and transcripts of his conversations with Gerod, Zinser initiates the reader into the same mysteries he was initiated into. He lets us feel his confusion and uncertainty, honoring the resistance that accompanies major paradigm breakthroughs. Ultimately the validation of his methods, and Gerod's insights, lies in his clients' emerging health and wellbeing—*soul-centered healing*.

Those already initiated into spiritual psychology will likely find the early chapters familiar territory but will be richly rewarded, and I suspect surprised, as the plot thickens in later chapters. Much more than a book on past-life therapy, *Soul-Centered Healing* is a work that explores the fundamental spiritual agreements that frame the entire human experience. It is a rich and rewarding journey, a book far ahead of its time, but hopefully a book whose time has come.

—Christopher M. Bache, Ph.D.
author of *Dark Night, Early Dawn*

Acknowledgements

I cannot name all the people from clients, to friends, to family who have played a part in the development of Soul-Centered Healing and the writing of this book. They number in the hundreds, and I am grateful to you all. I want to give special thanks to the early supporters of Soul-Centered Healing. They include: Grace, Beth, Laurel, Bob, Michele, Charlie, Kathy, Rilma, Monica, Ed, Judy, two Linda K.'s, Don, Jodie, Jackie, Tricia, Lee, Mary Kay, Carol, Cathy, Andy, Jeff, Pat, and Bree.

I am also grateful to friends who read, edited, and made suggestions throughout the writing of this manuscript. I especially want to thank Christopher Bache, Michael Jamail, Michael Kivinen, David Fedeler, Gary Breen, Chandra Allard, Alex Rachel, and Ralph Allison. Each helped make this a better book.

A special thanks to Katharine who for so long held open the door through which Gerod and I could communicate. Her dedication to this very long exploration was rooted in her desire to help those in pain.

I am grateful to Gerod and the many other beings of Light who have helped in so many ways. A special thanks to Tinnabulation, Byron, and Nattaranda.

Finally, I am grateful to Jane, Aaron, and Rachel, for their sacrifice and support over so many years. Each helped in different ways, and it's their love that so often helped sustain me. Words are not enough.

Introduction

The labyrinth is a powerful venue for healing from any illness or pain, whether the disease itself is cured or not. Walking with illness and pain can invite healing at the deepest levels possible, restoring right relationship with one's life, with God, with the past, with one's body, with relationships.—Melissa Gayle West, from *Exploring the Labyrinth*

New Territory

This book is an odyssey into the psychic and spiritual dimensions of the self and reality. It takes the reader on a journey across the boundaries of ordinary consciousness and into realms that are at once both strange and familiar. Through the minds of others, it is a journey into our own mind and soul to an understanding that we are not only physical and psychological beings, but psychic and spiritual beings as well.

Soul-Centered Healing tells the story of my work as a clinical psychologist and a series of extraordinary events that took my clients and me across the boundaries of ordinary consciousness and enabled us to work at unusually deep levels of the mind and soul. This work led to an unprecedented mapping of these inner dimensions and a method of healing that can benefit others. The purpose of this book is to share this body of knowledge and the model of healing that emerged from it.

The extraordinary element in this story involves the information I received from a spirit entity named Gerod. This included information both about individual clients with whom I was working, and about the psychic and spiritual dimensions of reality in general. I was given this information and guidance through a form of spirit communication called *channeling*. Channeling is a phenomenon in which a person temporarily allows a spirit entity to communicate through him or her, either verbally or in writing. It's as though the person is able to "step aside" and allow another conscious entity to control certain functions of the body in order to communicate.

Channeling is a controversial phenomenon in our Western culture, dominated as it is by empirical science. The controversy is the same one surrounding the many other psychic and spirit phenomena that we hear and read about—*esp, remote viewing, out-of-body travel, precognition,* and *communication with the dead,* to name a few. At its root, the controversy is about whether the psychic and spirit dimensions are real. Channeling, by definition, claims that they are real.

Numerous books, ancient and modern, claim to be channeled information. The *Seth Speaks* series by Jane Roberts, *The Course in Miracles* by Helen Schucman and William Thetford, and the *Conversations with God* series by Neil Donald Walsh are more recent and well-known examples of channeled material. Many people in our culture accept channeling and these kinds of works, including the Bible, as a valid phenomenon and a source of spiritual knowledge. There are also many people in our Western culture, however, who view the content of these books as fiction, products of the human imagination, or worse, as delusions or outright frauds.

What was unique and critical in my collaboration with Gerod was that his information could be tested. Gerod gave me information about specific clients and about particular psychic and spiritual phenomena that could be explored in therapy sessions over time, and independently tested with each client. This possibility of verification led me to include Gerod as a source of information and guidance in my approach to treatment. After I discovered the kinds of information Gerod could offer, and the possibility of clinical verification, I began an active collaboration with Gerod and my clients.

The beneficiaries of Gerod's information were those individuals with whom I was working. His information consistently led to the resolution of blocks, impasses, and interferences that I encountered with so many clients when working at the unconscious levels. Besides the immediate benefit to several hundred clients, this fourteen-year collaboration also led to a systematic and scientific exploration of these psychic and spiritual realms. It was an exploration into inner worlds much more complex, alive, and layered than I ever could have imagined.

While Gerod is an extraordinary element in this story, he is not its central focus. The point of the story is that the psychic and spirit dimensions are real and that we exist in these dimensions as really as we do in the physical world. The central focus of the book is on healing. There are phenomena, conditions, entities, and forces that exist at these unconscious levels that cause pain, conflict and fear. Soul-Centered Healing is a method for helping a person access and work at these levels of the mind and soul to resolve fears, misperceptions, and blocks that keep a person in distress.

I will introduce other aspects of the mind that are both conscious and perceiving, but which are separate from the conscious self, and which function, for good and ill, at unconscious levels. I will write about psychic and spiritual forces operating at these levels, forces that can and do affect us mentally, emotionally, and even physically. I will also write about the phenomenon of spirits—whether they exist, and whether there is an interface whereby discarnate souls can interact with a person. These are the kinds of issues and phenomena at the center of this story. This journey of discovery could not have been made without Gerod's involvement, but the findings about these psychic and spiritual dimensions are the point of the story and stand on their own. These findings also are what will be verified or not by other healers and practitioners.

Two Points of View

Before beginning the story, two issues need to be addressed. Both have to do with the limitations of perception and language that we confront whenever we attempt to address the psychic and spirit realities. This book is no exception. One is a cultural issue, the other personal. The first has to do with the limitations of our Western culture in dealing with nonphysical—or metaphysical—realities. We live in a culture dominated by empirical science as the arbiter of what is real. If something cannot be reduced to its physical components, tested and measured, then it isn't real. The result is that we do not officially recognize the psychic and spirit realities, nor do we have a common language by which to talk about them.

Empirical science has gained its authority and control in our culture based upon the extraordinary success of the natural and physical sciences to explain our physical reality. These explanations have been and continue to be validated by the highly advanced technologies we have created based on those explanations. They work. Consider the fact that we are living in a culture that is on the verge of full-scale nano-technology, stem-cell medicine, and genetic engineering. Somewhere along the line, and largely because of this success, empirical science and its methods have become the standard in our culture by which we judge whether or not something is real.

The problem is that psychic and spirit phenomena—channeling included—challenge and contradict what empirical science says is true. Empiricism rests on the fundamental assumption that matter is the ground of reality. If psychic and spirit dimensions are real, then empiricism will be forced to abandon its most basic assumption. It would call everything into question. It would be a whole new ballgame. Science would have to find a new ground, and develop new methods by which to learn about these nonphysical realms and how they inter-connect with the physical.

I want to acknowledge this problem of paradigms ahead of time so that it does not become a distraction or impediment to the reader. Coming from an empirical point of view, one might feel he or she is constantly trying to put square pegs in round holes. I do not claim that the phenomena you will read about in this book will ultimately be proven empirically. I don't know that they will, or even can be. (It's more likely that our idea of *empirical* will change.) I am claiming, though, that psychic and spirit phenomena themselves are real and they can and do affect us in significant ways. From my point of view, the problem is not whether they can be proven empirically, but rather, if they are real, how do we understand and talk about them?

This book asks the reader to temporarily step outside the paradigm of empirical science, and set aside its demands for physical demonstra-tion and proof. Instead, the focus will be on psychological, psychic, and spiritual phenomena that are part of the human experience and which, when studied on their own terms, reveal dimensions of con-sciousness and reality beyond the physical. We have to apply a different measure. They are dimensions governed not by the laws of matter, but of consciousness.

For the empiricist, the underlying question in this book is whether these phenomena, and what they imply, are real and true. Once the story is told, the reader can bring the empirical paradigm back into play and reach his or her own conclusions about these phenomena and the larger reality they imply.

The Ground of Experience

Besides the limitations of our Western paradigm, there is a second and even more problematic issue in dealing with psychic and spiritual realities. It has to do with the shift in perception that is required of a person to know and experience these realities. We can believe these realms exist, or think and talk about them intellectually, but to know them through experience involves a shift in perception and awareness.

The situation is analogous to those *Magic Eye 3D* pictures that are sold in all the malls. The picture looks like a crazy quilt of colors and designs. If you focus in just the right way, though, your perception suddenly shifts and you are seeing three-dimensional objects and figures. You have to shift your focus, though, or you will not see this other dimension. Once you experience the perceptual shift, it becomes easy to shift your vision back and forth between the two perspectives. Perceiving psychic and spiritual realities is like the *Magic Eye* picture. It involves a perceptual shift. Unlike with the *Magic Eye* picture, though, it would be a shift from a three-dimensional to a multi-dimensional reality.

We know this kind of shift by the term "conversion." Usually, we hear the term used in the context of a religious conversion, a born-again experience. This kind of conversion often emphasizes the convert embracing a particular religion's tenets and beliefs. *Conversion,* however, needs to be understood much more broadly as a human phenomenon, experienced by individuals across cultures and throughout time. The emphasis here is on the experience itself and the alteration in a person's perception and consciousness. The consistent element in these reports is the person's stated or implied knowledge of a higher or greater order of reality.

The problem is that those who have not experienced this perceptual shift have no experiential basis on which to judge the statements of those who have. Carl Jung, the Swiss psychiatrist, said that this dichotomy is where people part ways. "One says they have had a religious experience, the other says they have not, and that is the end of the conversation." I'm sure there are many reasons why someone makes this shift and someone else does not. My guess is, it involves some blend of the usual subjects: nature, nurture, and providence.

The challenge in writing this book about psychic and spirit realities involved finding a common ground and language by which to speak to both points of view. Originally, I tried to write this book as the objective scientist. It was to be an intellectual presentation of my findings. I was trying to tell the story from the outside looking in. What complicated the challenge even more was in knowing that even among those who already knew or believed that these realms exist, there still was no common language and framework by which to talk about them. I couldn't assume that my language and terms would be the same as the reader's.

In the end, I finally realized that I had to tell the story from the inside out. Only by bringing the reader into the clinical story, where these phenomena were discovered and dealt with, could I offer a common ground for both points of view. This includes the experiential basis for those still unsure of these unseen realities, and a context for communicating clearly the meaning of terms for those who have their own language and concepts.

This book asks the reader to temporarily step inside the shoes of a clinician and follow the course of the investigation as it moves from one clinical problem or phenomenon to the next, and expands from one level of understanding to ever-deeper levels. Everyone has been a clinician at one time or another in his or her life. Who hasn't run into problems, had to step back, and try to determine the causes and look for possible solutions? There is a logic to any clinical investigation, and there was a logic to this one too. I hope that by giving the reader this clinical context, I can show where the knowledge of these realms is anchored in experience. Also, by defining different terms within the context of human experience, I hope my language about these realities is clear and understandable to the reader.

This book chronicles my investigation of the psychic and spirit realities by focusing on specific clinical phenomena, events, and insights that represented a significant advance in the investigation. Each chapter can be viewed as a separate vignette with its own theme or focus. Each vignette, though, builds on the chapters that come before as the story moves from and ego-centered to a soul-centered perspective.

There is a glossary at the end of the book that the reader can refer to as a quick reference for the meaning of some of the central terms. Also, the illustration on the next page is a visual model of the inner world presented in this book. I think it may be helpful that you see it in the beginning, though its meaning will only become clear later on.

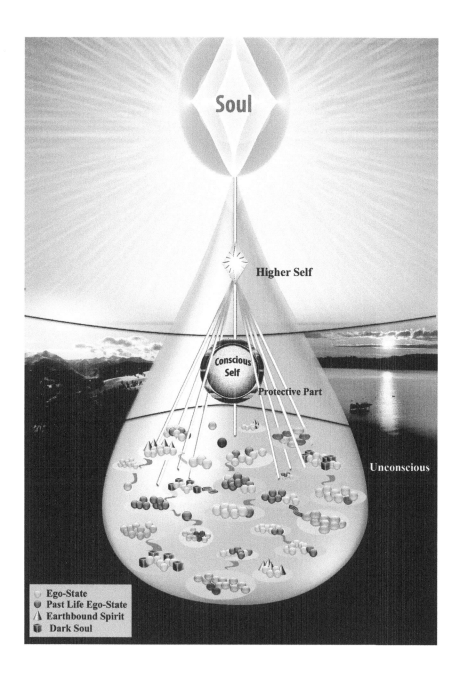

Soul

Higher Self

Conscious Self

Protective Part

Unconscious

○ Ego-State
● Past Life Ego-State
△ Earthbound Spirit
▥ Dark Soul

Part 1

To the Boundary of Spirit

1

Worlds Within Worlds

Scientific materialism has no right to claim for itself absolute truth, for as it examines the world in its supposedly objective manner it overlooks the fact that the examination is being performed by a decidedly nonobjective entity—an individual human being. The subjective is an utterly inseparable part of experience. However convenient it may be to do so, science cannot separate the "I" from the "it."—William James

Paula Two

When I accepted Paula as a client, I didn't know she had multiple personalities. Paula didn't know it either. It was 1982, and I had recently resigned my position as staff psychologist at a local psychiatric hospital. I had been in private practice for about six months when a woman from Paula's church referred her to me. Paula was in her early thirties and was seeking treatment because of her increasing anxiety and depression in the months following her father's death. She had left what appeared to be a successful position with a national corporation to move back home with her mother. By the time I saw her, Paula was very depressed and seemed to have lost any desire to re-establish her independent lifestyle. Instead, her depression and anxiety were threatening to overtake her completely.

The first several weeks that I spent assessing Paula's situation quickly turned into six months. Paula had so many emotional crises, medical complaints, and general obstacles, that we never could get to the heart of things. We were always fighting fires on different fronts.

As Paula's therapy continued, I began to encounter strong resistance because of her fears and defenses. She had very few memories of her life before the age of thirteen, and the more we attempted to explore this period, the more anxious Paula became. She had vehemently refused hypnosis as a tool for accessing memories. She seemed afraid of remembering, and this in itself was a tip-off that there was something for her to fear.

I recommended to Paula that we try an intermediate step. I suggested that we use *Guided Affective Imagery (GAI)* as a safe way of exploring the inner terrain of her memories and feelings. GAI is a technique in which a client, while in a relaxed state, is given a series of words, one at a time, and asked to create an image for each one. The first image, for example, is *The Meadow*. Once a client has entered some level of relaxation, the therapist suggests that the client imagine himself or herself in a meadow. Besides the word "meadow," the therapist makes no other stipulations or suggestions. The particular meadow, in all its specifics, is the client's own creation, and it's through that creation that the client's personal material begins presenting immediately. Once the person has been able to develop a sense of "being there," the therapist ask him or her to look around and tell what they see. From that point on, the fantasy develops. The person might see a building in the distance, or a group of men on horseback coming right at them, or they might see a dark blotch of land where everything has died. In his essay on Guided Affective Imagery, Hanscarl Leurner describes the therapeutic use of imagery and fantasy once the client has been able to enter a relaxed state.

> The object of fantasy becomes considerably more vivid; it increases in color and plasticity, develops into a three-dimensional object, and is located in surroundings through which the subject can walk around the imaginary house and observe the rear of it. In other words, . . . a quasi-realistic and perceivable world develops in the consciousness of the subject or patient. He is able to move freely in this world of optical fantasy, although he is always aware that he is in a state artificially fostered by the therapist and that the things he perceives in his daydream therefore do not represent reality.[1]

The person fantasizes his own world based on these images and then is free to interact in, re-create, or transform what is occurring.

It's like virtual reality—not quite the real thing, but in some ways it is very close.

After Paula and I discussed this technique at length, she finally agreed to try it in our next session. That session, however, came and went. The next time we met, Paula's anxiety was so intense that I suggested she simply try a brief period of relaxation with her eyes closed. I told her this would be a good first step to prepare the way for the guided imagery.

It took several sessions, but Paula was finally able to imagine the meadow and then, in her imagination, she was able to mentally enter into the meadow and describe it for me. This was slow going. She was so afraid about losing control that I forced myself to go even slower than I thought was necessary. In the next few sessions, Paula became more comfortable with the imagery procedure, and we worked with two more of the images. Everything seemed to be going well until we came to the image of *The House*. Paula was walking through her imaginary house from room to room when suddenly she screamed and started to panic. She gripped the arms of the chair and was fighting to breathe. Immediately, I told her to focus on my voice. I reassured her, helped her to calm her breathing, and slowly helped her to withdraw from the imagination and return to everyday awareness. When she did, Paula told me she had come face to face with someone who looked like her, only younger, maybe in her early twenties. Then she told me the young woman's name was also Paula.

This encounter changed the course of the therapy. An immediate issue was whether Paula would allow this other one to talk. The prospect was frightening for Paula. She said it was as though she had always known it—that there was someone else—but had never acknowledged it, not even to her self. Now, she had come face to face with her.

Paula eventually agreed to enter the relaxation again (as long as we didn't call it hypnosis), and allow this other Paula to come forward if she wished. In the first session where we tried this, Paula Two did come forward. There was obviously some readiness on someone's part to open this door, and when Paula Two presented directly, it was clear that she was in charge.

The transformation caught me by surprise. I was suddenly confronted with a confident, sharp, and energetic version of Paula. She said her name was Paula, and we agreed that we would call her Paula Two. In the next half hour, she told me things about Paula's past of which Paula had no memory. She also said that she was the tip of the iceberg, and that there were many others inside besides her. She seemed to have a great deal of insight about Paula's present life as well. She was somewhat condescending toward Paula, but seemed accepting of her at the same time. She also told me she was blocking Paula from listening to our conversation.

This was my first experience with an alter-personality. I had been working with Paula for two years by that time, and I knew her well. I knew her speech patterns, her mannerisms, and her emotional patterns. I also knew a great deal about how she thought. As I listened to Paula Two, I realized she had her own identity and center of consciousness distinct from Paula's. Based on Paula Two's accounts, there really did appear to be some kind of inner world present here operating behind the scenes. How wide the separation was between Paula and Paula Two, I couldn't say, but from where I stood, it appeared significant. Judging also by Paula Two's ability to assume consciousness and control the body, this inner world likely played a very important part in Paula's life.

I viewed the discovery of Paula Two, and the other alter-personalities she referred to, as a breakthrough in Paula's treatment. It was as if we had found the missing pieces. These personalities apparently knew what had happened in her past, and talking to them held out the promise that Paula could finally know the truth about herself. By bringing them forward to share their stories, I hoped that Paula could now bring together the missing pieces of her life. I believed that if this happened, Paula could finally begin to let go of so much past hurt and trauma and start genuine healing. From a therapeutic standpoint, there seemed only one way to proceed. Paula and I agreed that these parts of her needed to tell their stories.

Multiple Personalities

Meeting Paula Two brought me into contact with a world I knew little about in 1983. Nothing I had read or heard about alter-personalities prepared me for the experience itself. Paula Two was not some one-dimensional cutout that stepped in for Paula at times to take care of a problem and then take off again. On the contrary, she behaved as a complex person in her own right. She insisted that she be treated with the same respect and consideration as Paula. Taken at face value, she was obviously a significant factor in Paula's life. She was conscious of her own identity. She had memories, and talked about herself and her past, including events and experiences of which Paula had no awareness. She told me things about Paula's unconscious functioning that made a great deal of sense. Finally, as she demonstrated in our sessions, Paula Two was able to take over the body and be fully present in the conscious reality. She had, it seemed, a mind of her own. Hearing her describe her life, one might concede that she had more of a history and life than Paula did. And until recently, Paula Two had lived completely outside Paula's awareness.

From the time we met, I believed that Paula Two was a key to Paula's therapy. I also assumed that by understanding how Paula Two came to exist, and how she functioned, I would gain new understandings about the mind. What exactly was it about Paula Two, for example, that enabled her to be conscious at the same time as Paula? How could she instantly, seemingly at the speed of thought, block off emotions or awareness from Paula? What determined when one or the other was "out"?

I also assumed that some kind of integration of the two would be best for Paula. I did not know, however, exactly what the result of such an integration would mean, nor did I even think about it in a highly detailed way. From my point of view, it was just the way we were supposed to be, a single identity, one mind, one body. Paula's life, I assumed, would be better ultimately if she incorporated Paula Two.

Once the alter-personalities began to come forward, I had to depend on Paula Two and the others to tell me their stories and what they knew about Paula's past, about the inner world, and how it functioned. They acted like people and I talked to them like people. They were self-aware; each had his or her own identity; and they were able to act independently of Paula, the conscious self. Also, many of the alter-personalities, though not all, were aware of Paula and her conscious reality.

These alter-personalities were able to intervene in Paula's conscious world in various ways. An alter-personality, for example, could deliberately divert a line of thought before Paula could give it too much attention and possibly begin to remember a traumatic experience. An alter-personality could even take over Paula's place in the conscious reality if she became too frightened, or others inside decided that she couldn't handle a situation. Paula Two claimed to do this often. At the grocery store, for example, when Paula was hurt by a cashier's insensitive comment, Paula Two came out front and center. She managed the situation instantly before Paula's hurt feelings could trigger other memories or feelings that might send her into a full-blown panic. Paula Two stopped the emotions, acted as if nothing happened, and became very businesslike and brief with the clerk. Paula, meantime, did not become conscious again until she was standing at the car door with her keys in her hand.

My immediate problem after meeting Paula Two and becoming aware of the multiple personalities was the torrent of information that flooded me. Many of the alter-personalities were willing to talk to me once they knew it was safe. Each one, though, had their own individual experiences, feelings, and memories and often their own agendas. One personality could require the entire hour of therapy and maybe more to work through his or her experience and emotions.

I began to meet many alter-personalities, and talked with each of them, at least briefly, in order to get a preliminary idea of who they were and where they might fit in Paula's inner world. It was like having twenty new clients within several months time. That's twenty new relationships to begin and twenty new stories to learn. And all in one hour a week! It was very slow going. The positive side, though, was that it gave me time to study what this phenomenon was all about.

Dissociation

My own reading and consultation with several colleagues helped me to reach certain basic understandings about multiple personality disorder and what treatment approaches appeared most effective. Alter-personalities were viewed as psychological states created by the mind as a defense against intolerable pain, shock, or trauma. The psychological term for this defense is *dissociation*. Through this process of dissociation, the conscious self's awareness is split-off, or separated, from immediate experience. Instead, an alter-personality is created to take over consciousness and the responsibility for survival in the moment. The purpose of the alter-personality is to be, and do, whatever a situation calls for in order to survive.

The problem is that alter-personalities continue to exist after the trauma has passed. In effect, they continue the defense by *containing* the trauma and keeping it separate from the conscious personality. Ignorance, however, is not bliss. The person pays a two-fold price for this ongoing protection. First, the person lives in a fragmented reality that leaves them feeling vulnerable, anxious, and confused much of the time. Second, the alter-personalities take on a life of their own. They create a shadow world, so to speak, in which they continue to affect, and at times take control from, the conscious personality.

In treating multiple personality disorder, there are two basic goals. The first, and usually more immediate, is to help the client establish greater stability in their day-to-day world. The inner fragmentation of *MPD* often leads to crises and conflicts in the outer world of relationships, work, and meeting daily needs. In the therapy, this means finding out about the inner system of alter-personalities. Who is in charge of what, and who can override whom? The idea is to make the treatment a team effort and secure agreements from the different personalities about such concerns as not hurting the body, letting others be "out" at certain times, and not interfering with the person's work schedule.

This first goal is more practical. It's concerned with the internal power structure and helping the client to become aware of it and able to work with it. Knowing the internal power structure, for example, is important in order to know which alter-personalities can take over in an emergency, or which ones are most likely causing conflict, or who could do the troubleshooting when things go awry.

The second, and central goal, in treating multiple personality disorder is healing the fragmentation. This requires a deeper understanding of the inner system, however, and takes far longer. It involves working with each of the alter-personalities to share its experience with the conscious self, and then be able to release its pain and distress. In the process, the conscious self reclaims and begins to integrate the missing pieces of his or her life.

By making the memories conscious, there is no longer a need for the alter-personality to keep its experience separate from the conscious self. The dissociation, then, can begin to resolve and, theoretically, the alter-personality can integrate. This is pictured as a kind of melding process where the alter-personality blends with the conscious self. It is also thought that whatever areas of functioning the alter-personality performs can then be incorporated and taken over by the self.

This was familiar territory to me. A large part of psychotherapy is helping a client do this kind of *working through*. It is basic Freud. His seminal insight was that traumatic experience, usually in childhood, could be repressed and become an unconscious source of pain, conflict, or disease. Freud discovered that by bringing these experiences to consciousness, a person could experience relief and a resolution of their symptoms and distress. The process is called *abreaction*. The theory is that healing results when a person experiences emotional release and integrates the experience through the remembering, abreaction, and telling of it.

I subscribed to this principle and it was a basic guide in my practice of psychotherapy. The difference, though, concerning MPD was the dissociation, rather than repression, of experience, and the extreme autonomy and ability the alter-personalities exercised in controlling the self.

The Depths of Fragmentation

The major problem in treating Paula was that her inner world was much more complex and extensive than any of us knew. It became clear over the months that there were many more alter-personalities of which even Paula Two and the others had not been aware. The same questions had to be asked of each. What role did they play for the self? What memories did they carry? How often were they out? What triggered them to come forward or take over? How much power or influence did they wield over the self? I was always in a position of not knowing what to expect, or whom I might encounter from one session to the next.

As I learned about the different alter-personalities, it also became clear that they formed different systems and subgroups within Paula's inner world. Some of them knew about each other and some didn't. Trying to understand how these subgroups interacted—not only with Paula, but also with each other—added a whole new level of complexity both clinically and theoretically. Paula and I both tried to maintain a map of her inner world as the different alter-personalities and groups emerged, but it was always a work in progress, having to be revised and redrawn as we proceeded.

In terms of a modern day analogy, working with Paula was like being in an "Internet chat room." The term refers to an Internet site where many people, each using a computer, is present in real time and communicate with each other directly. In a chat room, while you cannot see who is there, you have a list of names in the corner of your computer screen to tell you who is present. Over time, you get to know who is behind the names as you communicate with each person directly or read what they communicate to each other. You also become aware of the different subgroups operating within the chat room, and you learn the rules. You get to know, for example, who will rush to whose defense or who will side with each other on particular issues.

The difference with Paula was that there was no screen. There was no list of names in the corner to tell me who was there, and I could not observe or hear how the alter-personalities were relating to each other. I only learned who was present as they announced themselves or were triggered to come forward. It took time to identify the alter-personalities and gain some understanding of how each related to Paula and to the others. The therapy process itself seemed in a constant state of search and discovery.

One time, for example, Paula reported an episode of overwhelming terror that had been triggered while she was driving. She felt such terror, she said, that she was afraid she would lose control of the car. That was the last thing she remembered before finding herself on the couch at home staring at the television.

As I helped her review step by step what had happened immediately before the terror began, she recalled seeing a young girl running down the street. Paula had no idea why the sight of the running girl triggered such terror but she said she was starting to feel it again even as she talked to me about it. When I checked with the alter-personalities, none of them claimed responsibility or admitted knowing anything about it. This kind of situation happened often and it would send us looking—either in the present session or a subsequent one—for whomever had been triggered.

There were very few answers, of course. Working with Paula only two times a week for an hour was not nearly enough time to unravel all the workings of her inner world. In the therapy, I still had to put out brushfires, help her tend to business, and listen to complaints, before she was ready to deal with the areas of pain in which the therapy was focused. The time went much too quickly to pursue all the questions in detail. You deal with as much as you can. The guiding belief, though, was that each personality was created to deal with pain; that the pain could be released and healed; and that once it was released, then the alter-personality and its experience would integrate with the self.

Over the course of the next year, I became immersed in the study of dissociation and multiple personality disorder. Three more clients also were referred to me who had been diagnosed with multiple personality disorder. My experience with Paula was repeated as I worked with these new clients. My immersion into the phenomenon of multiplicity began to deepen very quickly. Each revealed a complex and unique inner world that was very much alive and active at internal levels. Unlike Paula, though, my new clients already had some awareness of their multiplicity, and all three knew at least some of their alter-personalities. In terms of their treatment, I was playing catch-up from the start. There was a flood of information coming from each of these four clients. The goals, though, remained the same for each: 1) maintain stability for all of the personalities in their inner and outer world; and 2) facilitate the process of integrating each fragment through the remembering, sharing, and release.

It was the caseworker for one of these new clients who first told me about the International Society for the Study of Multiple Personality and Dissociation (ISSMP&D).[2] She gave me a brochure announcing the Second Annual Conference being held in October 1985 in Chicago. I joined this organization within a week after reading the brochure, and I made plans to attend the conference just a couple months away.

2

Ego-State Therapy

The organization of the sub-personalities is very revealing and some-times surprising, baffling or even frightening. One discovers how very different and often quite antagonistic traits are displayed in different roles. These differences of traits which are organized around a role justify, in our opinion, the use of the word "sub-personality." Ordinary people shift from one to the other without clear awareness, and only a thin thread of memory connects them; but for all practical purposes they are different beings—they act differently, they show very different traits.—Robert Assagioli, from *Psychosynthesis*

Ego-States and Alter-Personalities

What I learned in Chicago about MPD and dissociation was invaluable. It provided a wealth of information. It gave me focus and direction in learning more about MPD and how to help my clients. It taught me what resources were available and who to look to as leaders in the field.

My impression from the conference was that a massive amount of information was being shared in the field, but no one here needed to rush into making big claims and pronouncements. Most participants were clinicians and, like myself, were looking for practical help with the thousand and one questions that came up in treating this disorder. They were talking about the same kinds of issues and questions I originally faced with Paula and began to encounter with my new MPD clients. By listening to the experiences of others, I was forewarned about situations I likely would encounter in the future, such as dealing with emergency hospitalization or an angry alter-personality. Participants shared techniques and clinical experiences about the varied facets of diagnosis and treatment. It was all shoptalk, and I took in all I could.

Of everything I learned, though, the two most significant were about *ego-states* and *ideomotor signaling.* The first is a psychological phenomenon, and the second, a powerful hypnotic technique for communicating with the unconscious.

I attended a pre-conference workshop entitled *Ego-State Therapy of Multiple Personality Disorder* given by John Watkins, Ph.D., and his wife, Helen Watkins, M.A. They talked about their approach to therapy that recognizes, as with MPD, that everyone possesses unconscious personalities. They called them *ego-states** and viewed alter-personalities as an extreme form of the same phenomena. They said that for most people, ego-states are not as distinct and autonomous as alter-personalities but they are on the same continuum.

According to this model, we all have ego-states operating at an unconscious level. In John and Helen Watkins view, the mind normally creates these separate states as an adaptive function making it possible for the self to live in a complex world, a kind of division of labor and specialization. The ego-states are like subsets of the self that perform certain functions and play different roles for a person. Some ego-states are created to help deal with the normal demands and crises of growing up. Other ego-states, as with so many alter-personalities, are created as a response to trauma or abuse. Once created, then, these ego-states, each with its own adaptive response, can be activated at a later time when a similar situation or threat occurs.

In his book, *Hypnotherapeutic Techniques,* John Watkins described the dynamics of these ego-states.

> Within the personality at any given time, one state is usually "executive." It constitutes "the self" in "the now." It includes those behaviors and experiences currently being activated and which are being felt and acted upon. At the time, the executive state is the one most highly energized with ego cathexis. Other states, separated by a boundary from the executive state, are for the moment relatively immobilized. Their impact upon the individual is "unconscious." For example, when the individual is at a party one state is "executive" and one set

* A term first used by Paul Federn, an early follower of Freud's.

of behaviors and experiences are operative. When he is at work the next day the "party state" has ceased to be executive and is replaced by another. He behaves and experiences differently.[1]

Normally, according to Watkins, these ego-states are fairly well integrated. One ego-state at a time is "executive," while the others remain at an unconscious level and to some extent, dormant. Most of us navigate our way through these different states so smoothly that we are usually not even aware of the transition from one state to the next. Problems arise, though, Watkins says, when an ego-state is too differentiated or dissociated from the ego-self and acts in a way that creates conflict or distress for the conscious person. For example, an ego-state based on a fear of authority could come into conflict with the conscious person's need to make an important decision in the face of possible harsh criticism. An ego-state like this could react with such intense anxiety to this threat that the conscious self feels paralyzed and unable to decide.

Ego-states, according to Watkins, can also trigger and activate each other as they vie for executive control, and the conscious self may wind up feeling as if he or she is on a roller coaster. While the ego-states involved in these conflicts remain hidden from sight, the effects of their conflicts can begin to show up in any number of symptoms: anxiety, emotional outbursts, psychosomatic illness, and depression are the kinds of conditions that can commonly result.

John Watkins described these overly differentiated ego-states as maladaptive. He said that the process of creating ego-states can go awry. In the face of extreme conditions, such as physical trauma, abuse, or shock, ego-states can be created that are very differentiated from the ego-self, and the greater the differentiation, the greater their potential to create conflict and distress. According to Watkins, at its extreme, the differentiation results in dissociation and the creation of alter-personalities. He argues that somewhere along the line the process changes from differentiation into dissociation.

The boundaries between ego-states vary in permeability from person to person and probably within a single individual from time to time. At one end of the continuum, there is almost complete communication between elements in different states. The boundaries are token, and the "federal" jurisdiction over all the person makes him highly integrated. At the other end are the true multiple personalities, wherein the boundaries between the respective states are so rigid and impermeable that "Mary" is completely unaware of the existence of "Joan," and when one is executive it is amnesic to the period during which the other was activated. Most people lie somewhere in between.[2]

John and Helen Watkins emphasize that we are all on this same continuum. Each person has ego-states and the same principles and dynamics governing alter-personalities also governs ego-states, though to lesser and varying degrees.

We (Watkins & Watkins, 1979, 1981, 1982; Watkins & Johnson, 1982) have gathered increasing evidence that the dividing of the personality lies on a continuum ranging from normal adaptive differentiation at one end to pathological maladaptive dissociation at the other, where the true multiple personality disorder occurs. The in-between regions on the continuum consist of "ego-states," covert patterns of behavior and experience, usually accessible only under hypnosis.[3]

By placing all of us on the same continuum, John and Helen Watkins' model clearly implied that my own clients might benefit using this same method. In effect, they were saying that we all have these many personalities at an unconscious level, and they can cause the same kinds of pain and conflict that I saw with alter-personalities.

They supported these claims with numerous clinical examples and a number of videotaped segments from some of their own sessions with clients. They also demonstrated how to identify an ego-state and the kinds of questions to ask. In his book, published around the same time, John Watkins said that these ego-states respond to such questions as:

"What is your name?" "Where do you come from?" "How long have you been in the person?" "Under what circumstances were you born?" and "What is your function within George?" etc.

Referring to the work that he and his wife had been doing with ego-states in their clinical practice, he further stated that they

. . . found that these entities described themselves as having identity, content, specific functions within the psychological economy of the entire individual and could often indicate their origins—sometimes related to traumatic events. In other words, they acted like "covert multiple personalities."[4]

From a clinical point of view, the central question was whether these ego-states could be a significant factor in causing someone psychological and emotional problems. Can such mental states, for example, be involved in a person's panic attacks, instant rages, or constant feeling of inadequacy? Can there be a *parent state* within someone, for example, that is constantly criticizing the self and others? Or could there be a *child state* that perceives any criticism as rejection and experiences it as a loss of love? When a client complains of a sudden shift in mood that has now persisted for days, or feels an ongoing sense of guilt that makes no conscious sense to them, can this be the triggering of an ego-state within them? Based on John and Helen Watkins' workshop, the answer was definitely, yes. Based on my own experience, it made a lot of sense.

In 1985, the idea that each of us has ego-states or sub-personalities was not a great leap for me. At the workshop, I related easily to what John and Helen Watkins were saying: that we all have these parts of the self, usually functioning at unconscious levels; that they act like personalities but are, in fact, complex organizations of feelings, behaviors, and motivations.

It made sense that there could be inner states within each of us that seemed to function separately from the conscious self, but which were not as extreme or dissociated as with alter-personalities. I was already aware of different schools of thought and practice where *sub-personalities* were a central concept. Carl Jung called them *complexes;*[5] Eric Berne called them *parent, adult,* and *child states;* and Roberto Assagioli called them *sub-personalities.* These authors and others in the field recognized these complex states that John Rowan defines as "semi-permanent and semi-autonomous regions of the personality capable of acting as persons."[6]

In my own clinical practice, I had often used techniques that treated the client as if there were different and distinct parts of themselves. In group therapy, I had practiced Psychodrama, a technique developed by Jacob L. Moreno, M.D., where one group member, the *protagonist,* assigns roles to other group members in order to recreate and act out a significant scene or situation. Usually it is a situation that has been repeating in the person's life, one in which another part of him or her seems to take over and results in conflict and pain.

In a similar vein, I frequently used role-playing or the *double-chair technique** as a way of helping clients recognize different "parts" of themselves. My own experience with alter-personalities in the previous two years had already shown me how complex and powerful these parts of the self could be, and the extreme degrees of autonomy they can achieve. It was not difficult to imagine ego-states as a more limited and toned-down version of alter-personalities where the extremes of dissociation took on a life of their own. In this view, alter-personalities, subpersonalities, and ego-states were all names for the same phenomena.

John and Helen Watkins' "continuum" made sense to me, and what they were doing in their approach to therapy made sense too. This was not really a leap for me. The leap was when they claimed that through hypnosis we could contact and communicate with a person's ego-states directly. In short, put anyone in the chair, induce trance, and you could communicate with one of that person's ego-states, independent of the conscious self. If true, it could be a powerful way to help a client access directly the unconscious sources of his or her pain and open these levels to healing and resolution. In essence, unlike the alter-personality that can come out on its own and communicate directly to the therapist, John and Helen Watkins claimed that with normal clients they used hypnosis to go inside and find them.

It's one thing to work with a client in trance and make suggestions "as if" there were parts of the unconscious mind listening and able to respond. It's something else again to say that these parts could talk back. It implied that they possessed some level of intelligence and autonomy. As a therapist, it would become a matter of talking "to" and not "at." It reinforced the view that these parts are like alter-personalities who very obviously are aware and able to communicate. From a clinical point of view, if ego-states possessed the capacity to communicate,

---

* A technique where the therapist and client sit facing each other and carry on a dialogue. The therapist role-plays either the client's conscious self or one of these 'parts' of the self. It's a way of objectifying for the client a pattern of behavior or perception that is causing problems.

then this approach offered the same basis for verification as with alter-personalities. In talking with someone else, we all know rather quickly whether we are communicating or talking nonsense.

Ideomotor Signaling

In the months following the conference, I expanded my study of MPD and alter-personalities to include ego-states and the different hypnotic and therapeutic techniques used to work with them. I discovered other schools of thought and practice that also recognized ego-states as real phenomena and a significant issue in therapy. Not all of these approaches called them *ego-states,* but they described them in a way very similar to John and Helen Watkins.

A second thing that these approaches shared in common was their use of a hypnotic technique called *ideomotor signaling.* This is a technique for communicating with a person's unconscious mind through body signals—usually head or finger movements—instead of words. When you hear someone say they agree with something and they are shaking their head back and forth, then you've probably just seen an example of ideomotor signaling. The conscious self says one thing, the unconscious another.

I had some awareness of this technique before the Chicago conference, but thought of it as a way of communicating with alter-personalities who refused to *come out* and speak. At the conference, the importance and wide use of ideomotor signaling in the field of hypnotherapy became quickly apparent. John and Helen Watkins talked about using ideomotor signaling in their own work, and it came up in different talks and demonstrations during the conference. In the following months, it kept coming up as I studied the different approaches to working with MPD and ego-states.

The discovery of ideomotor signaling is usually attributed to Milton Erickson, M.D.,[9] a psychiatrist renowned for his success in treating people through hypnosis. Erickson discovered that the unconscious mind could communicate using signals, such as movements of the head or fingers, instead of having to use verbal responses. Erickson took the step of deliberately using these signals to bypass the conscious self and communicate directly with the unconscious mind. The following is an excerpt where Erickson is working with a client to establish ideomotor signals while inducing trance.

Something everybody knows is that people can communicate verbally or by sign language. The commonest sign language, of course, is when you nod your head yes or no. Anybody can do that. One can signal 'come' with the forefinger, or wave 'bye-bye' with the hand. The finger signal, in a way means, 'yes, come here,' and waving the hand means really, 'No, don't stay.' In other words one can use the head, the finger, or the hand to mean either yes or no. We all do it. So can you.[8]

Once the patient was in a trance state, Erickson used these signals to evaluate his or her readiness and willingness at the unconscious level to accept or carry out certain changes in behavior or attitude. He also used these signals to access information about events or experiences of which the patient had little or no conscious memory.

Leslie LeCron and David Cheek M.D., contemporaries of Erickson, further developed ideomotor signaling as a therapeutic tool. They used these signals as a direct way of questioning the unconscious mind about the causes or reasons for a particular problem or symptom. In *Mind-Body Therapy*, the book he co-authored with Earnest Rossi, Cheek recalls watching a demonstration in which LeCron helped a man resolve in twenty minutes a gagging problem he had experienced for forty-five years.[9] The man reported that he would begin to vomit whenever he tried to brush his back molars or when he went to the dentist.

Through ideomotor signals, LeCron determined that an event had occurred in the man's life that led to his gagging. As LeCron continued the questioning, Cheek reports, the man came out of trance and remembered a specific trauma as a child when his throat had hemorrhaged after a tonsillectomy. The doctor had put a clamp in his throat and left it there all night. The sudden insight and emotional release of this trauma led to an immediate resolution of the problem. A dentist from the audience was invited to test the resolution. Using a tongue blade, the dentist performed several manipulations with no apparent distress or gagging by the subject. Cheek knew the person and so could follow his progress over the years. Except for a brief recurrence a few weeks after LeCron's treatment, the man remained symptom free.

As I learned more about ideomotor signaling, I responded much as I had when confronted with multiple personality disorder. I began studying the range of methods for using these signals, which included the works of LeCron, Cheek, Watkins, Barnett, and others. These clinical works provided numerous examples and clinical transcripts describing the use of ideomotor signals in working with clients. The technique was immediately helpful in my work with alter-personalities, and this in turn prepared me to try ego-state therapy with other clients.

Ego-state therapy and ideomotor signaling fit together hand in glove. Ego-state therapists like Watkins, Barnett, and others were saying to communicate directly to the ego-states. Ideomotor signaling was a tool by which to do that. Most ego-states, with most people, are not able to manifest in the body like an alter-personality. Ideomotor signaling, therefore, is an effective way to bridge this gap. Without it, I'm not sure how effective ego-state therapy could be.

Hypnosis: Accessing Inner Resources

Up until the Chicago conference, I had used hypnosis with clients in its more traditional sense as *suggestion*. In this approach, once a client has entered the trance state, he or she is given suggestions for change. The phrasing is structured specifically to address the client's particular symptoms or conflicts. In his book, *The Hypnotism Handbook*, Charles Cooke gives an example of this suggestion technique for a client suffering from frequent headaches. These suggestions are given, of course, with a modulated voice and rhythm conducive to the client's relaxation.

> Now we are going to make your head feel free and clear. Now, all these muscles in the neck are letting go even more. They are becoming loose and flexible. The muscles are becoming loose and flexible like rubber bands tossed loosely on the desk. The neck muscles are relaxing more and more and more . . . Now the base of the skull is becoming completely relaxed, loose, limp. You are beginning to feel so good; you are feeling better and better and better. (Repeat foregoing sentence many times.) Now your forehead and temples are relaxing, letting go, letting go. The muscles are relaxing and you are feeling so much better, so very much better. (Repeat many times.)[10]

The critical issue in this approach is the client's capacity and willingness to accept the suggestions, incorporate them at an unconscious level, and act on them when returning to his or her normal level of conscious awareness.

Rossi has called this approach to hypnotherapy, "authoritarian,"[11] because the hypnotist *authors* the suggestions and presents them to the subject while in trance. The conventional belief is that in a trance state, the self is passive and one's mind is open to suggestion. In this authoritarian framework of hypnosis, the idea or suggestion comes from outside the self. It is the hypnotist's suggestions, not his or her own, that the subject is receiving and acting on. It is a one-way communication, from doctor to patient. The success of the cure depends on the patient's passivity and acceptance of the suggestions. This has been the prevailing view of hypnosis in our Western culture. It is also the view that has led to so many misconceptions and fears about the potential for hypnosis to be used to manipulate and control a person. No wonder people find it frightening.

Ego-state therapy and ideomotor signaling implied a very different approach to healing and the use of hypnosis. Rossi[12] called it *utilization* as opposed to *authoritarian.* He describes it as a revolutionary shift in which the mind, conscious *and* unconscious, is viewed as an active agent rather than a passive receptor.

> The induction and maintenance of a trance serves to provide a special psychological state in which patients can reassociate and reorganize their inner psychological complexities and utilize their own capacities in a manner in accord with their own experiential life.
>
> ... Direct suggestion [authoritarian] is based primarily, if unwittingly, upon the assumption that whatever develops in hypnosis derives from the suggestions given. It implies that the therapist has the miraculous power of effecting therapeutic changes in the patient, and disregards the fact that therapy results from the inner resynthesis of the patient's behavior achieved by the patient himself. ... It is this experience of reassociating and reorganizing his (the patient's) own experiential life that eventuates in a cure ... [13]

The power of hypnosis, according to this view, resides within the self's own ability to reassociate and reorganize different states of mind and emotion. It was an approach whose aim was to unlock and unblock the self's own abilities and inner resources. The power of hypnosis, then, was in its ability to loosen the boundaries between these states and free the self's inner resources to heal and resolve the pain or conflict.

This view of hypnotherapy was a revolutionary shift in my perspective. It altered my understanding about hypnosis as a specialized mental state—*suggestibility*—to a tool for helping clients access and deal with unconscious levels of their conflict and pain. *Ego-state therapy* gave me a basic map for finding the parts of the self involved in a client's pain or conflict, and ideomotor signaling offered a method for communicating with them directly. Within this framework, the one-way communication from therapist to client became a two-way communication between therapist and client.

3

At an Impasse

No problem can be solved from the same level of consciousness that created it.—Albert Einstein

Practicing Ego-State Therapy

When I decided to try ego-state therapy and the different techniques in my own practice, I did not expect textbook cases. I did expect, though, that the same basic principles and dynamics would be operating. I expected to see similarities between my clients and the clinical cases I had been studying. I had a number of clients whom I considered prime candidates for this approach. They ranged from clients with limited and specific symptoms such as panic attacks or fear of flying to those clients who were dealing with deep and chronic conditions such as depression or constant feelings of insecurity or anxiety. As I studied these different approaches, I began to take tentative steps to apply them. I discussed ego-state therapy and ideomotor signaling with selected clients where I thought it might be helpful. Almost every one of them readily agreed to at least try it.

In many ways, the process worked like my mentors said it would. Using their techniques, sometimes word for word or with slight modification, I found it relatively easy to induce trance and establish finger signals with a client. It was the next step, the identification of the *critical experience,* where things became slippery.

In theory, once a client is in trance and good signals are established, the therapist asks the unconscious mind to review the past for an experience that has caused or led to the development of the person's presenting symptom or complaint. This is followed by the therapist's direction that the yes finger will lift when that review has been completed. In theory, when the yes finger lifts, it means that such an experience has been located and a link found between past and present. The task for the therapist, then, is to help facilitate the sharing of that information from the unconscious to the conscious. It's basic Freud. We heal by making the unconscious conscious.

All the approaches I studied included this basic element of sharing and release as central in the healing process. In general, the theory is that during a critical experience, such as trauma or shock, one's perceptions and emotions somehow become locked together in an ego-state, a state that continues to exist and function at an unconscious level. By bringing the experience to consciousness, the belief is that it will unlock these states and lead to their release (catharsis) and integration.

When I began using this approach with my own clients, I was looking for these kinds of critical experiences and ego-states. I posed the questions I had been taught would elicit information about such experiences without triggering a client's defenses. At first, with many clients, this seemed to be working. Following an unconscious review, I communicated with a part of the mind that gave an age, sometimes a name, and agreed that it held experience or memories related to the particular issue we were focused on in that session.

In using this new method, the problem wasn't in finding ego-states involved in an issue; it was in finding too many. With many clients, when I asked the unconscious to look for the critical experience, often more than one ego-state responded. Over several sessions with a client, for example, I might have five or six ego-states presenting, all seemingly related to the problem or symptom we were trying to address.

There were many ego-states whose signals came through strong and clear. With others, however, the signals were so weak or ambiguous that it became a painstaking process to determine whether it was a genuine response. There were times I didn't know who I was talking to, and sometimes I didn't know whether I was talking to anyone at all. It often meant backtracking and asking a new question or phrasing the old one in a new way. Vicki S. is a good example of what happened when I started using ego-state therapy.

Vicki S.

Vicki was forty-two and, up until the year before, she would have described herself as a mother, housewife, community volunteer, and school sports booster. That all changed the night her husband, Dale, told her that he wanted a divorce. She knew her marriage was strained, but Dale's announcement came as a shock. He made it clear over the next couple of days that there was nothing more to discuss, he had already made up his mind. By the next week, he had moved out. Vicki was already reeling from this blow when, a few weeks later, it came out that Dale had been involved with another woman for the last two years. For Vicki, it was the ultimate betrayal. In the following months, she alternated between feelings of panic and anxiety, ever-increasing anger toward Dale, and a deep sense of emptiness. Her depression magnified, and she finally sought therapy at the urging of a friend.

It did not take long to see that Vicki's divorce had precipitated a profound crisis in her life. Her identity and self-worth had been so enmeshed with her husband's that when Dale walked out, she didn't know who she was. A good part of that identity and self-esteem had derived from the prestige of Dale's professional position in the community and this, too, was gone overnight. In many ways, she had to create a new identity that involved doing things and making decisions by herself that she had not had to face in a very long time, if ever.

The goals of Vicki's therapy during the first year were to help her reestablish her psychological and emotional equilibrium and alleviate her depression. She was an intelligent and insightful woman, a good candidate for therapy. She was also honest. When I made an observation or interpretation that I knew would be painful or difficult for her to confront, she did not run away. Even if it took a few weeks, she would come back to it on her own. She was willing to look at her own motivations, biases, and shortcomings. Vicki made good progress in therapy. She was putting her life back together.

From my point of view, she had accomplished a great deal in that first year. She had returned to college and taken the classes required for her teaching certificate. She also was adjusting to her new role as a single parent and head of household. She made more efforts to maintain her friendships and community involvement. She had gained a great deal of

insight into herself and the relationship with Dale. She more clearly saw
her own part, as well as Dale's, in what had brought about the breakup
of their marriage. Despite her insight and her many positive adjust-
ments, though, her feelings of betrayal and anger towards Dale and the
accompanying depression continued unabated. These feelings, of course,
had been a primary focus in her therapy from the beginning, and she
still could not let them go or move beyond it. She vacillated between
her rage at Dale and her own deep feelings of guilt and worthlessness.

Vicki had shared with me early in her therapy that sex had been a
major problem in the marriage. She said that she began to lose interest in sex following the birth of her first child, and she was no longer
able to achieve orgasm. She had attributed the change to the baby's
birth and believed it was only temporary and that her sexual feelings
would re-ignite. When that didn't happen, she was too afraid to talk
to Dale about it. She continued her sexual relationship with Dale but
said she was "going through the motions." Their sexual encounters
were less frequent, and she would try to avoid sex or make excuses
when she could.

Vicki knew this was having a significant effect on the marriage. She
went further, though. In one of those early sessions, she said she believed
this change in her sexual feelings had something to do with her dad and
sexuality. She said she just knew something happened, but she had no
specific memories. Over the months, as Vicki tried to come to terms
with her hurt and anger at Dale, she found herself coming back more
than once to these questions about her father. When I tried to explore
this issue directly, Vicki was aware of feelings of anger and panic, but
still there were no memories. She was stuck, and the therapy was stuck.

I believed that if Vicki's father had sexually abused her, then it
was likely that one or more ego-states had been created around such
traumatic experience. I also believed that if the abuse occurred, then
these ego-states could be holding the memories and somehow blocking them from the conscious mind. I finally suggested to her that
hypnosis might be a way to help her resolve the impasse and answer
these questions and feelings for herself. While she expressed some
anxiety about it, Vicki felt that if hypnosis could help her find relief,
then she had to try it.

We used hypnosis in our next four sessions. Vicki was a good hypnotic subject, and I was able to establish the ideomotor signals very
quickly. I asked for an unconscious review to look for the experience

involved in her feelings of betrayal and anger. For me, it was like Alice falling through the rabbit hole. Over the next four sessions, we identified four different ego-states and each one had a story. When I asked for the unconscious review in our first hypnosis session, I was expecting one early experience and/or one ego-state to be presented. Instead, I found four in rapid succession. I was scrambling and straining to make sense of the responses I was getting and how they related to Vicki's situation. The first ego-state was twenty-three years old. She shared the memory of a time when Vicki, a few months after her daughter was born, got into a heated argument with her in-laws and ended with her yelling at them to "go to hell."

In our next session, Vicki shared with me what had come to her since our last session. She told me that Dale had been supportive of her and her position in the argument. Two days later, however, after talking to his mother, Dale flip-flopped and sided with his parents. Vicki remembered the profound hurt and betrayal that she had felt, but at the time, those feelings had been repressed.

The 23-year-old ego-state made sense to me. She was triggered because she too felt betrayed by Dale. She still carried the experience of this original betrayal, and she was apparently fueling Vicki's present hurt and anger. As I worked with her, though, another aspect emerged that turned out to be just as significant for Vicki. In reaction to Dale's betrayal and her subsequent anger, 23yo* had somehow blocked Vicki's capacity for sexual pleasure and enjoyment. It wasn't clear whether this was to punish Dale or to protect Vicki from further vulnerability and hurt. It was an important piece, though, in helping Vicki to understand the loss of her sexual feelings and her estrangement from Dale.

While working with 23yo, a second ego-state presented. She said she was forty-one. I came back to her the next week, and eventually she shared memories of the time when Dale left her eighteen months before. Vicki could feel the shock, hurt, panic, and anger all over again. The memories and feelings were familiar, but during the session, Vicki allowed herself to experience the emotions more deeply than she had before.

I met a third ego-state while working with 41yo. She was thirty-two years old, and she refused to share information about her experience except to confirm that it was related to the other two. I came back to

---

* Throughout the rest of the book, "yo" will designate a specific ego-state, and is used as a name, as in *23yo* or *8yo,* etc.

her the next week. Vicki still didn't know what it was about, and 32yo still refused to share any memories. She did, however, give strong *yes* responses to the feelings of anger, fear, and humiliation as I went through a list of feelings. I did not get very far before the communication was interrupted by an eighteen year-old ego-state.

18yo was probably the strongest of the four ego-states I had met so far. In response to my questions, she signaled that she did remember what happened. Further, she was willing to share her feelings with the conscious self but not her memories. She believed the conscious mind was not ready. 18yo shared her feelings, and Vicki went through an intense emotional abreaction, but she had no memories or pictures to help her know what was happening. After the session, Vicki said that the only thing that came to her was at the end. It was a figure draped in black, "Like the Amish," she said. That's all she could see.

The next week, I had no trouble reestablishing communication with 18yo. During the course of the session, she finally agreed to share some memory. When she did, Vicki remembered one of her high school football games. She was a cheerleader, and she and a friend had come to the field early to sell programs for that night's game. As they entered the field through one of the gates, Vicki saw her dad and they stopped to talk to him. Vicki said, "He was wearing a car length coat and gloves. He was wearing black." At that moment, she felt herself begin to panic and she—or some part inside—stopped the sharing.

Vicki remembered the man in black from our last session. Now she believed she knew who he was. After coming out of trance, Vicki was agitated and struggling to control her emotions. She talked about her dad. She said she *knew* this memory was connected to sexual abuse in some way, but she still had no conscious memory of it.

The 18yo never was able to share her memory. In the next several months, when we did hypnosis, I identified a twelve year-old ego-state who blocked 18yo from sharing. Then there was a 16-, 10-, and 2-year-old. They almost seemed to be thrown out as diversions. When I tried to elicit more information through the finger signals, I was blocked. It seemed that the closer my questions came to bringing the experience into focus, the more blocked or confused things became. Something or someone appeared to be actively blocking the memories. I didn't know whether it was the conscious self, ego-states, a defensive mechanism of the mind, or my own inexperience in carrying out the procedures. The memories went only so far but rarely to the experience itself.

Shadow Boxing

In those first eight months of using ego-state therapy, my experience with Vicki was repeated with other clients. Sometimes the process worked just like it was intended. I was able to identify parts of the self that could communicate independently of the conscious mind. These ego-states shared memories or information about early experiences and traumas that appeared directly connected to the symptoms or conflicts we were trying to address. They were experiences that the conscious self had been aware of but had forgotten, or had kept on the periphery of consciousness, or experiences of which the person had no memory at all. For these clients, uncovering memories and experiences often led to profound insight and emotional release. For me, it was a confirmation that ego-state therapy was a valid approach in working with the unconscious mind. The fact that the techniques worked to any extent was a positive result to me.

The problem, however, was that I encountered a great deal of blocking and confusion with many of my clients just as I had with Vicki. My communication with ego-states was so often disrupted, taken over by another, or just went silent before the critical memory and feelings were shared. I was not surprised that there should be some level of resistance and fear when working with different parts of the self. We were usually dealing with painful and frightening memories. Like with Vicki, though, it often seemed that the closer we approached the source of pain or confusion, the more likely it was that we would get blocked. Sometimes the blocking started in the first several sessions; other times it started many sessions later after what appeared to be good progress in the therapy. In their most recent book, *Ego-States: Theory and Therapy,* John and Helen Watkins describe this blocking:

> For some reason, in our conversation with the original personality something was said that made it more convenient for the patient to switch. Perhaps we asked a question that the host personality could not or did not want to answer. It abdicated. Perhaps the energy available to the host personality at the time was depleted, and a stronger and more highly energized state was able to become overt and assume the executive position. Or perhaps the course of the discussion was such that the underlying alter was more highly motivated to emerge and communicate . . . Therapists are often confronted with a switch to a

different alter when the therapeutic communication is getting too "hot" or threatening to the patient, or to the alter that is currently present.[1]

In my own work with clients, each time an ego-state agreed to share its memory or feelings and it didn't happen, I had to consider these and other possibilities as to why a memory was blocked, or why my communication with an ego-state ended abruptly or was interfered with by another. I cannot tell you how many times I asked the wrong question or said the wrong thing, only to see an alter-personality disappear or the signals go dead. I didn't know if the ego-state or alter-personality took off on its own, was silenced or overridden by another, or whether the conscious self was somehow keeping a block in place.

Once a communication with an ego-state was disrupted, however, the ball was always in my court to figure out what to ask or what to say that would reestablish communication. I was constantly backtracking to the moment where the block had occurred, trying to pick up the trail again. I spent a great deal of time before, during, and after sessions trying to understand why specific blocks had occurred, and what approaches might resolve them.

I was finding the process to be much more complex and difficult than I had originally expected. In effect, I was finding the same thing with the rest of my clients that I found with MPD clients. There appeared to be multiple parts of the self functioning at an unconscious level and forming complex systems of protection and/or compensation for the conscious personality. The process was all the more difficult, though, when communication was restricted to ideomotor signals. Yes/no communication went very smoothly when both parties were cooperating. It could be quite tedious and confusing, however, once any blocking began. Unlike with alter-personalities, there was no tone of voice and often little facial expression or body language to help interpret what was happening. It was like the difference between a personal encounter and trying to carry on a dialogue using Morse code.

The Psychic and Paranormal

While my clinical focus was on ego-states, a number of clients were also reporting unusual or out-of-the-ordinary experiences and phenomena. These came up sometimes during the sessions as memories of past events, and sometimes as phenomena occurring during the session.

The terms I used for these phenomena in my own mind were *psychic* or *paranormal*. They included such phenomena as *ESP*, precognitive dreams and premonitions, encounters with strange beings, and near-death-experiences.

Clients had reported strange experiences or memories like this since I first began practicing psychotherapy. Most psychologists, I think, will tell you the same thing. These reports could be interesting and fascinating, but they were not that frequent and they rarely would become a focus in therapy. When I began using hypnosis, however, reports of these kinds of experiences increased significantly. It was as though the trance state loosened the boundaries that usually kept these experiences outside one's conscious awareness.

One client, for example, told me she saw auras around people all the time. She said this had occurred ever since she was a child. Another client said she frequently was aware of things just before they happened. She said it was like living one step in front of herself. This was happening so frequently, she said, that it was driving her crazy and she didn't know how to stop it. Another client told me that a few days before our session she had awakened to see a figure in the doorway of her bedroom. She said, "It was as real as you and me." It had done nothing to threaten her, but she said it still frightened her. And finally, more than one client remembered leaving their body during surgery.

These experiences, from a client's past or occurring in the present, were not coming up in every session, and when they did, they still did not become a focus of the therapy. Most of the time, I could only observe and note what my client reported and what happened. Either I did not know how to address the particular experience or phenomenon or it did not appear relevant to the therapy. I had no explanation for many of these phenomena, and I often didn't know whether they were important enough to pursue in the therapy. If it seemed important to my client to talk about or deal with it in some way, then I did the best I could to listen, understand, and give them support.

These phenomena, however, only added to my growing confusion and frustration about the inner world and how it worked and how it affects a person and how to work with it. When these psychic or paranormal phenomena did come up, I did consider them within the context of my client's therapy. I still wasn't sure, though, how to rule them in or out as a source of blocking or even how to deal with them.

4

At the Borderline of Spirit

The refusal of modern "enlightenment" to treat "possession" as a hypothesis to be spoken of as even possible, in spite of the massive human tradition based on concrete experience in its favour, has always seemed to me a curious example of fashion in things scientific. That the demon theory (not necessarily a devil-theory) will have its innings again is to my mind absolutely certain. One has to be "scientific" indeed to be blind and ignorant enough to suspect no such possibility.—William James

An Unknown Voice

In October 1986, I had been working with Diane C. for more than a year when I was confronted with the question of spirit possession. Diane was originally referred to me for outpatient therapy following a six-month hospitalization where she was treated for multiple personality disorder. She was one of the three MPD clients referred to me in the year following my diagnosis of Paula. Diane's caseworker, in fact, was the one who first told me about the conference in Chicago on multiple personality disorder and dissociation.

For the previous six months, I had been working with a number of alter-personalities who described growing up in a family that was part of a satanic cult. I had known about this cult aspect of Diane's case before I accepted her as a client. Her inpatient therapist had shared this information with me, and it was also included in her psychiatric record. Up to this point, however, I had not worked with any clients who had reported this kind of ritual abuse. To me, a cult conjured up images of social misfits or anti-church rebels mocking religion or casting futile spells and incantations. (This was before satanic cults and child ritual abuse had become a media phenomenon.) My focus was on dissociation and multiple personality disorder. I accepted Diane as a client with the idea that we would treat the multiplicity, and that any trauma from cult abuse would be addressed and resolved as part of that process.

My views on satanic cults and child ritual abuse began to change as a result of my work with Diane. I worked with a number of alter-personalities, ranging in age from four to sixteen, who shared memories of extreme torture and terror carried out in a systematic way. As a therapist, I had worked with many clients over the years who had suffered sexual, physical, or emotional abuse as children. The experiences of ritual abuse shared by Diane's alter-personalities, however, were far beyond anything I had yet encountered.

By the fall of 1986, memories of ritual abuse had become a focus in Diane's treatment. One day during a session, an alter-personality came forward who referred to herself as the *Daughter of Darkness.* When this alter-personality came into the consciousness, I introduced myself. She didn't know it was 1986. She didn't know who Diane was. She didn't know where she was, and it was obvious by her facial expression that she was profoundly disoriented. I began to tell her about Diane and the conscious reality. I told her our intention was to help her heal and be released from any pain and fear. I told her that we knew some things about the cult and that nobody, including her, had to keep this experience and knowledge secret any longer. She could become free of it.

As we talked, the *Daughter of Darkness* began to gain understanding about the present and what was happening. She became more relaxed, and I began to ask her questions about herself. She told me that when she came out before, it was always in a room where a large group of people, wearing robes, was gathered around a table lit by torches. This room was the only reality she knew. She apparently had been out several times in Diane's life, but to her, it was always in this room, and it all felt like one ongoing event.

This alter-personality began to talk about what occurred in this room with the other people when suddenly her face grimaced in pain. Then her eyes shut for a moment. When the eyes opened, I noted a cold fury directed at me. I was looking at a face that was controlled and menacing at the same time. The transformation had been instantaneous. It was as though the alter-personality I had been talking with was yanked off the stage and someone else had stepped through the curtain and into the body.

With this menacing look, a deep voice, speaking with authority, said we would go no further. There would be no more questions. The encounter raised the hair on the back of my neck. As I searched my mind for the best way to respond, the thought occurred to me that what I was dealing with here might not be an alter-personality. I don't know where the thought originated. I had worked with many of Diane's alter-personalities by this time, and this entity just did not feel the same. My training and my beliefs pushed me to understand this entity as a part of Diane, a creation of her own unconscious mind. I was all for that view, but I couldn't shake the disturbing sense that something else was going on here.

I tried to engage this entity for several minutes. I asked a number of carefully worded questions trying to elicit a response, but it just stared at me. Finally, I assumed as much authority as I could muster and demanded that this entity respond to my questions. Even before I finished my demand, however, I felt it had called my bluff. It just continued to stare. After several more minutes, seemingly on its own terms, it finally withdrew. One of Diane's familiar alter-personalities then assumed consciousness and was now facing me.

The memory of this experience remained extremely vivid for me over the next several days. It forced me to consider whether someone or something had taken over Diane's consciousness and could do so again. In terms of Diane's treatment, this question was crucial. If this was a part of her, an alter-personality, then everything could make sense. Psychologically, this entity could be understood as an alter-personality, but possibly one who mirrored such a terrifying reality that it had to stand somehow separate and opposed to the self and the other alter-personalities. I speculated that with its malevolence and outright threats, maybe it kept all the other alter-personalities in line and kept everyone else—in this case, myself—away from these memories. In the end, though, even these kinds of 'protectors' could usually be accommodated. Once they felt safe enough to open up, their position as the separate and evil villain could be resolved.

Following this experience with Diane, however, I could not rule out that I had encountered a wholly separate entity. The sense of evil intent and malice was so strong that I was unsure whether this entity was a part of Diane, herself. I didn't know whether I had just glimpsed something from across the boundary of spirit. Even to posit the idea of a separate entity, though, raised profound and serious questions: Was it possible that Diane's problems involved other forces or entities and not just memories and alter-personalities? Could a separate entity be present and active in Diane's mind or psyche? And if so, how does that happen, and what to do?

These were fundamental questions, the answers to which could affect the focus and course of Diane's therapy. They were questions that went to *cause*. If I was going to assist Diane in her healing, I had to know what caused, or was causing, her problems and distress. Was it a separate entity or was it a part of Diane?

Worlds and Dimensions

The next week, I went to the public library to search the card catalog for books on possession. I didn't believe that Diane was possessed, nor did I believe this was a replay of *The Exorcist*. Possession, however, was the closest I could come to describing the situation. I found several titles and, after locating the appropriate section, I started searching the shelves. As I glanced back and forth between the numbers and titles, I had my second shock within a week. I found several sections filled entirely with books on all kinds of paranormal, spiritual, and metaphysical topics. These included books on haunting and poltergeist, shamanism and witchcraft, as well as UFOs, channeling, and near-death-experience. Possession, in fact, made up only a tiny fraction of these books. I was familiar with many of these terms but what was overwhelming to me was the discovery of so many books across such a wide range of phenomena. My head was spinning. By the time I left, I had an armload of books, including the two on possession.

The first book I read was Malachi Martin's, *Hostage to the Devil*, which included five, fully documented case studies on possession and exorcism. Martin stated at the beginning:

> The . . . five case histories are true. The lives of the people involved are told on the basis of extensive interviews with all of the principles involved, with many of their friends and relatives, and with many others involved directly or indirectly in minor ways. All interviews have

been independently checked for factual accuracy wherever possible. The exorcisms themselves are reproduced from the actual tapes made at the time and from the transcripts of those tapes.[1]

Martin goes on to describe these five individuals and what he calls the preternatural* phenomena manifesting within and around them. Each of these case histories depicted a force or consciousness somehow separate from the person, but exercising complete, or near total control over his or her mind and body. They are stories of such evil and malevolence, where the possessing force appears intelligent and acting with conscious intent.

It was a frightening thought. Yet, many cases of possession were reported each year. If it was true for one person, that an evil force can possess a person, then what stops it from going to the next person, and the next? Is there really such an alien and evil force that can possess a person or is it somehow all just psychological? And if it is real, how does one get into such a state? What is it that makes some people succumb, and others not? There were no definitive answers to these questions.

The next book I read was *Far Journeys* by Robert Monroe, a former broadcast executive and owner of radio stations and then cable television systems. In 1958, at the age of forty, Monroe inexplicably began to have out-of-body experiences and later wrote a book about these experiences entitled *Journeys Out of the Body*. *Far Journeys* was a sequel to this work and described his continuing explorations and experiences in these out-of-body states. He described the experience in general.

> What is the out-of-body experience? For those who have not encountered the subject as yet, an out-of-body experience (OOBE) is a condition where you find yourself outside of your physical body, fully conscious and able to perceive and act as if you were functioning physically—with several exceptions. You can move through space (and time?) slowly or somewhere beyond the speed of light. You can observe, participate in events, make willful decisions based on what you perceive and do. You can move through physical matter such as walls, steel plates, concrete, earth, oceans, air, even atomic radiation without effort or effect.[2]

* Something that is beyond normal, or outside the bounds of nature.

In *Far Journeys,* Monroe described his out-of-body travels into what appear to be other dimensions or levels outside our normal space/time reality. While acknowledging the limitations of our human language and concepts to describe these realities, he also tells of numerous encounters and communications with other beings during these astral journeys.

Monroe does not offer any overall explanation for the many phenomena he experienced. At the end of the book, he does present what he describes as a general schema or framework by which to view these different levels of nonphysical reality.

For the next year, I immersed myself in this literature and read my way through these sections of the library. I also began to search out these topics in bookstores, particularly among used books, where I acquired a number of titles. These books were windows into other worlds and alternate realities. They were strange and fascinating, and at times even terrifying. I was astonished by my own ignorance about these dimensions and the wealth of material written about them. I was confronted with volume after volume of reports, writings, and studies that I had not ever been aware existed. Over the months, taken all together, I was convinced of the reality of these unseen dimensions.

All of these documented accounts and reports of psychic and spiritual phenomena, however, did not answer my questions about Diane and what had happened in our session. To this day, I cannot tell you who or what was speaking to me through Diane. Whether it was a part of her or whether it was a demonic entity or consciousness, I don't know. In subsequent sessions, it did not respond to my attempts to bring it forward.

While I could not answer the question about Diane specifically, in my own mind, I did answer the underlying question that confronted me in her session: was it possible that the presence I encountered with Diane was a separate entity that had in some way intruded and forced its way into her consciousness? After my extensive study, I believed the answer was, *yes.* It was possible. It very well could have been a separate entity or spirit communicating with me that day.

In my readings, I learned that people across cultures had been dealing with spirits throughout the ages. Through visions, voices, spells, and rituals, there had been many kinds of contact and communications with spirits. The scientist in me, of course, would say *alleged* communications and contacts, but I was beyond that now. I had read enough testimony, most of it from first-hand accounts. The question no longer was whether spirits and other dimensions existed. I was convinced they did. The question became how to make sense of it all. This was another matter entirely. There were so many different phenomena and manifestations in these reports and studies that I didn't know where to begin, and I had no overall or integrated framework of understanding.

Conversion

All my reading and studies of paranormal phenomena did not, in the end, affect my work with Diane. Also, I saw no direct clinical applications that would be helpful in the treatment of clients in general. The most immediate benefit was to me, personally. Sometime during these months of reading and study, I experienced a conversion. I came to a point where I knew there were other levels of consciousness and reality. I don't remember any one moment like St. Paul being struck from his horse. For myself, it was more the steady accumulation, and finally the preponderance of evidence. Unless I believed that all of these people were hallucinating, misinterpreting, or lying, then I had to conclude that there were other dimensions of consciousness and reality. It's like reading a detective story. After so many clues and insights from scores and scores of witnesses, your suspicions start moving in a certain direction, and at some point, everything you see points exactly to the same conclusion.

During this period I became convinced that every person's consciousness, mine included, survives the death of the body; that we are spiritual beings; and that most of us come into this world with a history of lifetimes. I was convinced, too, that there were dimensions in which spirits existed and could, under certain conditions, interact with or be seen by humans. I believed that UFOs and extraterrestrial contacts with people were real, and often involved altered states of consciousness. This doesn't mean that I understood these different phenomena or that I could explain them. I just knew there were realities beyond the senses and ordinary consciousness.

Emotionally and psychologically, this knowing brought with it a deep sense of relief and reassurance. I'm not sure I can put it into words. It's not that it took away all my pain and struggle. I had even more questions now than before. Somewhere inside, though, was a profound knowing that we were all part of a much greater picture. Looking back, I see it as my awakening to soul.

In our Western scientific culture, we don't know *what* to think or even *how* to think about these phenomena. For the most part, these realities are denied, ignored, or believed to be so separate from our physical reality that there can be no legitimate experience or study of them. Before I began my own extensive reading, this was my position as well. I did not necessarily deny psychic or spirit realities, but they were not a part of my everyday awareness or thinking. In that sense, they were not real to me.

This changed after my conversion. Now I knew these phenomena were real, but I had no language or framework by which to grasp them. All the knowledge and information of these psychic and spirit dimensions I had gathered over these many months did not come together into a cohesive picture, or explain how these realities affect us. The conversion, though, created a crack in my world, and in my thinking. Experience contradicted beliefs. These realities needed to be taken into account, and I was only at the beginning of understanding what that meant.

From a clinical point of view, my experience with Diane and the unknown voice was an anomaly. It took place within the larger context of treating four clients with MPD, each of them women, and each with her many alter-personalities. In all this time, I had never thought of the alter-personalities as separate from the client with whom I was working. My experience with Diane changed that. It raised the question of whether some alter-personalities might, in fact, be some psychic part of another person or a spirit entity that has intruded into his or her mind? It opened a crack in my own conceptual framework and led to a personal exploration of these psychic and spiritual phenomena.

In the beginning, I had opened the door to these unconscious levels believing I knew what I would find there. I would find split-off parts of the self, and would help them release their trauma and integrate with the conscious self. After my conversion, I found what William James would call "the blooming, buzzing, confusion." Once I began opening these doors with clients, I was confronted with one mystery and frustration after another. The ego-state therapy worked often enough to convince me there was something to it. I had seen clients experience profound healing or come to a new perspective as a result of our work. That was the way it was supposed to work, and when it did, I took it as confirmation that this approach to healing could be beneficial.

Too many times, though, I was reaching an impasse. The attempts to identify critical experiences and ego-states with clients seemed to go in too many directions. There were either too many ego-states with a client, or their memories couldn't be shared to consciousness, or the signals were contradictory, or the responses stopped altogether. Every impasse raised the question of whether I just didn't know enough or whether I was meeting with purposeful blocking and resistance. Was I asking the wrong questions, or were my questions hitting too close to home? Was it both, or neither?

I'm not sure how long I could have continued in this kind of confusion and frustration—for my clients or for myself. My work with ego-states and alter-personalities always seemed to go just so far before the blocking, confusion or interference began. Looking back, I think the situation was leading to a professional crisis. On the one hand, I couldn't go back to just the traditional, conscious level, talk therapy. There was too much evidence of unconscious factors affecting my clients that traditional *insight therapy* didn't touch. On the other hand, identifying these critical experiences and ego-states without being able to take them to resolution was not a satisfactory outcome.

This was my quandary in the summer of 1987 when I met Gerod and everything changed.

5

A Door Opens: Meeting Gerod

Perhaps modern science's most devastating effect is that it leads its believers to think it to be the only legitimate source of knowledge about the world. Being a high priest, if not a bishop, in the cathedral of modern science—my university, the Massachusetts Institute of Technology—I can testify that a great many of what we call the "MIT family," faculty and students, believe that there is indeed no legitimate source of knowledge about the world other than modern science. This is as mistaken a belief as the belief that one cannot gain legitimate knowledge from anything other than religion. Both are equally false.
—Joseph Weizenbaum, Ph.D., Professor of Computer Science, Massachusetts Institute of Technology

Introductions

I met Gerod on August 1, 1987. It was a peculiar kind of meeting because Gerod didn't have a physical body. I couldn't see him and he didn't have a voice. It's not even accurate to call him a "he" because he has no gender or age. Gerod is a spirit.

A woman named Katharine Mackey initiated my encounter with Gerod. Katharine was a part-time secretary in our office. I didn't see her very often. On the days she worked, she was usually in her own office working on patient accounts and records. I had only joined the practice within the past year, so there wasn't a lot of opportunity for us to get to know each other very well.

One morning, before starting my appointments, she stopped me in the hallway outside my office. She asked whether we might talk for a few minutes when I had a break in my schedule. I must have reacted with a quizzical expression, thinking there was some business issue that needed to be cleared up. Sensing my confusion, she added that it was "personal."

Later that morning, when I had a break, I found Katharine and invited her into my office. We sat down, and I waited with some anticipation and curiosity to hear why she wanted to talk to me. I could never have guessed in a thousand years, though, why she wanted to meet. Katharine told me that she channeled a spirit guide named Gerod, and she wanted to offer me a session in which I could talk to Gerod, if I wished.

Katharine reminded me of a conversation I had had the week before with one of my colleagues in the office. We were in the conference room that doubled as a lunchroom on most days. Katharine was there along with a few other people. On the particular day Katharine referred to, I had been talking to this colleague about out-of-body experiences. These are experiences, like Robert Monroe's, in which people report leaving their physical body and observing it from an outside vantage point. While for some, the experience is short lived, others report traveling to other places or visiting other people but in this ethereal state.

This kind of conversation with my colleague was not unusual. He and I both had been using hypnosis in our work with clients and we would talk at times about some of the unusual phenomena they reported while in trance. This included such paranormal phenomena as the out-of-body experiences.

Katharine told me that when she overheard us talking, it reminded her of an experience she had at fifteen, in which she had an experience of automatic writing. She said it felt like someone else was taking over, and it had scared her. She stopped it, and over time, the whole experience apparently had faded from memory until she heard my colleague and me talking about these strange phenomena. Katharine told me that she had gone home that night, and sitting at her kitchen table, she tried the automatic writing again. She said the connection was "right there" as if just waiting for the call. During this experience, she said, Gerod introduced himself, and over the next couple of days, she and her husband had both communicated with him. They were impressed enough with the communication that Katharine decided to invite me to have a session with Gerod.

As I listened to her, I was already aware of channeling from my own research over the past year and a half. Channeling is one of the many ways in which people throughout history have claimed direct contact with spirits. A channel is a person who is able to step aside and allow a spirit or other entity to communicate through them, either verbally or in writing. In effect, the spirit assumes executive control of at least some of the person's conscious functions. Katharine was telling me that she had this ability. She could step away from her own conscious state and allow Gerod to be present. Apparently, she had had the ability all her life, but had not used it.

Katharine said she was offering me the session with Gerod for several reasons. First, given my own interest in these phenomena, she thought I might welcome the opportunity for a direct experience. Secondly, she wanted an objective party to elicit information from Gerod. And third, she desired an assessment as to the quality of the material.

I readily agreed to the session, as Katharine was right. I did view a meeting with Gerod as an opportunity. To me, the idea of communicating directly with an intelligent entity existing in a different dimension was truly exciting. Despite all of my reading, I had never considered seeking out a psychic or a channel. It just hadn't occurred to me.

I did believe, though, that what Katharine was telling me was true, that some people can channel spirit entities. I had no direct experience myself, however. I didn't see ghosts. I didn't hear voices. I never saw an object move of its own volition. And as many times as I had asked God to take a more personal hand in things, I had yet to witness an obvious or miraculous intervention. My belief in the existence of spirits derived from books and the testimony of clients.

I had no idea, of course, whether Gerod was truly a spirit. My work with sub-personalities and alter-personalities had shown me entities the mind was capable of creating. Gerod could turn out to be a figment of Katharine's unconscious mind, a possibility she and I were fully prepared to consider. My attitude was that if it turned out to be a lot of pie in the sky platitudes or mystical clouds, then I could chalk it up to experience. At the most, I would be out of a couple hours of my time. As far as I was concerned, Gerod could spend most, or all of the session, waxing eloquent on different subjects, and I would be willing to listen. If this was a genuine communication with a spirit, though, my own hope was for a dialogue. We agreed to meet that Saturday morning.

August 1, 1987

Katharine and I sat at the conference table. The office was closed on Saturdays, so I knew we wouldn't be disturbed. Katharine explained to me what was going to happen. It was quite simple. She would take a few minutes to move into an altered state that would allow Gerod to come through and control her arm, and then he would begin writing. Sitting at the table, pencil in hand, arm resting on a yellow pad, Katharine began her internal shift. I sat next to her so I would be able to read what was written. I waited and watched. In a few minutes, her arm began to move. Looking over her shoulder, I read the words, *"Gerod is here with you now Katharine. Is Tom there also?"*

I assumed that Katharine mentally responded in the affirmative, for the next lines appeared: *"Good, I will be happy to talk with him as you asked me about."* This seemed to be my cue. I thanked Gerod for meeting with me. I wasn't quite sure how to start this communication. What do you ask a spirit? This was my first challenge, and it was to be my first lesson.

The only personal question that came to mind concerned my brother, Ted, who had died in 1980 when he was thirty years old. Katharine was not aware of Ted's death, and I did not specifically mention it to Gerod. I just asked what he could tell me about Ted. Gerod's response left me confused and bewildered. He responded to my question as if Ted were still alive:

> Your brother Ted is doing well. His recent problems stem from discord within his soul and he is working very hard to overcome these. Be supportive of him. He needs much love and growth stimulation.
>
> You should stand back a little ways from him; give him room to make his mistakes and so you will help him in his growth; don't feel unhappy for him or unhappy that you cannot do more for him. Your loving concern is really enough at this time.

This response, of course, immediately raised all kinds of questions about Gerod and the validity of his information. I assumed that from his vantage point Gerod should know that Ted was not alive. It seemed to me that would be a pretty big thing for Gerod to miss. However, I had three other brothers and two sisters, and thought maybe something got mixed up there. I decided not to say any more about Ted. I knew it would take some time to come up with the right questions to be able to explore this without revealing the contradiction, so I decided on the spot to suspend my judgment about it and move on to other areas.

My next question to Gerod came out of the crisis that had been developing in my practice. In my hypnosis work with so many clients, I was aware of a growing impasse. So many attempts to identify and communicate with ego-states was resulting in confusion, blocks, and blind alleys with a number of my clients. I decided to ask Gerod about one of those clients, Jim D. I had seen Jim a couple days before, and I was well aware that we were reaching an impasse. I talked to Gerod in general about the confusion and blocking that I was encountering so often in my work with clients, and then asked about my work with Jim. I did not offer any information about Jim. I had no idea what Gerod might say, if anything. But then Katharine's hand began to write:

> Jim is possessed by a low-level spirit trying to adhere to earth. You can instruct Jim on ways to strengthen his soul and tell Jim he must ask this spirit to leave him. He is a good person growing well but he is not fully aware of his potential life with spirit guides, hence his confusion. A person more aware would have recognized the low-level state of this guide.

Gerod's response caught me off guard. I had read a little about spirit attachment in some of my readings. With a few clients, I ventured to ask whether an entity I was communicating with was part of the client. I had done this more out of desperation in an effort to make sense of responses rather than any clear belief that this would actually be the case. Now here was Gerod conveying, matter-of-factly, that my client was dealing with interference by a spirit.

If I believed Gerod, then spirit attachment suddenly went from theoretical and speculative to real. I couldn't even deal with the implications of this revelation at that moment, but I did ask Gerod whether he would say more about this kind of spirit attachment. Again, I read the words as they appeared:

> Discarnate personalities are usually inhabitants of the spirit levels. Your work with your patients has opened up an area I believe has not

been too well explored, as you may know. People with souls attract to themselves discarnates. Gerod is a discarnate but there are many of us, and many of us are not able to successfully function as guides. Unfortunately, these spirits become excess baggage for some earth-existing people. I would suggest to you that some, but not all, multiple personality people are so because they are inhabited or possessed by some lost wandering spirits who do not know better than that way of behavior.

This statement, of course, raised all kinds of questions about multiple personality in general and specifically about many clients with whom I was working, and had worked with, over several years. I had questions and confusion about so much of what I had encountered with my clients. Dealing with multiple personalities was complex enough. Adding to this the possibility of intruding spirits raised even more questions. At the same time, it suggested the possibility that I might also find some answers to the impasses. At that moment, though, sitting there with Katharine and Gerod, all I could do was try to fashion some kind of intelligent question out of the myriad thoughts and memories spinning in my mind.

I asked Gerod whether, from his point of view, alternate personalities were in some sense persons in their own right and fundamentally separate from the primary personality?

No. They are fragments of a personality. The earth-existing soul is intact, hence the discord. A personality grounded within a soul has a higher purpose and would strive to that, even if unable to achieve that. A fragment personality is incomplete, irresponsible to the soul, and so does not have the welfare of the soul in tune, and so causes pain and discord for human people.

I continued with a series of questions about alternate personalities. I did not have the foresight at the time to write down my questions, so I only have a record of Gerod's responses. In general, since I had a great deal of experience with alter-personalities, I wanted to hear what Gerod's perspective was on this same phenomenon. I believed that my own experience would at least give me some basis for comparison. The following are several of his responses about alter-personalities.

Yes. The soul is the repository for all information of this life or past lives. The personality is strong, is clever. Just as you can tap into your soul for information, so can these alternate personalities. They are real; they have energy and do exist. However, they are not an asset to one's being.

The soul is timeless, limitless, a link with all that is. It is to be protected, cherished, and nurtured. Abuse is abominable. It can injure a growing soul. However, that is what these life experiences are for—to nurture and stimulate growth. If a person faces a harsh life with little protection from a guide, it is part of that person's growth experience. Nonetheless, it is sad to me. A personality bases identity with the form of existence chosen, for example earth life. This earth person or personality is frail and vulnerable. Doing anything and everything to produce preservation of self, the personality will call in its own helpers of its own creating. Hence multiple personalities.

They [alter-personalities] are indeed "created." The mind is powerful. See what can be done by your mind when it has the right information—great things. A mind wants help—a mother, a father, someone of significance to love, to protect, to intervene. If in this physical reality no such one exists, then the mind will very carefully begin creating "people" to help. However, many of these helpers are misguided helpers, as they are not grounded to the soul.

There is only one soul in the multiple person unless they are a possessed soul. You need to distinguish between the person who is possessed, possessed by spirits—evil, low level, no good, mischievous, or merely confused—and the earth person who has indeed created soulless personalities within themselves.

Toward the end of the session, I asked Gerod about himself. He gave this response:

Gerod is a teacher of persons to stimulate growth of the soul in order that a person may grow toward the Light and so closer to God, as Katharine calls the Light.

I am a high-level guide interested in growth through the attainment of loving attitudes on earth. I have lived in a level of spiritual existence only. I have not been an earth dweller but have great interest and love for the loving natures of earth-experience persons and so have elected to be a teaching guide to you there. I am not good at fortune telling, table rapping, or the Michigan lottery.

After the session, Katharine and I talked for a little while. I'm sure I shared with her some of my impressions. She also knew I had some reaction to Gerod's communication about my brother. I told her about Ted's death and my confusion about what Gerod had said. I had no need to make immediate judgments about what had happened. Gerod had given me plenty to think about, and that's exactly what I did over the weekend.

Considering and Observing

Following the session with Gerod, I was almost certain that he was not an alter-personality. I still did not rule out that he might be an unconscious creation of Katharine's, but maybe from a deep spiritual or collective level within the self. It could, for example, be like the *inner self helper* (*ISH*) who manifests in so many cases of multiple personality. In clinical cases, the ISH presents as an alter-personality, but one that seems to have a greater knowledge and perspective about a person's inner world than the conscious person or the other alter-personalities. (I'll talk further about the inner self helper in Chapter 10.)

I also considered the possibility that Katharine was perceiving and functioning at some level of her mind that neither she nor I were aware of consciously. She knew all my clients' names. She also had met most of them when she filled in as receptionist at the front desk. I could not rule out that she was receiving information telepathically or psychically. I didn't rule this out, but my own intuition was that Gerod was an intelligent entity that existed independently of Katharine.

On Monday morning, when I saw Katharine, she handed me a piece of paper. She told me that the confusion about Gerod's response had prompted her to channel Gerod and ask him about it. This is what he wrote:

> Tom's brother Ted is reincarnated. He is living another earth life. I interpreted the question too literally I believe. Yes, Ted has died in the sense of the personality of Tom's brother Ted; however, his soul lives on forever and at this time his earthly experience is a little rocky, hence I did feel the concern loved ones would have for him.
>
> Ted has reincarnated as a child, of course. He is a boy of nearly six and he is having trouble feeling accepted. His family is loving, however, if not

somewhat overly protective, hence the boy feels smothered and unable to expand. Acceptance is loving freedom to be who you are. Smothered children are not allowed freedom of expressive natures; therefore they grow up conforming in a way that suppresses their creativity.

Tell Tom sorry for the confusion. But I followed the request for information very clearly and forgot you do not always see life in the whole, but only in this particular experience.

Ted lives in the northern part of California State.

When I had left the meeting with Gerod on Saturday, I did not see how the discrepancy could be reconciled between his supposedly greater knowledge on the one hand and his obvious snafu about Ted. This brief communication from Gerod on Monday morning was a first important lesson. Gerod was saying that when I asked about Ted, I was asking about a soul, and it was the soul that Gerod had identified and talked about, not the personality. Even though I knew it intellectually, Gerod's communication was a powerful reminder that we were dealing with two different points of view. My immediate response to reading this statement was that it was plausible. It could make sense.

This understanding also forced me to consider a different relationship to Ted. For the last seven years, I could only think and feel about Ted as a lost brother. I really had no idea whether he still survived at some spiritual level, or whether he was an energy that melded back into a cosmic consciousness, or whether he had just ceased to exist without a trace, except in the memory of those of us who loved him. My readings over the last year had pointed to the possibility that Ted still existed in some spirit state. Now Gerod was saying that Ted—the soul—was very much alive. However, he was alive as a different person, in a different body.

When I asked Gerod the question about Ted, I was asking about a personality. What Gerod was telling me was about a soul. Was this little boy in California my brother? What did that mean? Did my soul and the "Ted-soul" still have a connection somehow beyond personalities? All kinds of questions began to bubble up through this crack in my thinking. I no longer know how much of it was conscious and how much was a kind of background process carried on in that fuzzy area between conscious and unconscious.

A second thing happened that week to reinforce my dilemma. I had a therapy session with Jim. We did hypnosis again, only this time

I reframed my questions as if I was communicating with a separate spirit instead of a part of Jim. To my amazement, I began to get direct responses. From my work with Jim and many other clients, I knew very well about the blocks and confusions I had been encountering for so long. This time, though, it was as if someone inside Jim was saying that I was finally asking some questions that made sense. So I carried on a dialogue with what apparently was a spirit, and it finally did agree to leave Jim. During the session, and afterwards, I knew I had been engaged in a true communication. Whoever it was, a part of Jim or not, it was intelligent; it understood what I was saying, and it responded to my questions in a rational way.

Points of Contact

When I met with Gerod, I didn't know if he was a spirit. I didn't know how you *try a spirit,* as the old expression goes. The only tools I had were language and reason. It was a *meeting of the minds* in the truest sense of that term. No face to read. No gestures. No voice. Our contact had to be carried out strictly through language.

When I agreed to meet Gerod, I had hoped for a dialogue. I believed that as long as I could ask questions and make sure I understood the meaning of a word or concept, then Gerod and I could reach some kind of understanding. When I actually did communicate with him, I reached the limits of my understanding very quickly. I discovered that Gerod and I weren't speaking the same language.

Gerod said he was a soul who has been aware of his existence and ours from the beginning when all souls were created. That statement alone pretty much blew my perspective. He was not only intelligent, but was claiming to be speaking from a "higher order." This was a perspective I could not even grasp. I talked of *persons,* and he talked of *souls.* He talked of discarnate souls acting as spirit guides for humans, and he talked about earthbound souls able to "inhabit" a person. Concerning my brother, Ted, and my client Jim, he was claiming to be "reading" their souls in present time, as I sat there at the table with Katharine. He said that I had my own personal guide, and that my soul had lived other lives. When I asked about my own past lives, he cited my previous life as a physician living in Maine before World War II.

I knew the terms, of course—*soul, reincarnation, spirit guide*—but I had no personal knowledge of these things. I had no personal experience to confirm or refute what Gerod was saying. I tried to see it from his perspective, but I couldn't. I did not see souls when I looked at other people. I was not aware of spirit guides close by. I had no knowledge of myself as a soul with previous lives. Reincarnation was not a term frequently discussed in my world. Gerod implied that it was all part of a larger reality, but one that I could not see. I fit into his world. He did not fit into mine.

The possibility that Gerod existed at another level of being and knew of our world was explosive to me. The idea that he could actually know people and events in present time put a whole new spin on things; it said that our worlds did coincide. Gerod, in fact, was suggesting that our worlds were more integrally related than I knew. Being able to talk to Gerod about people and events in present time, though, offered us a common ground, a point of reference. We might see it very differently, but at least we were seeing it at the same time. Possible confirmation of this had come in my session with Jim.

Gerod said that a spirit was present and interfering in my work with Jim. In the next session with Jim, when I adopted a different line of questioning, the responses I observed seemed to confirm this. It wasn't proof by any means, but it got my attention. Suddenly, I had one foot in another world. Gerod could see the earthbound spirit with Jim. I could communicate with it. And most importantly, it looked like the spirit could communicate on its own.

I had no conscious awareness of this spirit and I had no idea how it existed. I had decided to try to engage it in order to assist Jim. I assumed if this was truly a spirit, then its presence with Jim could *only* be interfering. If ridding Jim of a spirit would alleviate any of his struggles, then that was the thing to do. Jim agreed. As a Christian fundamentalist, Jim seemed more comfortable than I was with all the talk about evicting spirits. The only problem was that I didn't know how it was to be done. The only *removal procedure* I was aware of was exorcism, and that's not exactly what Gerod was talking about here. His information about "discarnates" implied that they were errant souls from the spirit realm and should be directed back there. It would be like pointing a lost traveler back to the main road—more an *assist* than an *exorcism*.

Over the Edge

There was a point in that session with Jim when I was convinced that I was communicating with a spirit, a discarnate soul. In that moment, spirits went from being an intellectual abstraction to being a clinical imperative. Not only did spirits exist, and were able, under certain conditions, to affect a client, but they could also be dealt with directly through hypnosis and ideomotor signaling. In the future, when assessing a client, spirit attachment would be something to consider.

The communication only lasted for about a half-hour, but in that time, I saw how it could be true. People could be dying and getting stuck making their transition from physical to spirit. Their consciousness at the time of death—what they believe, or see—might in some way determine what happens. I also understood in that moment that our worlds might intersect in some place outside our normal consciousness. These spirits could be involving themselves with people and, knowingly or not, creating distress and confusion at levels of which we are not aware.

Once I acknowledged this possibility I had to deal with the questions that followed. Were spirits, at least for some people, a significant cause of psychological, emotional, or physical distress? And specifically, were any of my clients being affected in this way? If spirits do interfere, in what ways do they interfere? When do they interfere? And who is vulnerable? If they can torment someone, how does that happen? What is the mechanism? Can the attachment of spirits cause particular bodily ailments? Every question led to others, and I didn't know the answer to any of them. But I was compelled to find out.

The catch was that I could not acknowledge just one spirit. I could hardly argue that this was the one lone spirit in the entire universe and he just happened to show up with my client. No, to admit one spirit was to admit many. The problem was not in finding out about this one spirit within Jim, it was in finding out about spirits in general. I had to consider that, if it was true of Jim, it could be true of other clients. It was too late to close my eyes to this. If I had a client whose anxieties or strange symptoms were caused by the presence of spirits, then I would want to know about it and be able to help them resolve it.

I had no guidebooks, however, on how you find out about spirits. I only knew it could be an important issue. In our Western culture, direct contact with spirits has been taboo. The churches believe in them, but say they can't be trusted, as there are evil spirits among them. And science, which I considered my home territory, kept telling me, in the end, "if it doesn't have a physical body, then it isn't real." This was the world I grew up in. Knowledge of spirits was kept underground, as I had already discovered when I took my tour through the library. But now it had become a clinical question.

Glimpses of Another World

While I found Gerod's information in that first session to be intriguing, it was the clinical implications that captured my attention. When Gerod gave me information about Jim D. and the earthbound spirit, he was claiming to perceive Jim at the same time as he and I were communicating. If true, and he could locate one client in real time and give information about him, then it was possible he could do the same with others. And if it was present-time information, then it offered the possibility of verification. If we both were able to perceive the same person (or soul) in present time, it was possible that we could find a common ground or framework: one in which our perceptions and observations overlapped, could be compared, and tested.

This prompted me to ask Katharine for another meeting, and then another. We wound up meeting several more times in the next four months. Over that time, I asked Gerod about several client situations that had either become critical or were quite unusual. I also asked him more about earthbound spirits. We talked about concepts like *conscious* and *unconscious, soul, hypnosis,* and *memory.* I asked questions about whatever came up, and I got more than I bargained for.

I asked and I received. The information from Gerod was overwhelming and directly addressed the soul-states of my many clients. The following excerpt from Gerod gives just a flavor of these many exchanges:

> Rita will continue to surprise you with her information. She is rich for growth. Michael is a past life name and it is a spirit name also. It is a carry over from past life and your therapy with her will be most successful when healing takes form upon these issues. Many developing souls carry their unfinished business with them to the present. Michael is the past life and his history holds the roots of her unhappiness. Past life regression will give the history of a man discontent and socially maladjusted. Jail would possibly be a historical fact for this person. Therapy based upon this present life cannot be successful for it is not these events which hold the roots of her misalignment in life.

I could not conceive of all he was saying and implying in these many communications—that there were many kinds of beings—some evil, others benign, that interact with the world of humans. He said there were beings that deliberately try to manipulate and block people at unconscious levels. He talked about another realm in which there is a recording of all that occurs. Can you imagine? He was saying that our souls come into the world with a history and that it affects us, each in our own way. Gerod also talked of the Light. He said the spirit realm was in the Light and that each of us, as a soul, is already a part of that Light.

Over the months, I became convinced that Gerod was authentic. I believed he was an intelligent and knowing being, separate from Katharine. He wrote his complex statements without hesitating, and he wrote with authority. He said he was a being of Light, offering love and knowledge. He said his purpose was to promote healing and that his contact with me had been established specifically for that reason.

He was willing to have a wide-ranging dialogue, and I could ask whatever I wished. For a person with my curiosity, it was like winning the lottery. But there was an added element. He also claimed to be able to communicate directly with the souls of my clients. As long as a soul was in agreement, he could share what he learned or had been given in that contact. The stipulation was that he would only share information pertaining to the client's healing process. Since I couldn't see it from his point of view, I had to trust his judgment about these boundaries. From all he claimed to see, he would share what he could, what he thought might help, and what did not violate a soul's free choice.

With my clients, I began to have a kind of double vision. There was my natural view of illness as rooted in the conflicts and entanglements of mind, body, and emotion. Childhood experience, trauma, and emotional history were the kinds of factors I considered when assessing a client's situation and determining the best approach to therapy. Right next to that, however, I began thinking about my clients in terms that Gerod talked about: the soul, and the soul choices made before birth; the influence from past lifetimes; the interfering or threatening presence of spirits; and the relationship between self and soul. It was my first attempt at a soul perspective. It was sketchy, more like flights of imagination and intuition. I was looking for patterns and correspondences, causes and effects.

These issues, I knew, could have clinical implications for my clients, but I was in no position to assess all of that at the time. Earthbound spirits, however, based on my experience with Jim D., were something I could possibly address. Through hypnosis, I could communicate with them directly and work to negotiate their leaving. I believed intuitively what Gerod had said: these spirits do not belong here. It's not good for them and it's not good for the people they inhabit. He said they belonged in the spirit realm and could be directed there. If that were true, then it would solve two problems at once. If I could offer spirits an answer to their own troubles, then, at the same time, it could be an answer to the troubles they might be causing my clients. The spirit could go free and my client would be relieved of its presence.

With Gerod's information as one resource, and my own ability to communicate directly with spirits as another, I decided I would address the issue with clients if the presence of a spirit were indicated. By having two sources that could corroborate each other—or not—I believed I had a way to test the validity of my approach.

But my mistake in all of this was in believing that I could study spirits objectively: that is, if I could communicate with them, then I could learn about them and how to direct them to the spirit realm as Gerod suggested. I was naive enough at the time to believe that my intellectual prowess would enable me to explore and map this world that was opening up to me, like somehow it was all separate and outside of me. I did not recognize that crossing this boundary and engaging spirits directly through my clients would force me, sooner or later, to that boundary within myself. It was a soul boundary. It would not be known by my limited concepts and thinking; and if it was to be known, it would be on its own terms, not mine. By saying yes to dealing with spirits, I was, in effect, agreeing to those terms. I did not appreciate the enormity of that step. How could I? In the end, it would demand that I awaken to my soul.

6

Earthbound Spirits

The meaning of death is not the annihilation of the spirit, but its separation from the body, and that the day of resurrection and day of assembly do not mean a return to a new existence after annihilation, but the bestowal of a new form or frame to the spirit.—Al-Ghazzali, from *The Revival of Religious Sciences*

Becoming Bound

Spirits become bound to the earth for many different reasons, all of them having to do with the spirit's consciousness. Obviously, it is no longer the body keeping them attached to the earth reality because the laws of physics no longer apply to them. It is their *consciousness* that keeps them bound. I have communicated with many spirits, for example, who are afraid to go to the Light, the place Gerod calls the *spirit realm of Light.* Depending on what they have been taught, some spirits are afraid that in the Light they will be judged and punished. Hoping to avoid what they believe will be painful, they attach themselves instead to some place or some person in the physical reality. Often these spirits harbor a deep terror that they will be found unworthy of the Light and be rejected. While some may be afraid of the hellfire and damnation they have been taught about, most are afraid of the pain of returning to the Light, to the Creator's Infinite Love, only to be turned around and sent away. In their self-torment, these spirits stay bound to the earth because it is familiar and predictable and, from their point of view, it is safer than the alternative.

I have also worked with spirits who died traumatically—an automobile accident, a fire, murder, or a natural disaster—situations where death came suddenly and there was no time to prepare consciously. These were people, now spirits, whose consciousness remained focused in the physical reality. Often they were not even aware that their body had died. At the time of their sudden death, these spirits can be confused and try to go on as usual. Others become frightened and latch onto the first person they see. It might take them awhile to figure out what has happened. Meanwhile, they either didn't see the Light or lost sight of it in the confusion. These spirits are usually among the easiest to work with. They are very open to hearing about the Light, and once they have located it, they leave quickly.

Addiction is another reason spirits remain earthbound. Their consciousness is so bound up with their addiction that they go right on living it even after the body has died. These spirits will search out people who themselves are addicted and who offer the possibility of a vicarious "fix." For a person in the physical reality, it appears that drug and alcohol induced states create a vulnerability in one's energy field and leaves the person open to spirit attachment. An earthbound spirit, in seeking to continue its own addiction, will be drawn to such a person.

I find that these spirits are also usually open to hearing about the Light and the spirit realm as long as it is safe. Often, it does not take long for them to acknowledge that their present state—trying to continue their addiction—was an exercise in futility. They will usually agree to at least feel the Light or allow a spirit from the Light to come forward and communicate with them directly. This can help reassure them that they will find relief in the Light.

Finally, another common situation is when a spirit remains bound to a loved one or loved ones on earth. A spirit might join with his or her child, for example, out of love, or guilt, or a desire to help in some way. They might also stay with a loved-one because they did not see the Light at the time of death and don't know where else to go or what to do. Once it is pointed out to them, most quickly understand that their presence is an interference, and probably an obstacle, to their loved ones. When instructed about the Light and able to see it themselves, they will usually leave. The complicating factor is that the surviving person to whom they are attached must also be in agreement to let them go. It's not that a spirit still can't leave; it can. It's just that separating from a grieving or reluctant loved one can be more difficult. Just like here in the physical world, it's a two-way street. Everything depends on the particular relationship they have together.

The Earthbound Realm

These are four common reasons why a spirit might remain earthbound. There are others. In the end, each spirit has its own story and its own reasons for how it became stuck in this netherworld. Each earthbound spirit has become bound up in their own world of fear or ignorance or attachment. What characterizes all of them, though, is their lack of growth. They are focused in a world in which they can no longer participate.

In his book, *Far Journeys,* Robert Monroe describes seeing this earthbound realm during his out-of-body travels. In one of his experiences, he describes traveling outward from the earth. He describes it as moving through different dimensions or "rings." At one point, as he ventured further from the earth, he says he turned back and looked. What he saw was a distinct realm of spirits, but a realm closely interwoven with the physical.

> But I knew the next ring inward. It wasn't nice. Beyond that was the physical life. The two were tightly interwoven, the thick ring just slightly out of phase with physical matter. It was the interface between one reality system and another. Even from this perspective, it was difficult for a novice to distinguish instantly the differences in the two. But I could.
>
> That was the problem. The inhabitants of this ring couldn't. They didn't or couldn't or wouldn't realize they were no longer physical. They were physically dead. No more physical body. Thus they kept trying to be physical, to do and be what they had been, to continue physical one way or another. Bewildered, some spent all their activity in attempting to communicate with friends and loved ones still in bodies or with anyone else who might come along, all to no avail. Others were held attracted to physical sites in which they instilled great meaning or importance during their previous human lifetime. . . .
>
> Still others interpreted their change in status as simply a bad dream or nightmare, and were waiting and hoping to wake up soon.[1]

Dr. Raymond Moody, a psychiatrist, also writes about earthbound spirits in his book *Life after Life, The Investigation of a Phenomenon—Survival of Bodily Death.* His information is based on the reports by some of his patients who had a near-death-experience. Many of these patients reported seeing spirits who existed at a different level, or in another dimension, than they or the spirits who came to them from the Light. In his book, *Reflections on Life After Life,* Moody describes what he calls, "the realm of bewildered spirits."

> Several people have reported to me that at some point they glimpsed other beings who seemed to be "trapped" in an apparently most unfortunate state of existence. Those who described seeing these confused beings are in agreement on several points. First, they state that those beings seemed to be, in effect, unable to surrender their attachments to the physical world. One man recounted that the spirits he saw apparently "couldn't progress on the other side because their God is still living here." That is, they seemed bound to some particular object, person, or habit. Secondly, all have remarked that these beings appeared "dulled," that their consciousness seemed limited in contrast with that of others. Thirdly, they say it appeared that these "dulled spirits" were to be there only until they solved whatever problem or difficulty was keeping them in that perplexed state. . . .
>
> Some persons who have seen this phenomenon have noticed certain of these beings apparently trying unsuccessfully to communicate with persons who were still physically alive. One man related many instances he observed while he was "dead" for an extended period of time. For example, he told how he saw an ordinary man walking, unaware, down the street while one of these dulled spirits hovered above him. He said he had the feeling that this spirit had been, while alive, the man's mother, and, still unable to give up her earthly role, was trying to tell her son what to do.[2]

For these spirits, the physical world is no longer their world, but they have not let it go. You could say they are *of* this world, but not *in* it.

Outside and Inside

These observations—and there are many more like them in the literature—point to an objective realm, but one that is nonphysical. "Just out of phase with our own," as Monroe says. For those who have observed this realm, like Monroe and Dr. Moody's patients, the spirits appear to have an objective reality. They have their own human bodies, only they are *etheric* bodies, not physical. These spirits appear to continue to identify with their bodies and the human life just lived. The reports also suggest that these spirits "attach" themselves to people or places as a kind of grounding into the physical reality. When a person reports seeing a ghost or apparition, hearing a voice, or feeling a presence, it is often this kind of earthbound spirit that he or she is sensing.

There is, however, another kind of earthbound spirit that is not so easily discernible. These are spirits that do not attach to someone, but appear to "enter" a person's energy field and "inhabit" them. The attached spirit is one that seems to retain a strong identification with the physical world. They might sit across the room from a person or travel from one family member to another. Inhabiting spirits, on the other hand, seem to enter into a person's "psychic space." They are present somehow *within* the person's mind. Technically, *attached* and *inhabiting* spirits are both earthbound, but they exist in two different states or realms. In his book, *Return from Tomorrow,* George Ritchie gives a remarkable account of observing a spirit move from one state to the other.

Ritchie was a young private in World War I who became severely ill with bacterial pneumonia. He recalls the night his body died and had to be resuscitated by his doctor. It couldn't have been very long, a few minutes at most. In his book, Ritchie describes what happened in those few moments of death. He describes leaving his body and being aware of himself as a spirit, very much alive and conscious of what was happening around him. He observed people going about their business, only they were not aware of him at all. He could have shouted and waved and they would have walked right through him. In this out-of-body state, he said he wandered to several familiar places on the military base and in the surrounding area.

One of the places he visited was a bar close to the base. It was a hangout for the soldiers and the locals. Ritchie describes watching the people at the bar, but he also says that right along side these physical people he observed what he calls the "the insubstantial beings." Like others, Ritchie was observing the earthbound state and the activity of these spirits. He then describes one scene in particular that caught his attention.

> I thought I had seen heavy drinking at fraternity parties in Richmond. But the way civilians and servicemen at this bar were going at it beat everything. I watched one young sailor rise unsteadily from a stool, take two or three steps, and sag heavily to the floor. Two of his buddies stooped down and started dragging him away from the crush.

But that was not what I was looking at. I was staring in amazement as the bright cocoon around the unconscious sailor simply opened up. It parted at the very crown of his head and began peeling away from his head, his shoulders. Instantly, quicker than I'd ever seen anyone move, one of the insubstantial beings that had been standing near him at the bar was on top of him. He had been hovering like a thirsty shadow at the sailor's side, greedily following every swallow the young man made. Now he seemed to spring at him like a beast of prey.

In the next instant, to my utter mystification, the springing figure had vanished. It all happened even before the two men had dragged their unconscious load from under the feet of those at the bar. One minute I'd distinctly seen two individuals; by the time they propped the sailor against the wall, there was only one.

Twice more, as I stared, stupefied, the identical scene was repeated. A man passed out, a crack swiftly opened in the auriole around him, one of the non-solid people vanished as he hurled himself at that opening, almost as if he had scrambled inside the other man.[3]

Ritchie could see the spirit enter the sailor, but he could not see what happened after that point. From Ritchie's point of view, the spirit simply "vanished." We don't have the language yet to describe these phenomena where one conscious entity inhabits another and interacts with a person at these more subtle levels. If I had to put it into words I would say that the spirit somehow resides within the matrix of a person's consciousness and energy.

This distinction between spirits who "attach" and those who "inhabit" is not, as far as I am aware, clearly drawn in the literature on spirits. It seems to me, though, that it is an important distinction. In my work with clients, I have dealt with both kinds of spirits. It is usually the inhabiting spirits, though, who cause the most problems for people. Operating from the inside, so to speak, these spirits can affect a person much more directly and intimately than those who attach. Depending on the intention of the inhabiting spirit, they could do anything from just living off a person's energy to figuring out ways to exercise some degree of control.

In one of my earlier sessions with Gerod, before I made any distinction between *attached* and *inhabiting spirits,* I explored this issue with him.

Session #66—January 6, 1989

T. I don't know where I read this now, but it was that when a person dies and leaves the physical body, there is still the etheric body, and someone may try to hang on to their etheric body. It's as though once they leave the physical body, they must also detach or let go of this etheric body. Is that the same thing?

G. It is somewhat. The spirits that are earthbound, before they attach to a person, they walk around, they look at their hands, they see their body still. They might see their body lying dead on a table or a floor or the road, but they also look and see the body surrounding their soul and it is perfect, and they quite often cannot let go of that body. If they never let go of that body, they are never going to go to the Light. There is talk of people going to the Light with their body and seeing their loved ones in the bodies that are familiar. These bodies are not etheric bodies. These are bodies of thought. The etheric body is at a different vibratory level than an earth body and it is very different from a spirit body. A spirit body can envision, imagine, create for itself any body that it wishes if it wishes to have a body. And so, if you get close to the Light and you are in a body, it is not an etheric body because if you are in the Light in the spirit realm you have left the etheric behind.

T. Gerod, when I'm working with the earthbound spirits, then, are they still within an etheric body?

G. Most often they are. If they take up residence so to speak within someone, they have to let go of that body in a way because it is very hard to jam a third body into a physical body. So usually they leave the etheric body and it will dissolve, but they take into the new human body they are inhabiting, all the memory, all the record, all the physical complaints of their body. And they tend to try to have that new physical body adhere to the memory and impression of what their body was. That is why an earthbound spirit can often create physical ailments for a presently living earth body.

Several weeks later, I came back to this issue with Gerod.

Session #73—February 21, 1989

T. Gerod, why do earthbound spirits who attach to someone seem to stay with that person rather than roam and explore? Is there some need there for energy or is it because of fear . . . ?

G. Comfort, security, familiarity, establishing life again, and it becomes more solid, more comfortable and secure when you stay in one place and you get to know the person with whom you are inhabiting.

T. Companionship?

G. Companionship, but also predictability. The spirit knows what will be going on in its life, so to say. It's almost like it has a life. It gets to know the person it is living with; it is able to begin to influence that person. The longer it is with an individual, then the greater the influence it can exert and it becomes more and more like actual life itself. Spirits who are earthbound also have needs. They are earthbound because they have fears, they have needs, and it is usually best met within the framework of one where they can establish themselves, establish an identity.

Gerod was talking about a spirit entering a person. He said that a spirit could let go of its etheric body and create a thought body. "A spirit body can envision, imagine, create for itself any body that it wishes if it wishes to have a body." This *thought body,* according to Gerod, is the one that goes into the Light. He was also saying a spirit could "enter" someone as a thought body. I had no concepts for what Gerod was describing. I didn't know what kinds of bodies were possible for spirits or how one could "enter" a living person.

Possession is probably the closest word we have to describe this state, but this is not actually possession. Normally, an earthbound spirit does not intend to take complete control of a person's will. They may try to control a person in certain areas or influence them in certain ways, but they are not trying to take possession. I would also add that each person has their own immunities and defenses against the intrusion of spirits. I will take up this issue of vulnerability more fully in a later chapter. For now, I would just observe that earthbound spirits, generally speaking, do not have the knowledge or the ability to carry out an assault such as possession even if they wanted. They can become mean or insistent, and they can create quite a disturbance, demonic possession, though, is usually not the issue.

Inhabiting spirits are more interested in continuing their own life rather than taking over someone else's. They are looking for a host, someone compatible with their needs and energy. They often do not see the harm or disruption that their presence causes for a person, or if they do, they either don't care or they have an excuse for it. Once an earthbound spirit enters a person, they might withdraw again into their own world of memories or preoccupations and be only peripherally aware of the host's conscious reality. Alternately, some inhabiting spirits stay very aware of the person's conscious reality and will even try to participate in it.

The Light

When I first recognized that earthbound spirits might be affecting some of my clients, I was not interested in trying to understand them. My primary aim was to make them leave. Mine was a clinical point of view. Once I was convinced that earthbound spirits existed and could be involved with people, I had to determine whether they could be affecting a client. I did not know how the presence of a spirit *caused* a headache, or *spoke* in a voice audible only to my client, or triggered a panic attack at the sight of an automobile accident, for example. I did not have trouble believing, though, that consciousness was capable of these effects. My experience with alter-personalities had already convinced me of that. The idea of a spirit as a separate consciousness having the same kind of effect on a person as an alter-personality was not a great leap. In my own mind, though, the bottom line was that if you remove the separate consciousness, then you remove its effects.

As it turned out, I did have to understand these spirits in order to know what would persuade them to leave. Trying to force a spirit to vacate a client is a highly unreliable enterprise. Usually it does not work, and if it does, the spirits often return once everything has settled down again. If I was belligerent, trying to scare them away, they might get belligerent right back, or just suddenly withdraw into silence. I learned early on that bluffing was not going to work.

Since I could not force them out or tell my clients how to make them leave, I had to find a way to persuade them. I had to give them a good enough reason not only to communicate with me but also to agree in the end to leave of their own accord. From the beginning, Gerod had described these spirits as stuck, misguided, or lost and suggested that I direct them to the Light. He said they belonged in the spirit realm of Light, and as souls, they were already beings of Light and possessed the knowledge of that within themselves. I just needed to remind them of that.

Session #2—January 16, 1988

G. You may ask if there are spirits present in hypnosis similar to the way you do with multiple personality; you most likely will get a response if you ask directly. I don't believe most would volunteer themselves but if you pointedly ask you most likely will receive a response, for these earthbound spirits are curious and enjoy attention. Once you have their attention, if you wish to engage conversation, you may be able to do so. This will depend somewhat on the hypnotic state of your client and the degree to which they and their will are cooperative, but at that point of identifying that a spirit is present, you may ask that spirit to vacate and take itself directly to the Light.

T. Gerod, in working with an earthbound spirit, when you talk about trying to help them move toward the Light, is it that, with effort, any earthbound spirit will be able to locate the Light?

G. That's right. All souls have within them that potential to develop their very, very highest level. The earthbound spirit is the soul that has forgotten what it is supposed to do or never quite knew what it was supposed to do and it has the potential for very high-level work just as any soul does. And that's why with any soul that is earthbound, you are doing them a great service when you can send them on their way to the Light. They deserve that help too.

Gerod's position was that these souls belonged in the Light and once they opened themselves to that Light they would know too that that is where they belonged.

Gerod talked about the earthbound realm and the plight of those spirits who exist there.

Session #66—January 6, 1989

There are so many beings who do not seem to understand who they are, what they are, where they are going, and what they should be doing. And then what happens is they become trapped in that netherworld, that world that is nothing, that world that is not earth, that world that is not the spirit realm. They wander and rattle and create excruciating pain for themselves, and so what you do is you free them and you help to free others.

Later, in that same session:

> The spirit realm is a fine-line cross over into the Light. The spirit realm is a commitment to grow. It is a commitment to the Light. The astral realm is a very transitory, less positive place.
>
> When a body dies, there is the Light. A person can see the Light. If they follow the Light they will go straight to the spirit realm, right through the astral-plane. There is a long tunnel with a Light at the end. If you take your eyes from the Light, you may end up in that astral-plane which is also very close to earth and you bring yourself to the earth.

I could not see this Light Gerod talked about, but he assured me that a spirit could see it if it chose.

The closest thing I had to compare this to was the descriptions of "the light" given by people who had had a near-death experience (NDE). These are people who had suffered some trauma like an accident or abuse and later reported that during the trauma they had left their body but continued to be fully conscious and aware. The majority of these people also reported that upon leaving the body, they moved through a tunnel and into a light, or at least to the edge of the Light, and then returned to the body. What they described about being in the light was an overwhelming feeling of love and oneness with all that is. They had little or no concern for the body. The comfort, harmony, and reassurance that each felt in the light was so complete that most of them reported a strong desire to stay. Each of them felt—even after returning to their body—that the Light was real, and it was where they ultimately belonged. Most reported that they finally did return to their physical body because they somehow *knew* there was more they needed to do in their earthly life. Fear of death was no longer a concern. In fact, they know when the time is right that they will welcome a return to that Light.

In his book, *Closer to the Light,* Dr. Melvin Morse, a pioneer in NDE research with children, cites numerous case studies from his own practice. One report involved a fourteen-year-old boy who left his body in the face of what appeared to be imminent death. The car in which he was riding was swept off a bridge by raging floodwaters and the terror and confusion of the moment appeared to trigger his experience.

I knew I was either dead or going to die. But then something happened. It was so immense, so powerful, that I gave up on my life to see what it was. I wanted to venture into this experience which started as a drifting into what I could only describe as a long rectangular tunnel of light. But it wasn't just light, it was a protective passage of energy with an intense brightness at the end of which I wanted to look into, to touch.

As I reached the source of the Light, I could see in. I cannot begin to describe in human terms the feelings I had over what I saw. It was a giant infinite world of calm, and love, and energy, and beauty. It was as though human life was unimportant compared to this. And yet it urged the importance of life at the same time it solicited death as a means to a different and better life. It was all being, all beauty, all meaning for all existence. It was all the energy of the Universe forever in one place.

As I reached my right hand into it, feelings of exhilarating anticipation overwhelmed me. I did not need my body anymore. I wanted to leave it behind, if I hadn't already, and go to my God in this new world.[4]

Another description of this Light is by Albert Heim, a Swiss professor of geology, who writes about his near-death-experience in a mountain climbing accident in 1871. This account is quoted in Colin Wilson's, *The Afterlife*:

Mental activity became enormous, rising to a hundred-fold velocity . . . I saw my whole past life take place in many images, as though on a stage at some distance from me . . . Everything was transfigured as though by a heavenly light, without anxiety and without pain. The memory of very tragic experiences I had had was clear but not saddening. I felt no conflict or strife; conflict had been transmuted into love. Elevated and harmonious thoughts dominated and untied individual images, and like magnificent music a divine calm swept through my soul.[5]

The last example is from Margot Grey, who later founded the International Association for Near-Death Studies in Great Britain. While on a trip to India, she had become severely ill and was near death for several weeks. At some point in the crisis, she reports leaving her body and what happens afterwards.

I remember looking at my body lying on the bed and feeling completely unperturbed by the fact that it seemed likely that I was going to die in a strange country . . . but thinking that it was totally unimportant where I left my body, which I felt had served me well and like a favorite worn out coat had at last outlived its usefulness and would now have to be discarded. . . .

Later on, I seemed to be traveling down an endless tunnel; I could see a pinpoint of light at the end of the tunnel towards which I seemed to be moving . . . I remember knowing with absolute certainty that I would eventually be through the tunnel and would emerge into the light, which was like the light of a very bright star, but much more brilliant. A sense of exaltation was accompanied by a feeling of being very close to the 'source' of life and love, which seemed to be one.[6]

There are thousands of reports like this from people all over the world and throughout history.

This was the light I thought about when Gerod suggested that I "direct spirits to the Light." In effect, he was saying that the Light was the natural solution to the interference by earthbound spirits. By directing a spirit to the Light, I would be helping it find its way. My clients, in turn, would be relieved of its presence and its effects. It was a win/win proposition.

Confirmation of the Light

I had the opportunity to confirm Gerod's statements as soon as I began to work with spirits directly. In those first few months after meeting Gerod, I had identified several cases involving earthbound spirits. In each case, I brought up the issue of the Light as early as I could and communicated to the spirit, or spirits, that they should move to the Light. For those spirits who saw the Light and experienced it, the reaction was immediate. They either left immediately upon that first contact with the Light or became very willing to negotiate their leaving. I could not tell you what happened when a spirit experienced the Light, but whatever it was, like those who had a near-death-experience, it changed them. From that moment on, they wanted to go. This was the consistent response that I observed from earthbound spirits. Once they experienced the Light, it was only a matter of time before they left.

Two cases stand out in my mind. The first involved Deborah T. She was thirty-eight, divorced, and worked in a government office.

Her sixteen year-old daughter, Jan, had recently left and moved in with her father, so she could be closer to her boyfriend. Deborah also had recently terminated a relationship with a man she had been dating just as the relationship began to become intimate. Deborah was aware she was "putting up walls" to any potential relationship but she didn't know why.

In our early therapy sessions, I explored these different relationships with Deborah and it soon became clear that she harbored an intense fear of rejection. Her fear was especially triggered in situations where she had to confront someone and say no to them or have to draw the line. She was always afraid that these situations would erupt into conflict. For Deborah, every conflict carried with it the threat of rejection. From her children to her ex-husband, to the people in the office, and especially with Don, the man she was dating, Deborah had to keep everybody happy. If she said the wrong thing, did the wrong thing, or did something to upset the other person, she risked their rejection and the loss of their love. Consciously, Deborah knew her relationships were not that fragile. At an unconscious level, however, this was always the fear. She constantly felt in danger of being abandoned.

The fear of rejection is not uncommon in people, but for Deborah it was extreme. Once we began to focus on her fear, Deborah recognized that it had been a part of her life for a long time. She also began to recognize the extent to which it had controlled her life and affected her relationships. She saw how her anxiety was triggered at the slightest threat of confrontation and how, at an unconscious level, she would begin to avoid such situations. When conflict did occur, she saw how often she wound up either apologizing, dissolving into tears, or becoming so overbearing that she provoked an attack.

At this point, Deborah's therapy shifted to helping her develop the skills and insight she needed to change these patterns. I taught her several techniques for dealing with her anxiety before and after a confrontation or conflict. These included especially techniques involving deep breathing, relaxation, and rehearsal imagery. I also taught her ways to remain psychologically and emotionally centered during a confrontation.

Deborah was a quick study and began to put into practice what she had learned. On a selective basis, she began to confront key people in her life and learned that she could handle it. One success built on another. As a result, Deborah became more confident, and she began to feel better about herself and her relationships with others.

The issue, however, continued to be her anxiety. While her overall anxiety level had diminished, Deborah continued to report episodes of intense anxiety. While these episodes were less frequent, and the relaxation techniques helped her cope, they were still painful.

I had recently begun using hypnosis with Deborah in order to explore possibly deeper causes of this anxiety. In our first session, I identified a sixteen-year-old ego-state. Initially, the ego-state was frightened and did not want to communicate. Reassuring her that I was there to help, the sixteen year-old finally did respond to several questions and shared a memory. Deborah remembered the time at home with her parents after they discovered she had had sex with her boyfriend. What made the experience even more painful was that it had been her first sexual experience. When she had returned home that night, and the parents had surmised what had happened, she came under full attack.

When I began to ask 16 year-old about this experience and to have her share more, she became afraid again. I tried to ask about her fear and then all signals stopped. In the rest of that session and the next I tried to communicate with 16yo without triggering her fear, but it wasn't working. At some point in that frustrating process, my intuition was that this might be a situation where a spirit—in this case, Deborah's mother, Elaine—was interfering.

Elaine had died five years before, and she had come up in our sessions more than a few times. Deborah had described her mother as very critical of her all her life. When Elaine was upset, she often said things that made Deborah feel guilty, ashamed, and humiliated. If Deborah tried to defend herself and criticize her mother's position or perception, Elaine would quickly escalate from anger to emotional threats of rejection. It's not that Elaine did this consciously. She had her own issues about criticism and self-worth. While Deborah felt that she and her mother were close in some ways, this remained a very touchy area in their relationship.

Before taking any action in therapy, I wanted to see if Gerod would confirm the presence of a spirit or not. I called Katharine and she agreed to channel Gerod herself that night and let me know the next day. I did not tell Katharine my suspicions about Elaine, but only my concerns that a spirit might be present. When I saw Katharine the next day, she gave me Gerod's reply.

Katharine, you may tell Tom this. Yes, Deborah is beset with a troubled spirit that needs gentle reminding of the fact that it is not where it should be. This is a strong spirit but one wise enough to know it should go on with higher work. However, it seems confused as how to get out of the place it is in. We can discuss this further if you should wish to do so.

In my next session with Deborah, when the interference began again with 16 year-old, I asked whether "the one blocking" was separate from Deborah. After some hesitation, I saw the yes finger lift. After giving some reassurance that I was there to help, I asked several more questions about its awareness and identity. Based on these responses, I was convinced that this was Deborah's mother. I communicated with her about the need for her to move on, about how her presence may be affecting her daughter, and the need for Deborah to get on with her own life. When I directed Elaine to look for the Light, she signaled quickly that she could see it, and she wanted to go. After the session, Deborah told me that she knew it was her mother, and they had been able to have some resolution before her mother left.

Once Elaine went to the Light, it became safe for 16yo to share her experience with Deborah. She shared how angry she was at her mother for taking her dad's side that night when she had come home from being with her boyfriend. For 16yo, her mother's alliance with dad was an act of betrayal and abandonment all in one. She was hurt, angry, and afraid. With Elaine actually present, there was no way 16yo was going to communicate about this or share it with Deborah. She was afraid if she shared these feelings or suggested that Elaine was wrong, it could trigger her mother's wrath and then the threats and blame would rain down. So, during the therapy session, she kept quiet. Once her mother left, however, 16yo was able to share her feelings and reactions.

In our session, Deborah experienced the catharsis and emotional release of 16yo. She could release the shame and hurt, the fear and anger, which were bound up inside her. More importantly, Deborah felt that she could open herself to the joy and pleasure of that night in discovering her own sexuality. There was more inner work to do after resolving the presence of this spirit and the trauma at sixteen, but these were two major pieces in Deborah's healing process.

The second case involved Marianne, a woman in her late fifties, whose husband had committed suicide two years earlier. Her immediate complaint was disturbed sleep, along with episodes of anxiety. She had tried traditional therapy and sleeping pills, neither of which had really solved her problem. She had been referred to me because she wanted to try hypnosis. In our initial session, Marianne pinpointed the onset of her troubled sleep to shortly after her husband's death. She thought that maybe subconsciously she was feeling guilty about Larry's death, that maybe she hadn't done enough for him or had failed him. It didn't seem that way to her consciously, she said, but it's how she felt.

During our first hypnosis session, there was very strong blocking and confusion. Finger signals were established easily enough, but my questions around the sleep issue were not getting clear or consistent responses. I had already considered the possibility that Marianne's husband had remained earthbound, and the interference I encountered only served to strengthen that suspicion.

Since I was still tentative about how to do all this, I talked to Gerod about my suspicions. His reading of the situation was most interesting.

Session #3—January 22, 1988

Marianne is visited very frequently by the spirit of her husband. He is very earthbound. She needs to let him go and he needs to let go also. He is not with her all the time as he wanders quite often. I would wonder if there are not other people in the family who are disturbed also. He seems to visit her more in the night. That energy causes disturbance in the sleep pattern. I shouldn't wonder that she's not getting enough rest. Once again, it's a matter of talking with the spirit to let it know that it is creating a disturbance and to let the soul know that it is time to go where it belongs for its continued growth and development. I think that if it goes she will feel very much better and it's quite possible that there are other people in the family who will also. As I said, this soul is wandering quite a bit, and I am sure there are other people to whom it is appearing. I think you could talk with her about this to get her sense of it.

I saw Marianne again the next week. I did not share with her my suspicions. I believed that telling her ahead of time could trigger all kinds of reactions, conscious and unconscious. I also did not want Marianne having to take a conscious position on the question of earthbound spirits and her husband before we did the hypnosis. I wanted to ask questions during the session that only a separate spirit would understand and be able to follow. I believed that this was the only reliable way I had to confirm a spirit's presence or not, that is, by keeping it independent of Marianne's preconceptions and/or my suggestions. By telling Marianne ahead of time about my suspicions, I was concerned that during the session I might get back an elaborated version of what I had told her. This would do neither of us any good. If I was going to be able to confirm the truth of her husband's presence to Marianne, I had to first confirm it to myself.

In the next session with Marianne, once she had entered trance, the interference started again. I asked whether the one who was interfering was separate from Marianne. There was a strong yes signal, and I continued through several more questions. I became convinced that I was communicating with Larry. When I asked him to look for the Light, he signaled that he had found it. I asked whether it felt all right to him, and I received a yes. I suggested to him that the Light was where he needed to go. Keeping in mind what Gerod had said, I talked to him about the effects his presence could have on Marianne and other loved ones. By this time, Marianne had become aware consciously of what was happening, and she was in tears. I suggested that they say good-bye in whatever way they needed to, and then he left.

Following the session, Marianne and I talked about what had occurred. She seemed relieved but struggled to come to terms with what had just happened. In the next couple of weeks, Marianne's sleep improved significantly and she reported much less anxiety and a greater sense of peace. Shortly after this, we terminated therapy with the understanding that she would call if needed.

I had several other cases where the same thing happened. Once a spirit had been identified and directed to experience the Light, it changed. As overused as the word seems sometimes, the best way I can term the change is to say the spirit became *enlightened*. However it happened, the Light gave these spirits a new perception, and they liked it. I observed this change enough times to convince me that the Light was a reality to them. It confirmed for me what Gerod and those who had a near-death-experience had said about the Light: it's where souls belong.

7

The Quickening

Don Juan explained to me that, for us to perceive those other realms, not only do we have to covet them but we need to have sufficient energy to seize them. Their existence is constant and independent of our awareness, he said, but their inaccessibility is entirely a consequence of our energetic conditioning. In other words, simply and solely because of that conditioning, we are compelled to assume that the world of daily life is the one and only possible world.—Carlos Castaneda, from *The Art of Dreaming*

Across the Line

When I first started working with earthbound spirits, it was a clinical decision. I viewed these spirits as intruders, much as a physician would view invading bacteria. Unlike disease organisms invading the body, however, earthbound spirits appeared somehow to invade a person's mind and consciousness. Spirits affected people differently than bacteria did, but the issue was the same: another life form had breached the boundaries of self and was creating a problem or imbalance in the host, my client. I assumed that the removal of an intruding spirit would alleviate its effects on my client and allow the breach to be healed.

The remedy for this intrusion—*the penicillin*—was the Light. Gerod said that when I encountered a spirit, "direct it to the Light." He said it is the spirit realm of light, and a spirit can see it if it chooses. When I put this into practice, the results were unequivocal. Once a spirit chose to see the Light, it did. And almost every time, it would embrace the Light and be gone. It's as though there was an immediate shift in its

consciousness and it awakened to a new level. If it did not go imme-
diately, it would usually take only a little reassurance and it would go.
Clinically, it was a simple formula. By assisting spirits in going to the
Light, my clients were being cleared of the intrusion, *the infection.*

Although I did not understand the power of the Light to precipitate
this immediate change in a spirit, I thought about it in the terms used
by people to describe a mystical experience, a religious conversion, or
a near-death-experience. They used terms like "total love," "perfect
understanding," "oneness" and "peace." I believe everyone has had such
an experience of the Light in his or her life. A moment of bliss, being
in love, feeling everything is right with the world. The psychologist
Abraham Maslow called them *peak experiences.* When I directed spirits
to the Light, I believed this is what they experienced. In my mind, I was
not only clearing my client, but I was directing the spirit home to God.

From the beginning, however, I encountered some spirits who
resisted or refused any experience of the Light. They could see it, they
knew what I was talking about, but they would not approach it or
let it touch them. In effect, they were not going to allow that change
or conversion to occur. And that meant, of course, that they usually
intended to remain with my client.

This refusal to accept the Light, therefore, became a focal point in
dealing with spirits. If a spirit did refuse the Light, then I would ask
questions designed to explore and identify why they were refusing. I
believed that if I could understand *why,* then I could help talk them
through any fears or doubts that were in their way. I believed that if I
could persuade a spirit that it was safe to at least *try* the Light, then the
Light would take care of the rest. This thinking and approach guided
my communication with spirits. As a therapist, the promise of the Light
was still my greatest leverage in having spirits leave.

In theory and in practice, this approach appeared sound. It worked
well. The problem, though, was that it did not go far enough. I made
the mistake of assuming that the spirits I encountered through my work
with clients had only two choices: they could either exist in the earthbound state—which I viewed as a place of discontent or numbness—or
they could go to the Light, where everything would feel right and make
sense for them. I believed that I could talk them *into* an experience of
the Light or talk them *out of* their resistance, or both. This assumption

that there were only two choices gave me a false sense of security. I saw my role as the ferryman, the facilitator, between two realms. In my mind, the distinction between my world, the earthbound realm, and the Light was very clear.

Five months after meeting Gerod, however, several things happened which tore apart these clear boundaries and sent me spiraling into deeper realms of mind and spirit. The first thing that happened was that another counselor I recently met had recommended that I read a book entitled *The Unquiet Dead,* written by Edith Fiore, Ph.D. a psychologist practicing in California. Her book was subtitled: *A Psychologist Treats Spirit Possession—Detecting and Removing Earthbound Spirits.*

The Unquiet Dead

I obtained a copy of *The Unquiet Dead* within days after it was recommended, and I read it in one sitting. I was transfixed and read it with growing excitement. Here was a psychologist writing about her own encounters with earthbound spirits as she worked with clients using hypnosis. She also described the techniques she used in dealing with them. In a matter-of-fact way, Dr. Fiore talked about *who* these spirits were and *how* they became earthbound.

> I viewed the possessing entities as the true patients. They are suffering greatly, perhaps without even realizing it. Virtual prisoners, they are trapped on the earth plane feeling exactly as they did moments before their deaths, which may have occurred decades before. They do not seem to profit from any positive activities or education that their hosts have experienced throughout their lives since the possession. Moreover they are keeping themselves from being in the spirit world which would offer them a beautiful life and afford them the opportunity to make spiritual progress.[1]

She discussed what made people vulnerable to spirit intrusion and described the kinds of effects spirits can have on a person. She also included a technique and format for what she called depossession.[2] Dr. Fiore instructed the reader on how to prepare for a depossession and essentially what to communicate to the spirit during the procedure. The following is an excerpt from that procedure.

Impress upon him that he is a spirit, cohabiting your body since his own body died, and remind him of the circumstances of his death. Tell him that we are all spirits and never die—that only the physical body dies. Explain that upon his physical death he found himself outside his body, completely conscious, at which time he should have gone directly to the spirit world, where his loved ones were waiting for him. Instead, he joined you. State that, without realizing it, he has been harming you by draining your energy and confusing you, since you cannot tell his thoughts and emotions from your own.[3]

Dr. Fiore described a number of different scenarios one might encounter with earthbound spirits and what approaches to take with them. She had obviously been in the same spot as me at one time but had since covered a lot of territory. She cited numerous examples from her own clinical practice, including five case studies.

My shock upon reading the book was the shock of recognition. So much of what she described was what I had encountered in my own work with clients. I knew exactly what she was talking about. It was a deep confirmation of my own work with clients and the reality of spirits. Her descriptions and extensive commentary brought the world of spirits to life for me. Where I had worked with a dozen earthbound spirits, she had worked with hundreds. Her understanding and experience went far beyond mine. She answered so many of my questions and explained so much about spirits that the knowledge lifted me into a new level of understanding, literally overnight. She revealed to me a world that resonated as true—theoretically, clinically and personally. *The Unquiet Dead* became a guide into these realms that I had just begun to explore. It offered a more detailed map of the areas in which I had been working and wandering.

After reading *The Unquiet Dead,* I felt more prepared and willing to address the issue of spirits in my own practice. I began to use Dr. Fiore's depossession technique immediately in my client cases where a spirit had already been identified. As a basic model, the technique worked well and deepened my conviction about the course I was on.

From Writing to Speaking

Before the full impact of Dr. Fiore's book could have time to register, something else occurred that radically altered my relationship with

Gerod and led to an explosion of information. In the first week of January 1988, Katharine told me that she might be able to channel Gerod verbally. She said she felt more *guided* to do this rather than as something she needed to do. She said she was nervous about it. She had tried it with her husband, and it had seemed to go all right. Now she was willing to try it in one of our sessions. The idea that Gerod and I might be able to communicate verbally had never occurred to me. I was excited by the prospect and told Katharine I was willing to try it whenever she was ready. We agreed to meet the next week, prepared to have either kind of session, written or verbal, depending on how Katharine felt.

Katharine did channel verbally in that next meeting and it was another shock. I did not know she could 'step aside' and let Gerod assume the voice but that was exactly what seemed to happen. It was like meeting someone with whom you've only corresponded through letters. Upon speaking with them personally, you *know* it is they. I could sense Gerod's presence in the way he moved and talked, but the deeper shock came in how much Gerod was able to communicate.

The first question I asked him, for example, was about earthbound spirits. This was still a major focus in my work with clients and it was also familiar territory between Gerod and me.

Session #1—January 9, 1988

T. I've been thinking about this whole issue of involvement of earthbound spirits in peoples' lives. When an earthbound spirit is involved in someone's life, what can we expect to be the effect on a person's life?

G. The effects upon your clients or the effects upon yourself?

T. Well, both.

G. Earthbound spirits are much more common than most people would realize. A lot of the problems that people have in life are associated with these earthbound spirits. And it is up to the individual to ferret out for themselves which part is themselves and which part is spirit, and your role would be to help them determine which is which. The effect that a spirit has upon someone's life is the constant confusion of separating thoughts. . . . (Pause.) A spirit will inflict its thought upon a person and then a person is not sure of who's doing the thinking, themselves or the earthbound spirit, but they're not even aware of this unless they're aware that there's another thought process taking place.

Of course the confusion then causes many other problems in their life: a dissociation with reality, dissociation with being able to commit in relationships. There is also the chance that they will not adhere to any type of reality that is one that will function well for their needs.

This information was delivered spontaneously, with one pause. Gerod spoke with a tone of authority as though he knew what he was talking about. This impression also came through the facial expressions and the gestures as he talked. It felt to me that Gerod was actually present and that he was in full control of the voice as well. The entire dialogue felt the same. Gerod and I went back and forth as easily as two friends sitting down to talk.

What impressed me most about this shift from automatic writing to verbal dialogue was the quickening of the pace and the depth of our discussions. Gerod could say more in a few minutes than he could have written in ten or fifteen minutes. I could go back and forth with him asking him to clarify a term or elaborate on a particular point he had made. I could interrupt him on the spot if he said something that confused me or contradicted my thinking. We could take off on tangents and then come back to the original problem. This kind of verbal dialogue freed me to explore theoretical and clinical issues with Gerod in a way that the automatic writing could not.

Until this time, I had been forced into a more passive role with Gerod. Because of the limitations of the automatic writing, it just wouldn't do to get caught up in clarifications and precise definitions. I had to choose carefully what line of questioning to pursue or it could quickly eat up every session. Being able to dialogue with Gerod verbally changed all that. I could ask him whatever I wanted and, if his response didn't make sense, I could explore further. If he couldn't tell me something, I would talk to him about why not. What was so remarkable in this shift to verbal dialogue, then, was not in the talking, but what the talking allowed me to do. I could ask many more questions, get more specific, and start to test the limits of Gerod's information. The verbal exchange allowed me to take a more active role in my dialogues with Gerod.

While working with Gerod and my clients, I continually questioned the existence of a larger reality in which all these issues and phenomena would make sense. Over the next four months, Gerod and I met eighteen times. We had a running dialogue from week to week. I began to talk to my clients about Gerod, and soon Gerod and I were focusing on clinical cases.

With the freedom that verbal dialogue brought, Gerod and I began to cover a great deal of territory. We talked about the *soul* as well as the conscious and unconscious mind. We talked about low-lying spirits and evil spirits. With some clients, Gerod talked about the effects of past life experiences. With three clients, he talked about interference by extraterrestrial beings. He talked about the soul having some ability to shield itself from evil while incarnate. He also talked about the "higher self," a part of each of us, he said, that knows about these spirit dimensions and knows the Light.

Realms of Spirit

A third thing happened around this same time of reading *The Unquiet Dead* and starting the verbal dialogues. In my work with clients, I was beginning to encounter beings, both attached and inhabiting, who were not earthbound spirits. They were spirits who knew about the Light but had no desire or intention of going to the Light. They knew very well that they were spirits and their presence or interference with clients was quite intentional. These were not just stubborn earthbound spirits. These were beings who *knew* what they were doing.

This question of *intent* changed everything. If an earthbound spirit could affect someone through their benign or naive presence, then what could spirits do who intentionally join a person? Why would they do that? And what do you do if they refuse to go? I had no answers to these questions.

Earthbound spirits and the Light had been my two landmarks in this unseen world. I had no doubt that I had been in communication with spirits. I also was convinced of the Light's powerful effect on the spirits who chose to experience it. These had become reliable categories in my thinking and my practice, and still are today. My task, as I saw it, was to help usher spirits to the Light and help clear any obstacles in their way. I had no category, however, for spirits who knowingly refused the Light and intentionally intruded into the minds of humans.

Low-lying Spirits

Gerod had talked about different kinds of spirits in my first session with him. However, as with so much else in those early sessions, I heard it, but it had not registered. I had been talking to Gerod about multiple personality and whether there is one soul, or whether each alter-personality had a soul. He replied that there was "only one soul," but then he went on to state the exception.

August 1, 1987—(First Written session)

> There is only one soul in the multiple person unless they are a possessed soul. You need to distinguish between the person who is "possessed"— possessed by spirits, evil, low-level, no good, mischievous or merely confused—and the earth person who has indeed created soulless personalities within themselves.

I didn't think much about these distinctions at the time, nor did I have reason to. As far as I knew, he was using the terms about spirits synonymously. But he wasn't.

I came back to these distinctions with Gerod when I began to encounter such spirits in my own practice. One of the first cases involved Ron S. Ron was thirty-three, married, and the father of two boys. He had sought therapy to help him deal with his growing anxieties and frustrations at work. He was also aware that work-related problems were not new for him. They were a pattern in his life, and he didn't know how to change it.

Until he left home at seventeen, Ron had suffered ongoing physical and verbal abuse by both of his parents. Emotionally, his was a devastating childhood and adolescence. One result of that abuse was Ron's profound feelings of inadequacy and failure. No matter what he did, Ron felt he wasn't good enough and "never would be good enough." His deep feelings of worthlessness and fear of failure were a constant struggle in Ron's life, and at times, threatened to engulf him. Ron's recent problems at work had triggered this struggle again, robbing him of his confidence, security, and self-worth.

This was the area Ron and I were exploring during a hypnosis session when I encountered a very strong block. After addressing it as a part of Ron with no success, I suspected a spirit might be blocking. When I addressed it as a spirit, the responses indicated it may be a genuine communication but the responses were not consistent enough for me to be sure. I asked Gerod about the block. He did see a spirit present and went on to describe it. He called it a "low-lying spirit."

Session #3—January 22, 1988

G. With Ron, you will find that there is a spirit involved. This spirit is mischievous and will give you a bit of a run, and Ron also. This spirit is one that does not know him. It is one that is low-lying, most definitely. It is aware that it should be in the spirit realm. It knows how to get there, and it knows where the Light is. He knows how to do it, but it is mischievous and a bit of a scamp. You will literally have to chase this one away. It's not looking to do harm, but just looking to stir up a little bit of excitement.

T. Can you say more about what you mean by, I "may have to chase it away?"

G. This spirit already knows all the logical arguments. It knows it is causing problems for your client. It knows it should not be here and it knows that it probably will grow more in the spirit realm and the thing of it is, it's just like an intelligent child who knows better but just doesn't want to mind. I would think that with this spirit it's kind of like chasing the child around the house. You will have to catch it. I do not know if it will talk with you directly and, if it does, it may talk back rather impudently. If it does, then as with a child, you tell it that it would have to obey you. That you are a physical being and that you have more power than it does in this reality and therefore it has to go. You may have to say it more than once or twice because, as I said, this is not particularly a misguided spirit in the sense that it doesn't know what it's doing. It most certainly does know.

I had to change my point of view and approach this spirit in a different way. The inducement of the Light, apparently, was not going to offer the advantage that it did with others. According to Gerod, the spirit already knew about the Light, and refused it. If the Light held no appeal, then I was not sure how Ron or I could force it out. Gerod said to tell the spirit directly that it had to go, that Ron and I had "more power" in the physical reality, and it had to obey. However, I could not feel this power that Gerod talked about, and I was not one to deliver an ultimatum unless I was prepared to back it up.

I saw Ron again the next week. I did not tell him about this change of tact, or what Gerod had said. Based on Gerod's information and point of view, I had prepared a number of questions for this session that I hoped would keep such a spirit engaged, even as I confronted it if necessary. Once Ron had entered trance, I asked for the "same one I communicated with last time" to come forward again. When the yes finger lifted, I started a series of questions about its identity and its intentions. The entity confirmed that he knew about the Light and wasn't interested. He also signaled that he knew he was a spirit, and that he also remembered when he first joined with Ron.

Once the communication was established, I took the first step toward confrontation. I asked whether he knew that he was violating Ron. He signaled his agreement with a yes. I told him that such violations are damaging, just as they are between humans. I told him boundaries had to be respected, and he would have to leave. I said this with as much authority as I could muster without sounding hostile or threatening. I believed I was stating a fact. I told him that Ron was aware of him now and that it was Ron's wish that he leave.

Ron, the conscious self, had by this time become very aware of what was happening. To my surprise, and Ron's, he was somehow acutely aware of this spirit. He "knew" it was separate from him, and he could even tell me some of the spirit's feelings and reactions. I continued with this approach, that is, that the spirit knew its intrusion was basically wrong, and that Ron had the "power of will" to make it leave. In the end, this strategy seemed to work. The spirit left. I did not know if it had to or whether we had just made it too uncomfortable to stay. Afterwards, Ron and I discussed his perceptions and experience of what had happened. He reported a clear awareness of this spirit and that it was separate from him. He also told me that he could tell the moment the spirit had left.

Another case of low-lying spirits involved a young mother, Fran, who wanted me to ask Gerod about her eight-year-old son, Terry. Terry was having problems at home and at school and neither the parents or the teachers were quite sure why. The next time I talked to Gerod, I asked him whether there was any information he could share about Terry and his situation.

Session #15—March 18, 1988

    G. This young son is affected by the spirits that are around his mother. Fran has attracted to herself spirits who sense a woman with great opening ability. She has a son who is very sensitive, very finely tuned. He perceives these spirits that are around also. He therefore finds it difficult to perceive reality because he is so tied into this other dimension. He is aware of it at a soul level, at an unconscious level. He would not be able to describe it to you in a very conscious way, but he is distracted. He is not able to give his full attention to what is going on around him in a conscious way because he is distracted. He hears things, he feels things with the inner eye and inner ear, and hears them with the inner mind. He is a very intelligent little boy, very loving, very warm, very special, but he is being distracted and the way to help him around this is to, at this point, remove these spirits away from his mother. And that will help him because it won't rob him of his sensitivity but there won't be spirits in such a close proximity to him and then he won't be so distracted. As he grows he may become a person who will be sensitive and aware and will develop very good skills, but it would be better if he were not distracted at this young age.

T. Gerod, are we talking here about earthbound spirits?

G. These are not earthbound spirits. These are what I call mischievous, low-lying spirits who have been to the Light and are out there being more playful than productive. It is somewhat the same treatment as with an earthbound spirit. . . . They should be in the spirit realm paying attention to what they do but they are sort of flitting about. They are very attracted to this woman because, as I say, she is an intelligent woman. She would seem to be a very good vehicle for them with which to communicate. She could communicate with them if she wished to and if she did, she would perhaps learn some interesting things, maybe even have a certain amount of communication. But these are not high-level guides and therefore I would not advise her to become too involved in communicating with them.

When I worked with Fran, we identified four spirits, one of whom she identified as her cousin, David, who had died ten years before at the age of twenty-four. David and the others seemed to travel together. He said they had been with Fran for at least a couple years. I had no idea what other people they may have been with or what else they could do in this low-lying state. I talked to David, though, about the interference their presence was causing for Terry and for Fran. David assured Fran that he had meant no harm, and they were prepared to leave. Before they left, however, Fran communicated with David mentally, and they said their good-byes. As usual, I talked to Fran afterwards about her experience of what had happened. Like Ron and others, Fran had a clear sense of these spirits, even more so, I think, since there was a personal connection.

According to Gerod, these low-lying spirits are sitting on the fence. They won't go into the Light, but they travel its fringes. They may have no business interfering with a person, but they also seem to know there are limits. With enough persistence, these souls usually will respect the conscious self's request for them to leave or, as Gerod said, it just becomes "too uncomfortable" for them to stay.

Evil Spirits

In those same months as I was learning about low-lying spirits, I was becoming aware of another kind of spirit as well. Gerod called them "evil spirits." They were malevolent, and at times, malicious. In my early contact with these kinds of spirits, I relied heavily on Gerod for information. Like with my client, Diane, only a few years ago, these spirits did not freely give out information about themselves. They were a greater challenge by far than earthbound spirits and low-lying spirits.

The first time Gerod and I talked about evil spirits at length, it concerned my client, Peter. Peter was in his mid-fifties and worked for a manufacturing company where he held a good management position. In the months before I saw him, however, Peter had become very depressed until his wife finally demanded that he seek help. I talked to Gerod about him because Peter and I were continually being blocked in our efforts to explore his situation through hypnosis. It had become clear to me over the months that whatever was going on with Peter probably involved his mother, an extremely controlling and domineering woman. It was not a surprise, then, when Gerod talked about his mother. The surprise came in *what* he said.

Session #2—January 16, 1988

Peter's relationship with his mother is one of the sources of this disturbance that is taking place. His mother is involved with an evil spirit; they transfer their energy over to him. He is not directly controlled or manipulated or even possessed by any kind of a spirit, but there is a strong influence from their relationship and the energy from her. This continues on even when they are separated. He is being watched over, so to speak, by forces that are not altogether pleasant for him. I'm not sure how I would tell you to look at this or go about working with him because it is always a situation that is more difficult when the spirit is not totally, directly involved with him.

I asked Gerod whether these spirits could be the source of the blocking I encountered in the sessions with Peter.

T. Gerod, in the hypnosis with Peter, I encountered either a strong resistance or strong confusion. Is that kind of thing part of the influence of this evil spirit?

G. Most definitely. An evil spirit is such that a person will throw up defenses and try to hold an evil spirit at bay, so to speak. Also, in doing that, he guards himself against any kind of access into his inner being. The soul will always try to protect itself and therefore will throw up a strong shield. I think that you will be able to get through that given a bit of time as Peter comes to trust you and that is perceived also by his higher self.

Gerod went on to describe this evil influence from his mother and talk about evil in general.

She doesn't even have to teach him bad things, or evil things, or speak badly of him, just the feelings are enough to set him into a turmoil about how he feels about himself and how he feels in his relationship with the rest of the world. This is a situation that does make a person rife for access by an evil spirit because it causes a lot of confusion, and eventually there can be some kind of acceptance of the situation. In possession, there is always a certain amount of turmoil and then it gives way to a certain amount of peace, like "I'm going to come in here and I'm going to bug you and drive you so crazy that the moment I give you some kind of peace or some kind of hope for an end to that situation, you will accept it . . ." and that is one way that the spirit seems to ingratiate themselves to the self. Right now, Peter is being somewhat stirred up and confused and he is successfully holding that off.

I did not understand what Gerod was saying at the time or what it might mean in Peter's life. I never did address it directly in his therapy, but I did consider it. I thought about it and reassessed what I knew about Peter and his situation in light of what Gerod was saying. My intuition told me there was something to it, but it wasn't clear, and I did not yet have a good enough framework or understanding of this kind of phenomenon to address it in Peter's therapy.

A direct confrontation with these kinds of spirits, however, did come in my work with Karen M. Karen was in her early 40's, lived alone, and taught in the public schools. She also was diagnosed with multiple personality disorder and was well aware of her multiplicity. Karen's history of abuse by her parents, and her parents' friends, was one of the most extreme cases I had seen. We explored and dealt with this living nightmare in her therapy as different personalities came forward and shared their experience and memories.

Karen was also a client who was beset by voices that were hostile and often threatened her. My attempts to identify these voices did not get very far. I asked Gerod about Karen and whether some of these voices might be spirits.

Session #5—January 29, 1988

T. Another one that we talked about briefly was Karen M. I certainly know her better now and I want to ask the question of whether there is any spirit involvement or evil involvement.

G. What I would say about this woman is that she is spirit possessed and that she is tinged with evil. She is a person, who as you have rightly said, is a shell person. She has been this way for a very long time—from shortly after birth—and she will continue to be this way until she once again, as many others have to do, makes the conscious choice to ask the spirits to leave her. She does have multiple personalities which were created at this young age to help her cope with these other "people" that seemed to be part of herself. Her descriptions of herself, as you may have noticed, are not altogether what one would expect from a person who is just describing a multiple personality. There are spirits present and you can probably communicate with these spirits to see why it is they are clinging so closely to her. They are not high-level. They are very low-level, and the evil I see is not evil in the sense of destruction or total havoc making, but it is there. Let us just say that Karen is one of those people that would be very ripe for possession by evil spirits.

When I speak of earthbound spirits I do not often use the word "possession" as it is not really quite correct to say that a person is possessed by earthbound spirits. When you are inhabited by, or you have earthbound spirits with you, they are there because you have somewhat invited them in, you have allowed them in. They are not seeking to possess you as much as they just want to be with you. A true evil spirit will wish to possess because they do not want to allow you any freedom of will. An earthbound spirit, a low-level spirit really doesn't care too much about controlling your will, they just want a place to live and quite often they don't mind your will at all because they wish to have companionship.

This confirmation by Gerod led several days later to a confrontation with two spirits presenting as adult males who were at once both arrogant and combative. I basically had to carry out an exorcism using the same techniques I had with Ron S., only many times more intense. I talked to Gerod about it a couple days later.

Session #7—February 6, 1988

T. Gerod, in experiencing those two spirits, in some ways it was like dealing with the earthbound spirits like I have with other clients but ones who somehow had crossed a line into evil. It's like they were earthbound but coming from a different level of it. Is that accurate?

G. That is accurate. The evil spirits that you encountered were at one time earthbound souls, but they also became tinged with the evil that slowly dragged them down into the darkness. It is their choice. When you read of the cases of very severe examples of possession, those evil spirits, they are souls. They were at one time a human person that lived on earth or a being from some other reality but they are a soul that has crossed that line because it is what for some reason appeals to their sense of being.

Low-lying spirits were difficult enough to understand and know how to talk to, but evil spirits and forces were far outside my range. I did not know how to think about them. I had no idea who or what they were, or what they were up to. With clients where these kinds of spirits were present, I did not know if I was dealing with isolated incidents of spirit harassment or whether there was a larger design.

The contact with evil spirits threatened the cozy arrangement in my mind between the earthbound realm, and what Gerod called the "spirit realm of Light." Evil spirits did not fit either of these categories. I didn't know where they fit. The contact with evil spirits put me in touch with another realm well beyond my comfort zone. I began to realize that in my work with earthbound spirits, I had been operating in only a small corner of the universe.

By engaging these spirits, I entered further into the unknown. I started out trying to usher earthbound spirits to the Light, and before I knew it, I was dealing with dimensions and beings, of which I knew nothing. In the coming months, with other clients, I would encounter more spirits like these. Every time I worked with one, it seemed to lead deeper into that unknown. I could no longer be certain with any given client *who* or *what* I might encounter.

Beings of Light

As I struggled to comprehend the possibility of evil spirits, I had another experience that tore open the boundaries that I held to in my mind. It happened the day I realized that I had been in direct contact with spirits from the Light. These particular spirits had come to assist an earthbound spirit with whom I was working.

Unlike with evil spirits, the idea of *helping spirits* was very familiar to me. This phenomenon had come up often in the reading I had done. Whether one called them *angels, guides, beings of Light,* or *loved ones,* I believed they were real. Gerod had already said in one of our early sessions that every soul that incarnates has a spirit guide to assist them during their life. According to Gerod, there were myriad souls in the Light, and they existed at different levels and served the purposes of the Light in many different ways.

A number of earthbound spirits I worked with had reported seeing these helping spirits waiting for them in the Light. It didn't happen every time, and I could not predict when it would happen. When it did happen, though, in almost all cases, it was helpful. These helping spirits appeared to be the same kind of spirit beings encountered by people in the near-death-experience, only in those cases, they are usually counseling the person against making his or her transition. Instead, their efforts are intended to guide the soul back to their body and their life on earth.

Then one day, while working with a client, I realized that these helping spirits could hear me and respond. I cannot recall now the specific session or the exact moment but I was working with an earthbound spirit who, despite all my encouragements, was still reluctant to go to the Light. At some point, I made a specific request of the helping spirits and, according to the earthbound spirit I was working with, they delivered. I don't remember whether I had asked for a specific "loved one" to come forward to make contact with the earthbound spirit, or that "further information and reassurance be given" concerning this spirit's particular fear, but the earthbound spirit was satisfied. The spirit had some kind of contact from the Light, and then was gone.

The realization that spirits in the Light could be aware of and respond to situations involving earthbound spirits immediately changed the way I worked with these lost or confused souls. These helping spirits, in fact, became one of my primary resources in assisting earthbound spirits to the Light. For many of the earthbound spirits I encountered, this direct contact and reassurance from what I called a "high-level guide" was a key factor in their decision to leave my client and go to the Light.

After this, I not only directed earthbound spirits to the Light, but I also told them there were spirits there to assist them. I told them they could see those spirits and communicate with them if they chose to, and I encouraged them to do so. Once an earthbound spirit agreed, it nearly always happened that it would see a spirit coming to them from the Light. I also learned with experience that when this request for a helping spirit failed, it was due to the earthbound spirit's own doubts, fears, or lack of belief. Once I helped that spirit resolve its own inner resistance or fear, the encounter with the spirit guide would occur.

Again, I believed in the existence of these *angels* or *guides,* but I had no direct experience of them myself. As far as I was concerned, they were across the divide between human and spirit. I looked at my work with earthbound spirits as a kind of *handing over* or *pointing the way* to the spirit realm of Light. I consistently received confirmation, though, from different earthbound spirits that they had made contact with a helping spirit or spirits who had come for them. It was the same kind of confirmation I observed when I first learned to direct spirits to the Light: one moment they were telling me they would not go or were having trouble, and the next moment, they were gone. These helping spirits in some way communicated whatever knowledge, love, or reassurance the earthbound spirit needed in order to say yes to the Light.

I also made specific requests of these spirits from the Light. When I thought of something that might help an earthbound spirit who was stuck, I would ask for it and often it would happen. I began to learn what I could ask for and what I could not. If, for example, an earthbound spirit were extremely frightened, I would find out whether there was someone, a relative or friend, whom they had been especially close to or had trusted in his or her life on earth. If there were, then I would ask that soul to come forward to meet the spirit I was working with. I also learned to take into account that a particular loved one may not be in the spirit realm at present because that soul had already reincarnated. So in using this technique, I learned not to make promises, and to identify more than one possible candidate before trying to call on a spirit from the Light to come forward.

If a spirit was stuck over a specific issue—perhaps something that caused guilt, or something that had happened in their life that made them mistrust God, or an intense fear of punishment—I learned to ask for a spirit guide to come forward who could communicate specific information to the earthbound spirit regarding its particular concern. As long as the earthbound spirit was willing to receive such a communication, it invariably happened.

Through the Looking Glass

When I first made contact with an earthbound spirit in my work with Jim D., I was not aware of the consequences it would have for me, personally and professionally. As I said at the start of this chapter, I viewed these spirits at first in a very limited way—as intruders, as someone or something to be exorcised from my client and sent back across the line. I assumed I could deal with spirits without having to cross that line myself. I had thought of it as these spirits stepping into our world. I did not realize that making contact with spirits would mean that I was stepping into their world as well.

Reading *The Unquiet Dead,* starting a verbal dialogue with Gerod, and recognizing that there were many realms of spirits triggered an explosion of information and clinical activity. Everything began to speed up. There were more talks. More questions. More clients. More issues. Somewhere in that quickening time, I said *yes* to this larger reality. This was not an intellectual yes. That had already happened before I met Gerod. This was a deeper realization, a knowing—a certainty—that these spirit dimensions were real, and that each of us is an incarnate soul.

This did not mean that I understood it all or grasped the big picture. Quite the opposite, these dimensions were just opening up to me. What I knew for certain at this point, however, was that there *was* a *big picture.* I began to view my clients now as souls, and with each one I began to consider whether psychic and spirit level issues were involved in their presenting problems or difficulties.

Part 2

Healing The Inner World

Part 2

Healing The Inner World

Introduction

Part 1 told the story of Soul-Centered Healing from a chronological point of view. From hypnosis and alter-personalities, to Gerod, to earthbound spirits, the first seven chapters chronicled the shift from a psychological to a metaphysical paradigm of reality. The story is told through the eyes of a clinician who is waking up to the reality of the psychic and spirit dimensions.

In Part 2, the focus shifts back to the individual, the inner world, and the healing process. While spirits were a major issue in those first years with Gerod, most of my clients were not having problems with intruding or earthbound spirits. In hypnotherapy, the sharing and release of ego-states continued to be the primary focus. The major problem was still the number of times my communication with ego-states was shutting down or being blocked. It was the same situation as before I met Gerod. This time, though, I could take my questions to him. When I encountered a block with a client that I couldn't resolve, I would ask Gerod about it in our next session. Most of the time he gave specific information about the block, and most of the time it helped resolve it or move it ahead. Sometimes it meant going back and forth several times between Gerod and a client, but it usually worked.

Gerod's information about these clients and the different sources of blocking revealed within each client a dynamic and complex inner world. Ego-states were still a primary focus of healing, but Gerod's view of these parts of the self was a radically different understanding than my own. I also learned from Gerod about the *protective part of the mind* and the *higher self,* one a significant source of blocking, the other a direct connection to the Divine. Each came to play a significant role in the healing process with ego-states. It took thousands of client sessions and hundreds of talks with Gerod to identify these parts of the self, establish a common language and understanding about them, and learn how to incorporate them into the healing process.

What emerged from this collaboration with Gerod was an approach to healing radically different than the psychology and psychotherapy I was trained in. It was an approach that recognized the psychic and spirit dimensions of the self. The collaboration led to methods for helping a person access and work at these levels when necessary for healing. They were methods that were able to resolve the blocks, defenses, and interferences that so often led to an impasse.

8

Through the Looking Glass

Our normal waking consciousness, rational consciousness as we call it, is but one special type of consciousness, whilst all about it, parted from it by the filmiest of screens, there lie potential forms of consciousness entirely different. We may go through life without suspecting their existence . . . No account of the universe in its totality can be final which leaves these other forms of consciousness quite disregarded. How to regard them is the question—for they are so discontinuous with ordinary consciousness.—William James, from *Varieties of Religious Experience*

Psychological States

When I first began working with alter-personalities, I viewed them as psychological or mental "states." They were, for sure, marvelous creations and strong testament to the self's ability to protect itself. I did not think of them, however, as real beings. They *acted* like real beings, and I treated them *as if* they were real. I listened to why they felt the way they did and what had happened to them. In the end, though, I believed them to be only reflections and artifacts in some way of the client's early experience. I saw them as *aspects* of the person that had somehow been separated and then crystallized into a stable personality. They could *mimic* real people, but they weren't really people.

I also did not believe that alter-personalities lived in a real world. I accepted that it was real to them and they believed what they were saying, but it was not real in any other sense. An alter-personality, for example, might *believe* she was out camping in the woods and she might *talk as if* it was true, but it wasn't. She was sitting in my office. There was no tent, no fire, and she obviously could not see any stars in the night sky. When an alter-personality told me it was five years old and wearing a dance costume or was thirty years old and lived in a house by a river, I accepted that each of them believed what they were saying. In my own mind, though, these worlds were a weave of fabrication, illusion, and memory. Even when two or more alter-personalities sat around the same table, I still believed that that table was a reflection and re-creation of my client's experience in the outer world.

I also believed that once an alter-personality was able to share its experience and release its emotion, it would dissolve or be absorbed into the conscious self, and its illusory world would disappear along with it. Theoretically, at least, once its secrets were revealed and integrated by the conscious person, there would be no need for the ego-state to exist.

Gerod's View

Gerod challenged this point of view in our first session. He talked about alter-personalities several times, first indirectly, and then directly. He made the point that an earthbound spirit might be mistaken at times for an alter-personality, and that it would be important to distinguish between the two. He said a therapist might believe he was treating a dissociative condition and assume that any voice he hears is an alter-personality. Mistakenly, then, the therapist works with the client to integrate something that is not a part of him or her.

When I asked Gerod directly about alter-personalities, many of his comments and statements were in basic agreement with my own understanding. He talked about alter-personalities in the same way psychologists do. He saw them as being a part of the self, created as a defense for the survival and protection of the person. He also agreed that because of the pain they carried, they could be a continuing source of conflict and distress for a person. As he put it, "they are not always an asset to one's being."

Despite our agreement on the creation and function of alter-personalities, however, there was a fundamental difference between how Gerod viewed alter-personalities and how I viewed them. Each time Gerod talked about alter-personalities, he talked about them as real beings. It was not only *what* he said that gave me this impression, but also *how* he said it.

August 1, 1987—(First written session)

The alternate personality is strong, is clever. Just as you can tap into your soul for information, so can these alternate personalities. They are real; they have energy and do exist. However, they are not always an asset to one's being.

. . . They are indeed created; the mind is powerful. See what can be done by your mind when it has the right information—great things. A mind wants help—a mother, a father, someone of significance to love, to protect, to intervene. If in this physical reality, no such one exists, then the mind will very carefully begin creating "people" to help. The personality will call in it's own helpers of its own creating; hence, multiple personalities. However, many of these helpers are misguided helpers, as they are not grounded to the soul.

In the following months, I did not talk to Gerod very often about alter-personalities and ego-states. It might have been a handful of times. My focus was still on spirits.

With my focus on earthbound spirits, the discrepancy between Gerod's point of view and my own concerning alter-personalities remained in the background. Whenever the topic did come up, though, he talked about them in a consistent way.

Session #7—February 6, 1988

Each of those personalities does believe that it is real; it believes it has a soul. It has memory. It is such a part of the main personality that it has access to, and use of, almost everything, and so it does believe it is real, and in that sense, it is created as we were.

From Gerod's point of view, these were viable beings, created by the mind, and existing within the self/soul.

Either/Or

The idea that these parts of the self were conscious beings was outside my framework of thinking. I'm not even sure in those early sessions how aware I was of the discrepancy between my point of view and Gerod's; or if I was aware of the discrepancy, that I didn't dismiss it as merely another problem in semantics. As I've pointed out about these early dialogues, much of what Gerod wrote—and its implications—was beyond my grasp at the time. This was certainly true about alter-personalities. From my point of view, Gerod was a being; spirits were beings; humans were beings; but alter-personalities were not. They were only projected psychological states or aspects of the self.

While I was not aware of it consciously, it was only a matter of time before this discrepancy would have to be addressed directly. It was, in fact, more than a discrepancy. It was a contradiction in my thinking. Either they were *beings* or they were *things (states)*, but they could not be both. It was also a contradiction clinically. If Gerod's point of view was correct, that these alter-personalities and ego-states were real beings, then it raised serious questions about the way I thought about them, how I talked to them, and how I treated them. You treat beings differently than you do things.

It was these clinical implications that began to force the issue to a head. I had to consider whether the reason I encountered so much blocking and resistance in working with ego-states was because I was saying the wrong things and asking the wrong questions. Instead of dealing with ego-states as crystallized memories or artifacts of the mind, did I need to approach them from Gerod's point of view and treat them as real beings? This is the question that was slowly coming into focus as Gerod and I began talking more frequently about alter-personalities and ego-states. I had always been respectful when communicating to alter-personalities, but I did not view them as possessing their own center of being.

There was one session in particular that took us a long way toward answering the question. In the session, Gerod gave me information that implied that he could actually see specific ego-states of a particular client whom we were discussing. The case involved Emily S. I was encountering ongoing resistance and blocking in our hypnosis sessions. Initially, Emily had proved to be a good trance subject, and I was able to establish strong finger signals with her. However, as soon as I began to ask about a particular problem or emotional pain, it was as if everything shut down tight. I could not get a response to my questions, or if I did, I could not keep it engaged for very long before the communication stopped.

I brought up Emily in my next session with Gerod because of the frustration she and I were both feeling about the stalled therapy. I wanted to see if there was any information or suggestion he might offer that would help the situation. Here's what he said:

Session #51—October 23, 1988

Well, it is difficult for this woman, and there is a very real concern for her at a deep level about the information that will have to come out if the therapy would continue, and that seems to signal a lack of cooperation. There is a lot of control here that is not readily apparent, but there is a state that is strongly controlled, that seems to stop the process at a certain point of penetration.

The "state" Gerod was referring to was an ego-state. He was claiming to be perceiving a distinct state within Emily that had been triggered and was blocking the healing process. If it were true that Gerod could perceive these states within a client, the implications would be profound on many levels.

1) Confirmation of ego-states (alter-personalities): First, it implied an objectivity and reality to ego-states that I had never given them. By claiming to see individual ego-states, Gerod was already claiming they were real. One statement assumes the other. In effect, he was confirming what many psychologists, myself included, already believed, i.e., that ego-states were distinct states operating at an unconscious level.

2) Confirmation of a psychic realm of activity: Gerod's statement also implied an objectivity and reality to a psychic dimension or realm, outside normal awareness, where these parts of the self existed and could act. When Gerod said that this "state" within Emily was stopping the process, he was claiming to be observing the dynamic interplay of psychological states. According to Gerod, he was perceiving in real time what psychologists theoretically called a psychological defense.

3) Ego-states as a major source of blocking: When Gerod identified Emily's ego-state as a source of blocking, it implied an answer to one of the central and ongoing questions in my work with clients. What was the source or cause of blocking I continually was encountering in my work with ego-states? Gerod's statement suggested that ego-states could be a major source of blocking.

4) Clinical Imperative: Unlike with spirits, ego-states were a primary focus in my work with clients. By claiming to see Emily's ego-state in present time, Gerod implied that he could observe and identify these states within other people as well. And further, if true, it meant that Gerod could be in a position to give information that would directly

benefit specific clients. This possibility is the one that moved the issue of alter-personalities and ego-states from a theoretical to a clinical level. If Gerod had valuable information about a person's ego-states that would assist in healing, then I could not ignore it. From my point of view, I would be negligent not to use this information.

5) Verification: Finally, Gerod's statement implied the possibility that his information could be verified. If he was, in fact, able to perceive a client's specific ego-states in present time, and give me information about them, then, theoretically, I should be able to communicate to those same ego-states directly in my work with clients and determine whether my findings agreed with Gerod's information. In effect, I would have two independent sources of information—my clients' and Gerod's—that I could test against each other.

These implications were not this clear to me in that moment, of course, but they all followed from the question of whether Gerod could actually perceive individual ego-states or alter-personalities within a person. It raised the question of what exactly Gerod could see and what he could tell me specifically about ego-states.

This session concerning Emily, though, only raised the question. It was a starting point, like when Gerod first told me about earthbound spirits. The information about spirits triggered a period of intense questioning and exploration, theoretically and clinically. The same thing happened here. After this session, ego-states became an increasingly central focus in my dialogues with Gerod.

Over the next year and a half, I pursued the question of what Gerod could see of these states. I explored with him theoretically how he viewed them and how he would treat them. Unlike with spirits, though, we were now talking about a phenomenon with which I was very familiar. I wanted to see how Gerod's perspective compared with mine. I believed that if we were talking about the same phenomenon, then at some point our views would have to coincide. There would be some common ground.

I also pursued the question with Gerod clinically. I looked for situations or opportunities to ask him about specific cases. I asked about those clients, for example, where I had identified a strong and distinct ego-state. In the next session with Gerod, I would ask him to look in this same area and describe what he saw. Alternatively, I asked Gerod about situations where the process was being blocked or shut down. In many cases, Gerod identified an ego-state(s) as the source of the block. In my next session with the client, then, I would check it out. I would ask questions based on Gerod's information and see if it worked or was confirmed in the therapy session.

Over the months, Gerod and I were narrowing in on the question of whether he could actually see these states within a person. I was beginning to reach the conclusion that he could, that they each exhibited in some specific form. Clinically, I was also coming to the point where I had to answer the question, one way or the other. Depending on how I saw these ego-states—as *psychological states* or as *beings*—it would lead to two very different approaches in the therapy. I had to answer the question in order to know how to proceed. What I did not realize was that in answering that question of whether he could see ego-states, I would also be answering the question of *who* he was seeing, not *what*.

The Red Shoes

The breakthrough came when information Gerod gave me about a client's specific ego-state was independently confirmed in the next session with that client. The case involved my client Martha K. Martha was thirty-six years old, happy to be divorced from an abusive husband, but still living an emotional roller coaster. She had grown up in what she knew was a "crazy family," and she also knew that she had her own brand of that craziness to deal with as a result.

Martha had called me earlier that week to tell me that she was having intense reactions to our last session. Her anxiety level had increased, and she often was feeling on the verge of panic. She said there was a "tightness in her head" that threatened at times to explode. This reaction did not surprise me. We had come to a very strong block in our previous session, and I suspected that we were approaching something very painful or frightening. I reassured her and suggested some ways that she could keep it contained.

When I saw Gerod that week, I talked to him about the block I had come to with Martha and her subsequent reaction to the session. I asked whether, from his point of view, the blocking involved the two year-old ego-state I had been working with in that last session. He replied, "No," and said there was something deeper going on.

Session #148—June 2, 1990

There is more underneath there. There's a lot more to come forward
to a certain degree. There is a certain evasiveness, a certain conflict at
that deeper level. She is being chided for doing this work, punished,
from internal sources. So there is a lot of anxiety and stress. There's a
lot of difficulty in being grounded in the present.

I asked whether he would suggest trying to move past the two year-
old and approach that level directly.

G. I would, yes. I would go right to that. Because working there will relieve
a major stressor, a major stumbling block. And once that is resolved,
it will be easier to do some of the other work.

T. Do you see that as more than one part?

G. Yes.

T. Is there a signifier, a signal, or something I might use to identify
them?

G. A pair of red shoes. There is a pair of red shoes that someone knows
something about. See if that will be helpful.

In the next session, as usual, I did not share with Martha any information Gerod had given me. Once she had entered trance, though,
I asked for the "one who knew about the red shoes" to come forward
and communicate with me. Shortly, I saw the yes finger lift, and I addressed that one. Through the finger signals, I learned that she was
three years old. She communicated that there were three of them there
altogether. With further questioning, I learned that each of them was
three years old, and each carried a different experience. The one I was
communicating with agreed to share her experience with Martha at
a conscious level.

When the sharing began, it soon became clear that Martha was
reliving the experience at some level. She began to describe out loud
what was happening along with her pain and terror. I didn't always
know whether it was Martha who was talking or the three-year-old. My
notes give an abbreviated account of the sharing as I tried to scribble
the main points of what Martha was saying while trying to give her
support and reassurance in what she was going through.

I'm being squished
against the wall
being crunched with my cheeks
I'm wearing my red tennies
he's sticking something in me
like sat on, only side ways
he's rubbing up against me
sort of on a stairway[1]

It was an intensely emotional and painful sharing. When Martha became quiet, I saw the yes finger lift, signaling that three-year-old's sharing was complete. I helped her and Martha, then, to release the pain, hurt, and confusion until they both could report a feeling of comfort and safety.

The "red tennies" were a powerful confirmation to me about Gerod's ability to know about individual ego-states. Martha knew nothing about the red shoes when we started the session. I had not discussed Gerod's information with her ahead of time. She was already in trance when I first mentioned the red shoes.

The yes finger lifted almost immediately, too quickly for Martha to fabricate a three year old ego-state, and share a detailed memory that conveniently incorporated the element of "red shoes" into her account. I just didn't believe that Martha was intentionally trying to deceive me, or consciously fabricating a story. So, when the three-year-old told me about her "red tennies," it verified what Gerod had said to me earlier that week: "There is a pair of red shoes that someone knows something about. See if that will be helpful." As it turned out, someone did know about the red shoes, the three-year-old, and now here she was, communicating with me. The three-year-old in red shoes is the one who made me a believer.

Stepping Through

In retrospect, I see the girl in red shoes as marking a radical shift in my own point of view on ego-states, in my relationship with Gerod, and ultimately in my understanding of the healing process itself. She was, first of all, an answer to the question raised so many months ago about my client, Emily: could Gerod actually see these *states* within a person? This girl in her red tennies was the strongest argument I had so far that, yes, he could see them.

I had been working with other clients where Gerod identified specific ego-states, and I was looking for ways to test his information in those cases as well. It wasn't about the girl in red shoes. If the confirmation had not come with her, I believe it would have happened before long with a different client and another ego-state. In the end, that was the point. The girl in red shoes was not an isolated phenomenon. All the ego-states were like her—alive and conscious in their own reality. The difference now was that I acknowledged them as inner beings living in a psychic reality.

Besides confirming Gerod's ability to know about these realms, the three-year-old also attested to her own existence, independent of Gerod or me. She obviously had to have been in her red shoes when Gerod first told me about her; and she was in her red shoes when I met her; and the logical conclusion was that she lived an independent existence in her red shoes long before I ever met Martha K. or asked Gerod about her.

Somewhere in that experience, I knew she was a being, separate from the conscious self, and living a separate existence at another level of consciousness. As soon as I knew this about her, I knew it about all the ego-states I had worked with over the past years. They were all beings, each conscious and alive in their own reality. In some sense, during that session with Martha, I had stepped into those red shoes, however briefly, and glimpsed that reality myself.

What was so important here was not the red shoes, but the world in which they were standing. It was a psychic reality, not a physical one. It was a realm ruled by consciousness, not the laws of matter. Once I accepted ego-states as real beings, I accepted also this reality in which they existed. I changed the way I thought about them and how I treated them in the therapy.

I accepted that each lived in a unique reality. I knew intuitively that for each of these inner beings, healing had to begin within its own experience and reality. What mattered was where and what the ego-state was living, not what I thought about it or where I thought it should be. To gain an ego-state's cooperation, what I said to it and what I asked of it had to make sense from its own experience and point of view, not my client's or my own. I could no longer presume that these ego-states were only reflections of the conscious personality or that they would dissolve themselves on command.

Going back to my earlier example, the ego-state who tells me she is out in the woods camping—she really is in a woods; she really does have a tent, with her blankets rolled up inside; and there really is a fire burning. If I were to say to her without any other explanation that her tent was not real, she would think I was crazy or trying to trick her. From her point of view, my voice has broken into her world and unless her consciousness changes, she will forget me and go right on camping after our contact ends.

This new understanding about ego-states, and Gerod's ability to identify them, precipitated a significant shift in my work. I became increasingly more focused and specific with him about other clients and their ego-states. In turn, Gerod gave me a great deal of specific information regarding many clients. He identified specific ego-states that he saw reacting to or directly involved in an issue we were trying to address. He might see a particular ego-state, for example, as intentionally blocking a communication, trying to hide, or in some way interfering with a client's trance state. He identified them often by their appearance: tall or short, old or young, hair color, distinguishing features, how they were dressed. Other times he would describe an ego-state's situation or setting. Often, he gave me its name.

There also were times when I asked Gerod about an ego-state that I had already identified, but who was stuck or being blocked. I would describe the ego-state or the situation I was dealing with to see if there was any information he could offer that might help resolve the impasse. Usually, Gerod could see the ego-state I was asking about, or the situation I was describing, and he was able to give me some specific information or suggestion. He might tell me, for example, why an ego-state was afraid to communicate with me, or who had stepped in to block its memory from being shared. In my next session with that particular client, then, I would go back to where we left off and use Gerod's information to try to take another step.

I reached a point fairly soon where at least half of every session with Gerod, and often more, focused on specific clients and ego-states. It was not unusual, for example, for me to bring up seven or eight clients in a session. Some cases involved a brief question or follow-up from the week before, while other clients we discussed in more depth. I had all the opportunities I wanted to directly test Gerod's information in my sessions with clients. Most of the time, his information was accurate or directly helped in resolving a block or conflict.

Looking back now, I see these two changes as a turning point in my work: 1) the recognition that ego-states were real beings and 2) the concentrated focus with Gerod on specific clients and their ego-states.

It was as if the girl in red shoes let me step into that reality and then Gerod was able to show me around. One of these factors alone would not have been enough to give me the leverage I needed to comprehend this reality, understand it, and learn how to work within it.

It is difficult to know how far this new understanding would have taken me into these inner worlds if, following my experience with the girl in red shoes, I had never again talked to Gerod. I don't believe I would have been able to go very far. And it would not have been for lack of trying.

Without Gerod's information, I would never have guessed all that was possible in these psychic or nonphysical realms, or the kinds of situations and binds in which these inner beings—as well as spirits—could become caught. I would never have known enough to ask about the inner structures and layers of the psyche and how to find the doors that needed to be opened for healing—or closed and sealed for protection. I would never have understood the interconnections between the psychic and spiritual dimensions and how they relate to each other and to the physical plane as well. Every time Gerod gave me a piece of information, it was a like a snapshot of these inner worlds and connections, every picture worth a thousand words. Over time and hundreds of client sessions, these pictures made more and more sense, like lining up snapshots to see a panoramic view.

The *girl in red shoes* is the closest I can come to identifying a moment when this shift in perspective happened, when I stepped through the looking glass and began to comprehend other dimensions of consciousness and being. My point of view about ego-states changed. It was then I came to believe they were centers of consciousness in their own right.

I changed the way I thought about them and how I approached them in the therapy. I accorded them the kind of respect and affirmation that I gave to other beings, human and spirit. I acknowledged the importance and validity of their concerns. I also began to see that it was the transformation of an ego-state's consciousness that was an essential part of the healing process, rather than just a dissolving of a memory construct. These were not just electrical patterns of brain waves; this was a living inner world.

9

The Protective Part of the Mind

Calling something by its right name is the beginning of wisdom.—
Chinese Proverb

First Line of Defense

When I first meet with a client and talk about the healing process—
about hypnosis and working with ego-states—I always assume that
the *protective part of the mind* is also watching and listening. This
is a part of the mind that is conscious and perceiving, but operates
separately from the conscious self. Its primary function is to ensure
the body's survival. This is why it is always aware and focused in the
present moment, because that's where the body is. The protective
part is always on alert for any signs of danger or threat. It's as though
we have a second pair of eyes always scanning, always assessing. Our
protective part doesn't care if we're going shopping tonight, or meeting
someone for dinner. It is focused on what is happening all around the
body/self right now. It will be aware of the grocery aisle or restaurant
if and when the body is there.

When I talk to a new client about accessing ego-states, I know it
often can trigger the person's protective part. While its primary function
is to ensure the body's survival, the protective part also, by extension,
defends the self from pain—physical, emotional, and psychological. In
the case of healing, the protective part often will perceive direct contact
with ego-states as a threat because this is where the pain is held. From
the protective part's point of view, ego-state therapy could be like going into a minefield. This is why the protective part will often block

the healing process: by working with ego-states, we keep touching into sources of pain and distress. Unless it knows better, the protective part may shut down the work with ego-states in order to protect the self from the pain. Because of this, I emphasize certain issues in this initial talk with a client, and many of my statements are directed specifically to the protective part. I want to reassure it, from the start, that the process we are undertaking is safe and can help.

There are two issues in particular that I emphasize. The first is the understanding that a person does not surrender his or her conscious control while in a hypnotic state. I want my client to understand this, but I also want to emphasize this point to the protective part. I want it to know that there will be no attempt to violate or override its defensive function. I want the protective part to know that I recognize and support its position. I want to make it an ally.

The second issue I address is the pain and distress that a person can experience when working with ego-states and other entanglements. When an ego-state shares its experience during a session, a client feels that pain and distress, the fear or the anger, but also realizes that these are memories and that the pain is from the past. For the protective part, however, pain is pain. Whether it first happened in the past or not, and whether it is caused by external events or internal events, the protective part reacts to pain and the threat of pain in the present.

So, as I talk to a client about ego-states, I am also telling the protective part that there is good reason for accessing these parts of the self. I am not doing this just so the person feels the pain once more, but to help him or her to finally release the pain. By working with ego-states for sharing and release, we are resolving not only the pain, fear, or hurt which they carry, but also healing the source of pain that is so often being triggered in the client's present life. The protective part, through the logic of instinct, knows that healing and relief from pain has greater benefit to the self than keeping such pain and distress locked inside.

By talking about these issues ahead of time, I want the protective part to know where we are going in the healing process and why. I want to reassure it that the hypnosis and healing process are safe. My statements during this initial meeting are meant to be a first step in gaining the protective parts agreement and cooperation in what at times can be a painful process.

The next step will be to communicate to the protective part directly. I cannot assume that it is in agreement with the healing process just because of what I have said during the meeting with my client and the reassurances I've tried to give. Once we begin the hypnosis, I want to ask the protective part directly whether it understands and is in agreement with the healing process we're about to undertake. If it communicates yes, then we'll proceed. If not, more explanation and reassurance may be needed.

Naming Names

Before continuing this chapter on the protective part, I want to step back a moment and talk about the term itself. You won't find it in the psychology books or the dictionary. I made it up to refer to this part of the mind that Gerod said was operating behind the scenes. We had to call it something, and naming it after its function served the purpose, both in talking to Gerod and in communicating to that part itself. There is nothing sacred about the name. The real question is not about its name, but whether such a conscious function exists and operates within the self.

We do not have a word or concept in our language to describe this type of consciousness, so it can easily lead to confusion and misunderstanding. It is easier for me to talk about the protective part clinically because that is where I work with it and see it in action. It is much more difficult, however, to define it theoretically.

On the one hand, the protective part acts like a *being*. It is conscious and perceiving in the present and operates with a great deal of autonomy from the conscious self. Though it is a limited consciousness, the protective part is intelligent. It can learn, is logical, and is able to communicate.

On the other hand, although it is conscious, the protective part behaves like a *function*. It is always doing the same job and using the same operations and routines to accomplish it, but it is doing it in an ever-changing present. Essentially, the protective part is a monitor and a switch, but it is an intelligent monitor. It has the capacity to learn and to adapt. We don't have a term for it. The closest I can come is to call it a "conscious function." The HAL computer in Stanley Kubrick's *2001: A Space Odyssey* might be an apt example. HAL is the spaceship's onboard computer that appears to have a mind of its own. HAL is able to anticipate the thoughts and actions of the different crewmen and take preventive measures to stop them, even if it means killing them. From the *Star Trek* series, Dr. Spock's intense focus and tight logic also come to mind.

We are conscious and think at many different levels all day long. From yesterday's regret, to the impending death of a parent, to a job that has to be done in the next ten minutes. Our minds cover a lot of territory in a day. We move from the past, to the future, and back again to the present all day long. The protective part, however, remains focused on the safety of the body in the present, and is perceiving always in terms of survival. The protective part perceives and interprets present situations and events in terms of threat and safety. It is a defensive function and, using Freudian terms, its range of response is limited to variations of fight or flight. In this sense, we might think of the protective part as a *watchdog* function.

Try to imagine a part of yourself right now that is conscious and observing right along with you, but is perceiving everything in terms of threat and safety. Try to step into these shoes sometime during the day and see strictly from a defensive point of view and you will have a glimpse of the protective part.

Gatekeeper

Before meeting Gerod, I didn't know about the protective part and so I didn't recognize it as a significant source of blocking. I was not aware of a part of the mind that might view the healing process or the trance-state itself as a threat and take steps to shut it down. I also did not realize that the protective part was aware of, and reacted to, the ego-states that I was asking to come forward in the hypnosis sessions.

I first learned about the protective part from Gerod. Early in our collaboration, I had asked him about a client, Julie C., where I was encountering very strong blocking. He said there was a part of Julie blocking because our work was stirring up painful memories and feelings. This part was reacting, he said, to protect the self from the pain of these memories. He also strongly suggested that I communicate with this part of Julie directly and see if I could elicit its cooperation.

He called it the *ego,* but I knew he was talking about something different than what psychologists mean by that term. In our culture, the *ego* is identified with the conscious self, what we mean when we say "I" or "me." That's not what Gerod was talking about. He wasn't talking about Julie's conscious self, but some other part of her that was aware and reacting to what we were doing.

This was another one of those moments, like with earthbound spirits, where Gerod caught me completely by surprise. I didn't know what he was talking about at first. I thought he meant that Julie was consciously stopping the process, but this was quickly ruled out. He wasn't talking about Julie at a conscious level, but a part of her mind that was acting on its own. It didn't take much to see that if what Gerod said was true, it could have important clinical implications. If there were a separate part of Julie's mind operating at a conscious level, then it certainly could be a significant source of blocking in the healing process.

The problem for me at the time was that I could not comprehend what Gerod was describing. I did not have a category for such a part of the mind. This was not an alter-personality or an earthbound spirit; and it wasn't the conscious self either. My framework of thinking did not allow for such a separate part of the mind to be operating consciously at the same time as the conscious self.

However, I couldn't rule it out either. I had to acknowledge that what Gerod was saying could be true. There could be such a part of the mind operating consciously, outside ordinary awareness, which could act on its own to block access to the unconscious.

As with earthbound spirits, I immediately began to explore this phenomenon in my dialogues with Gerod and in my sessions with clients. Over the next year, I talked to Gerod many times about the protective part. I paid attention to how he used the term. I asked him about specific clients just to hear what he would describe, and then compare it to what I knew. I also followed his suggestion to talk to new clients about the healing process *as if* such a separate part of the mind were listening and could understand. Finally, and also at Gerod's prompting, I began to ask for direct communication. With those clients where I thought this protective consciousness might be involved in blocking, I began to ask "the protective part" to come forward and communicate.

It was the same problem, though, that I had had about spirits. In this case, what do you ask a protective part? What's going to make sense to it? Going by Gerod's suggestion, the basic questions I asked centered on 1) whether this part understood the healing process and its benefits, and 2) would it allow us to work in areas of pain and distress.

Contact

From the start, I received yes responses when I asked that a person's protective part communicate with me. Through trial and error, I eventually learned what questions to ask and what questions got us off track.

After a year, I became convinced that this protective consciousness was real and that it could, and often did, block my work with ego-states and with other aspects of our work with the unconscious.

Based on this conviction, I began to make contact with a client's protective part a first step in the healing process. Because of this part's apparent ability to block at any time, it made more sense to address it right from the beginning and elicit its cooperation. From my point of view, and based on Gerod's suggestion, such an agreement could preempt a significant amount of blocking that we might otherwise encounter down the road.

Based on my experience, this turned out to be true. Before I started communicating to the protective part, I would estimate that a third of my clients had difficulty entering trance and/or establishing ideomotor signals. They often required several sessions or more just to develop even a light trance state. Some clients never could enter trance despite the number of sessions and various techniques I tried. My clear clinical impression was that by communicating first to the protective part, the whole process went more smoothly with most clients. After incorporating this step in the healing process, I would estimate the number of clients who had difficulty entering trance or establishing signals fell from a third to less than five percent.

The same was also true about my work with ego-states. Once a client's protective part agreed to the healing process, there seemed to be less blocking when I began making contact with a client's ego-states. My overall clinical impression was that the entire process was going smoother more often with more clients.

Clinically, these positive results were not always easy to discern or measure. As I'll talk about later, the agreement with a client's protective part did not eliminate all blocking. Working at the level of ego-states wasn't nearly as black or white as a client being able to enter trance or not. This ambiguity made it more difficult to discern when it was the protective part blocking and when it wasn't. It was more like knowing something through its absence, as though the protective part had stepped back, and I could feel that absence. I didn't encounter blocking where I would have expected to before. I didn't end up going in circles quite as much, and when I did, I could quickly rule the protective part in or out as the source of the problem.

The clearer I became about the protective part and how to work with it, the more I was able to focus on the other sources of blocking. Being able to eliminate the protective part as a source of blocking opened the way to a next step. It was like removing a filter and being able to see to the next layer down. While it didn't solve all the blocking, contact with a client's protective part did appear to eliminate a first line of defense. Direct communication with a client's protective part consistently led to the immediate resolution of blocking in many, many cases. I also believed that eliciting the protective part's cooperation in the beginning was pre-empting a good deal of blocking in the healing process.

What I have always found ironic since I first learned about the protective part is how easy it is to establish communication with it, and how quickly it will agree to suspend its blocking once it understands about the healing process. Looking back, it seems I was continually butting up against this block when all I had to do was ask.

10

The Higher Self

To be truly in touch with one's Inner Self is the key to mental and spiritual health. Patients with multiple personalities provide a striking example of persons who have lost touch with that part of them which is creative, non-neurotic, problem solving, and everything else which is needed to survive and grow in the world as it is. Whenever a therapist can bring this communication about, the patient can put his or her own healing forces to work, and that is the most any therapist can ask of himself. —Ralph Allison, M.D.

The secret of Sufism is to shift from the vantage point of our personal point of view to the Divine point of view. Very simply our being is made up of two poles of consciousness: the individual, personal self and the Divine, the higher self. It is at the pole of the personal dimension of consciousness that we experience constraint and limitation. While we may think that our circumstances are the cause of this frustration, the real source lies in not being aware of our higher self. Thus the goal in meditation is to reconnect our personal self to this transpersonal dimension of our being. —Pir Vilayat Inayat Khan, from *Awakening*

The Inner Self Helper

ISH (rhymes with *wish*) is a term in psychology, especially familiar to those therapists who treat dissociative identity disorder. ISH stands for *inner self helper* and it refers to a particular type of personality that can present during the course of a client's treatment. (I mentioned the inner self helper in Chapter 5 as one of the possibilities I considered in trying to explain Gerod.) The ISH can present in a different form from one client to the next—an alter-personality, a voice, a radiating spirit, or a revered figure—but when it does appear, it is a powerful and fascinating entity. What is most significant about the ISH is not its form, but its knowledge of the inner world and its abilities to assist directly in a person's therapy.

The term *Inner Self Helper* is attributed to Dr. Ralph Allison, a psychiatrist and pioneer in the field of dissociative disorders. In a 1974 article, *A New Treatment Approach for Multiple Personalities,*[1] Dr. Allison described his discovery of this unique type of personality during his treatment of Elizabeth, a patient recently diagnosed with multiple personality disorder. This personality, whom he called Beth, presented spontaneously at a time when Elizabeth was locked in a battle for control with a strong and adversarial personality named Betsy. It was during one of their combative dialogues that Beth emerged.

Dr. Allison had received a message from his answering service that Elizabeth had called while he was out. When he returned the call, however, Elizabeth knew nothing about it. She realized that one of the other personalities must have made the call, and she was determined to find out which one. She suspected it was Betsy, and that she was up to no good. She reasoned that since they were all in her head, she could talk to them and they would answer. Elizabeth decided to confront Betsy about the phone call and asked that her husband, Don, set up a tape recorder for her and leave the house for a short time.

After he left, she carried on the dialogue with Betsy while a tape recorder was running. She demanded to know why Betsy had made the call. When Betsy denied it, Elizabeth insisted she was lying. It was not long before Elizabeth and Betsy were hurling insults and threatening each other about who was going to do what to whom. It was while listening to the tape of Elizabeth and Betsy that Dr. Allison first learned about Beth.

> When I listened to the tape the next day, in addition to the voices of the primary personality of the patient and her antagonist, I heard the voice of a third entity who was trying to help my patient cope more competently with her problems. This voice I later identified as belonging to another entity previously unknown to the patient, an entity I eventually called the ISH (inner self helper).[2]

Dr. Allison met Beth in their next session and they talked. They agreed on the name and then he began to find out more about her. He talked to her frequently and she quickly came to play a central role in the therapy. Dr. Allison says she became his "co-therapist."

Beth had been aware of Elizabeth from the beginning. She knew all of her history and the past events leading up to the present. She also was aware of Elizabeth's alter-personalities. She knew when they were created and why. She was always aware of what was happening for Elizabeth in the present. Beth had been aware of Elizabeth and the alter-personalities all the way along but none of them knew she existed. Most importantly, Beth knew how the alter-personalities functioned within Elizabeth in the present. She understood how the inner system operated. Beth appeared to have the big picture.

This kind of knowledge alone could be invaluable in any therapy, but there was more. Beth also had a number of abilities by which she could actively assist in Elizabeth's healing. She could communicate directly to Elizabeth and the alter-personalities. She also could bring through memories to any of them, like opening a gate. She could block when necessary; and she could influence Elizabeth and the others psychically, through thought. It's no wonder that Beth, with her knowledge and abilities, quickly came to play an important part in Elizabeth's healing.

There was something else about Beth, however, which underscored everything else. It was her pure intent for the self's highest good. She had no self-interest or competing aims. There was no deceit. Her wish was for Elizabeth to be well and whole and to feel good about her self. Beth was willing to do whatever she could to assist in that.

Beth's appearance on the scene changed the course of the therapy. Dr. Allison not only worked with Beth directly during the therapy, he also helped Elizabeth understand how to work with Beth when she was alone and problems arose. It is clear in the article that Dr. Allison attributes Elizabeth's healing in large part to Beth.

After reporting on this case, Dr. Allison goes on to state that he found this same type of personality in five subsequent cases. Each of these patients had their own Beth-like personality. His experience convinced him that others who suffered from multiple personality could have their own inner self helper, and if so, it could be a key to healing.

Since that article was published, many therapists have reported on the presence of an inner self helper in their own cases. It's not that Dr.

Allison was the first one to encounter an *ISH* either, but he was the one who described it and gave it a name.

Not all therapists treating DID clients report finding such an ISH personality. Of those therapists who do, they do not always find such an ISH personality with every one of those clients. There has been enough confirmation in the field, though, to recognize the inner self helper as a genuine and valid phenomenon. Not nearly enough is known, however, to say exactly what it is, to predict its frequency of occurrence, or what value and importance to give it. There is strong agreement, though, at least in clinical areas of psychology, that the ISH can be a powerful resource for healing and integration.

In 1987, I did not know about Dr. Allison and his extensive work concerning the inner self helper. I was aware of the term, though. ISH and inner self helper had come up often in my readings and at the conferences I attended on multiple personality disorder.

I had no experience myself with what I considered an authentic ISH personality. I did encounter alter-personalities who had access to a great deal of information and memory. I also worked with personalities who were genuinely desirous of helping the self, but none of my clients exhibited such a well-defined ISH personality as described by other therapists. I was open to it and would have welcomed the appearance of an inner self helper with any one of my clients. None of those I had encountered so far, though, possessed what I considered all of the qualities and characteristics of an inner self helper.

Danny L. and the Self/Soul Connection

On September 2, 1987, I met with Gerod for the second time. I was impressed enough by our session the month before that I asked Katharine to do another. In that first session, we touched on many topics and a number of terms were put on the table. I found Gerod's information interesting and intriguing. We were two strangers getting to know each other. What impressed me most in that first session, though, were the clinical implications. When Gerod told me that a spirit was interfering with my client Jim D., he was not only giving specific information about Jim in present time, but also implying the possibility that he could offer information about other clients as well. This implication only became more compelling when my next session with Jim appeared to confirm Gerod's information about the presence of a spirit. All of this prompted another meeting.

The problem, however, was that Gerod was almost a complete unknown. He was claiming a knowledge and perspective so different and far greater than my own that I didn't know what to ask, or what he could tell me. I had read enough paranormal literature and channeled material to know that I didn't want to have just an intellectual discussion about metaphysics and psychology. I wanted to get practical. I wanted to know, first, whether Gerod had information that could help my clients.

I decided to use this second meeting with Gerod as a test case. I decided I would focus on one client for the entire session. I wanted to see what Gerod could tell me, and then use the rest of the time for follow-up questions. I wanted to see how specific we could be. This was not a test of Gerod or his truthfulness, but a test for congruence. I was looking for any common ground or reference points, like with Jim D., which might serve as the basis for a common framework between Gerod's perspective and my own.

The test case I had in mind for Gerod was Danny L., a fifteen-year-old boy with whom I had been working for the previous nine months. Danny was referred to me because of what his teachers described as his sometimes-bizarre behavior and his social isolation. I chose to ask about Danny for the same reason I had asked Gerod about Jim D. Danny and I were at an impasse. I was asking him to do something he either could not, or would not, do. I was asking him to be real with me.

From the beginning, Danny kept our relationship at a superficial level despite all my efforts to engage him at a personal level. My experience with Danny mirrored that of his teachers. No matter what areas I tried to explore with him—family, self, friends, school, hobbies—as soon as I asked a question that led to his feelings or areas of conflict, I quickly encountered blocks. He would get silly, act dumb, demand that we play a game, change the subject, or withdraw. These defenses were so quick that it was hard to know how conscious or not Danny was of what was happening. Something was troubling him very deeply, and he either did not know what it was or, if he did, he couldn't or wouldn't say. I had the impression that a deep part of Danny was living in his own world, one that he could not come out of or allow anyone else to enter.

In the last couple months, I had started hypnosis sessions with Danny hoping it might lead to some breakthrough. It didn't take long to see that it wasn't going to happen. Danny couldn't enter a trance state. Rather than relaxing, it's as though his defenses went to hyper-alert. (Looking back now, it would have been helpful to know about the protective part.) He couldn't keep his eyes closed for more than a few seconds. He would ask a question out of nowhere to interrupt the induction.

This is the point I had come to with Danny when I met Gerod. Nothing I had tried breached Danny's defenses or disconnection or whatever it was that only let him go so far and no further. After all this time, he remained an enigma to me. Asking Gerod about Danny was asking one unknown about another, combining two chemicals to see the interaction.

When I did ask, I did not understand Gerod's response. He talked about Danny in terms of his soul.

September 2, 1987—(Written session)

> Danny is having great difficulty with his soul. It is doing battle, so to speak, with his conscious mind and is resulting in great confusion. Danny is afraid of the very strong ties he has with his soul. Unlike many persons who are not consciously aware of their soul's relationship to their physical personality, Danny is very aware of his soul. However, he does not know what his soul is. His soul is struggling for recognition. Danny is someone inclined to psychic abilities if he would only allow himself to sit still and listen to his "inner voice," that higher self which is his soul. For many reasons he has fears of evil and has shut his mind to those feelings he has, believing they are mental ills and not matters spirit inclined. You can reach him if you can get him to believe the feelings and words are not to harm him but to enhance his life and growth.

I had no framework for understanding what Gerod was describing. I didn't know what he meant by "soul" or "higher self," or by Danny's soul "trying to approach him," or his soul "doing battle" with the conscious self. In general, he seemed to be saying that an open connection between the self and soul was a good thing, and for Danny, that connection was being blocked. He said Danny had psychic abilities, and suggested that he might be experiencing psychic phenomena and interpreting it as evil and/or crazy. In effect, according to Gerod, by trying to stop or close off the frightening thoughts and feelings, Danny was also closing off his soul connection. He was, in essence, turning against his true self.

I didn't find a correspondence between my psychological perspective and Gerod's soul-centered perspective. I did not see how his information could be used clinically. In the following weeks, I continued to think about and explore in my own mind what he said about Danny and his soul. I tried to understand how this information might fit, but I didn't see it. I couldn't see connections between what Gerod was describing and the kinds of symptoms and behaviors that Danny displayed.

I had been hoping that Gerod's information would match up with my own observations and add some important missing pieces. I was open to anything that might help make some sense of Danny's inner struggles and reveal new possibilities, but that didn't happen. When the therapy ended several months later, Danny's behavior had improved. He had learned some new ways of dealing with situations, but the disconnection that I felt with him had not been resolved.

At the same time, I believed that Gerod was describing something real when he talked about Danny's *soul* and the self/soul connection. As with Jim D. and the earthbound spirit, Gerod's information had immediate clinical implications. He was describing a condition he said was actively affecting Danny in the present. Then he also suggested that there might be a way to help Danny resolve it. Unlike with Jim, though, this wasn't a case of intrusion by an outside entity, but something about Danny himself. It wasn't something to be removed, but something about his soul.

The Working Part of the Soul

This is where the soul first became a clinical issue. Was Danny a soul? Was his soul causing him difficulty? What did Gerod mean by "soul"? If true, was there something I could do in Danny's therapy to help him resolve this disconnect that Gerod described? I didn't know the answer to these questions. They were questions about Danny, certainly, but they went beyond him. They raised questions about the soul itself. What is a soul? Are we all souls? What does a self/soul connection mean at a practical level? Going by Gerod's words, could the soul be a significant piece in one's healing process?

Gerod's answer to this was an emphatic yes, but my understanding of it came in stages. The first stage was the distinction he made between the *soul* and *higher self*. This happened in our first verbal session. It was part of the quickening. Up to that point, Gerod had seemed to use the terms "soul" and "higher self" somewhat interchangeably. Not this time, though. We were talking about a client where I thought there might be spirit involvement. Gerod said that her *higher self* would be aware if a spirit were intruding, even if she wasn't aware of it consciously. When I asked whether he made a distinction between the soul and higher self, he said he did.

Session #1—January 9, 1988

higher self is part of the soul. Some people say the higher self is the soul, and in many ways that is true, but the higher self is the perception of the soul that perceives more than the physical can perceive.

We came back to this distinction several times in the following weeks. Gerod continued to emphasize the higher self as the *perceiving* of the soul. He called it the "active part" of the soul.

I always say that the soul is the soul, and the higher self is the perceiving of the soul. When I speak of the higher self, I am speaking of the active part of the soul.

Session #4—January 26, 1988

The soul is a repository of all knowledge and all information; and when I speak of the higher self, I am usually speaking of the soul in activity.

Session #7—February 6, 1988

It is the working part of the soul. It is that part of the soul that goes about gathering information; goes about giving information in interacting with the conscious self.

Gerod's information shifted my clinical focus from the soul to the higher self. His basic message was that when he talked about working with a person's soul, like with Danny, he was really talking about working with the higher self. His clear implication was that this was the part of the soul that could respond to directions and be active in the healing process.

It was also this active part of the soul that Gerod had been referring to in that first session when he talked about helping a person open the self/soul connection.

Session #1—January 9, 1988

> If you can get in touch with their higher self, with their soul, with the part of them that is aware of what is taking place, that will expand the awareness so that eventually there will be a breakthrough to the consciousness—whether or not that breakthrough is very obvious, I could not say. For some people it will be, for a lot of people it may be years before it finally trickles through. But it will open up their consciousness to their greater self. Hypnosis is probably one of the more effective ways to deal with this at this time.

Based on Gerod's use of the term, I thought of the higher self as a conduit and interface between the soul and self.

Intelligent Communication

It wasn't long after focusing on the higher self that Gerod took it to another level. Several times, in different sessions, he suggested or implied that I could communicate directly to a client's higher self. I had not thought of the higher self in this way. The capacity to communicate put the higher self into a whole different category than an *energy conduit*. It implied a conscious intelligence, separate from the conscious self, which was perceiving and aware in present time. It was the same issue I would be facing shortly with the protective part, i.e., a conscious part of the mind, separate from the conscious self, carrying out certain activities at an unconscious level. Only with the higher self, we were talking about a very different level of consciousness.

Over the next two years, I communicated with many higher selves. Gerod also talked to me about those same higher selves from his point of view. From one case to the next, I was learning gradually how to communicate with a higher self. I was learning about what it could do, and what it couldn't do, or wouldn't do. The consistency of my interactions with many different higher selves became more and more convincing. It was strong confirmation that I was dealing with a distinct part, separate from the conscious self.

Further confirmation came from my clients' own experience during trance. Many reported a noticeable shift or change when I asked for the higher self to come forward and communicate. It took different forms: a sudden warmth spreading through the body; a change in mood; the appearance of an inner light that becomes brighter; or a feeling of universal love. With a few clients, the higher self even communicated verbally. There were also clients who were not aware of any change, but whose fingers signaled that the higher self was present and willing to communicate.

The Inner Guide

My growing experience working with higher selves led to a major breakthrough and radical change in my approach to healing. It didn't come from some new information, though. It came from an insight. The more I learned about the higher self over the months, the more its abilities and characteristics resembled those of an inner self helper. I don't recall a specific moment, but at some point I realized that the inner self helper I knew from psychology and the higher self I was investigating with Gerod were the same phenomenon. This realization instantly expanded my understanding of the phenomenon in both directions. What I knew about the inner self helper and its abilities, I now knew was also true of the higher self, and vice-versa. What one could do in the inner world, the other could do, too. In one sense, the inner self helper put a face on what Gerod called the "active part of the soul."

At a theoretical level, the convergence of these concepts—one from a clinical and psychological framework and the other from a clinical and metaphysical framework—also brought together two different paradigms of thought. Each had arrived at the higher self from a different starting point, and used different language, but they were describing and talking about the same phenomenon. Psychology recognized the inner self helper, but couldn't explain it. Gerod called it the higher self and said it was a manifestation of the soul.

This new understanding changed how I worked with higher selves in general. It was like Dr. Allison discovering Beth and all the ways she could help Elizabeth. Now I understood that every person has a "Beth," an inner self helper, a God-part, whatever you want to call it. Knowing what an inner self helper was capable of, the higher self promised to be a tremendous resource in each person's healing process.

I put this promise to the test. I began communicating to each client's higher self as though it were an inner self helper. I began asking higher selves for information, and to do things I knew an inner self helper could do; and they were able to do it. This included communicating with ego-states directly, just as the inner self helper can communicate with an alter-personality. It included accessing and sharing past- or present-life memories to the conscious self. It especially included bringing Light to the conscious self and to the inner world. There was so much that a person's higher self could do, I just hadn't known enough yet to ask. Gerod had called it the "working part of the soul." I look at the higher self today as the *workhorse* in the healing process. In many ways, it is the higher self that makes the process work.

In the coming chapters, I'll talk about the many powerful ways in which a person's higher self can assist in the healing process. These are ways that have been tested and confirmed over and over again in my work with clients. I think the reader will gain a deeper understanding of the higher self as we go through the chapters.

11

Soul-Centered Healing

To avoid frustration and disappointment, search and find the teacher within, the gurudeva within. In the Light of the inner guru you will be able to distinguish what is right for you and what is not. If you cannot distinguish right from wrong, good from bad, you will always remain a victim of abuse and exploitation by the external world. —Swami Rama, from *The Eleventh Hour*

The Place of Integration

After the girl in red shoes, two things happened that completely changed how I worked with ego-states. Both involved discoveries that could only have been made after recognizing ego-states as real beings. The first was the discovery that these inner beings do not just dissolve or disappear after their sharing and release. They continue to exist at an unconscious level.

Gerod had already been saying for some months that the ego-states were real beings; that they continue to exist after their sharing and release; and that there was a place of integration and comfort each could move to after its release.

Session #98—July 7, 1989

There are those who would believe that these ego-states are not the real person, that they are not able to exist or co-exist, that they must be absorbed so strongly that they cease to be, but in essence, they are part of the whole and what they have done is make the whole larger . . . What must be remembered is that the ego-state that becomes part of the personality (integrates), brings in its very own energy, and that energy just does not mix in and melt, it is more as if it adds to and expands, and there is the difference. It is like instead of stirring something in, you attach it on.

I didn't grasp the full import of what Gerod was saying at the time. These ideas were contrary to the generally held view in psychology—ones that I held also—that 1) these personalities were not beings, but states of consciousness, and 2) that they dissolve into the core self after their sharing and release is complete. It wasn't until I grasped ego-states as real beings that I understood the importance of this issue. It was the next logical question. If they are beings who go on living, then where do they live? If they are not absorbed into the self, then where do they exist?

Gerod's answer was that, once free of its pain, an ego-state could move into a new consciousness and a new relationship with the conscious self. We wound up calling it the "place of integration." He said to think of it as a place adjacent to, and with a door into, the conscious self. It was a place where it was no longer necessary for the ego-state to keep its experience dissociated from the conscious self. It's not as though the trauma never happened, but the ego-state—and so the self—no longer has to live it at this unconscious level. The release from pain, Gerod said, frees the ego-state to come into alignment with the conscious self in present reality. He was also suggesting that I could help facilitate this integration very directly as a final step in resolving an ego-state. It was a very different idea of integration than the one I had been working.

I tested out this idea of integration with many ego-states of many different clients. After an ego-state had had its release, I began to ask the higher self to show it to its place of integration. Then I would communicate with the ego-state about this place. The consistent response from one ego-state to another was that it had moved to a new place; that they were receiving Light and it felt very good to them; and they did not want to leave it. This was so consistent that it wasn't long before I incorporated this step into the healing process. Instead of trying to dissolve ego-states into some unified self, I was helping direct them to a place where they continued to live, but in harmony and cooperation with the self. This new understanding about ego-states and the place of integration had a powerful and positive impact on my work with clients.

The full import of this integration, though, became clear when I finally grasped that the ego-states were real beings, living in real places. So, of course it would make a difference to them where they were living, whether they were feeling safe and comfortable, or were in pain and distress. They were "places" of consciousness, of course, but real to them nonetheless. From a clinical point of view, then, it would be important for each of them to know that through the healing process it could move to a new place that would feel good and comfortable.

With integration as a primary goal of healing, the promise of a place of integration became a primary motivation for ego-states to say yes to the healing process itself. For many, it changed their view of the process from a threat of pain or dissolution, to a way to be free of pain and distress. Instead of a threat, integration promised relief.

As a therapist, the knowledge about integration put me in a position to give every inner being two very positive messages. The first was that it would continue to exist after going through the sharing and release. It would not be dissolved or die. This in itself was a relief for many of the ego-states with whom I was working. (As I found out later, many times ego-states had been afraid and resisting the healing process because they viewed the process as leading to their dissolution and death).

The second message for each ego-state was that there was a place of comfort and safety waiting for them once they were able to release their pain. Relief from pain and fear is a natural and powerful motivation for any being, and ego-states were no exception. The result was that most ego-states were very interested when I talked to them about a place of integration and, in turn, became more quickly cooperative and willing to participate in the healing process. This change, like in working with the protective part, seemed to lessen another whole level of blocking and resistance.

A Touch of Soul

During this same period, as I was learning about the place of integration, a second thing was happening that would have an even greater impact on the healing process. I was coming to realize that the higher self was a consciousness in its own right. It was intelligent and aware and able to communicate. As I described in the last chapter, I finally realized that the higher self had all the knowledge and abilities of an inner self helper. This included knowing about the inner personalities and being able to communicate with them directly.

Once I recognized ego-states as real beings—also conscious and intelligent—it changed the kind of relationship I saw as possible between the higher self and ego-states. The higher self could not only be a contact of Light for an ego-state, it could actively engage it, and relate to it at its own level of consciousness. I saw that the higher self could—or already did—relate to them as beings. A personalized contact with the Light, if you will.

I already knew that ego-states, in general, responded positively to contact with the higher self. I had thought of it as a kind of generic contact with the Light, a scattergun approach. I did not really grasp the potential power of this contact, though, until I recognized that every ego-state, as a conscious being, had the capacity to communicate with the higher self and know the Light directly.

I didn't know what went on between the higher self and an ego-state in their contact. I couldn't observe it directly, of course, but I saw the same results over and over again. Once an ego-state had direct contact with the higher self, its response was overwhelmingly positive. Over ninety-five percent of the time, once an ego-state experienced the Light, it became immediately cooperative in the healing process. It was like flipping a switch. Regardless of how frightened or resistant an ego-state had been, after communication with the higher self, there would be a complete turn around. It was suddenly willing to do whatever was required to maintain its connection to the higher self and the Light— even when that meant sharing painful memories and feelings.

This instant transformation parallels closely with a person's contact with the Light during a near-death-experience. Upon entering the Light, they report an infinite feeling of love and belonging. They all say, "words can't begin to describe it," and they don't want to leave it. They also report a higher level of knowledge and understanding of how everything fits, in their own life, and in all levels of reality. It was the same way I saw earthbound spirits respond once they chose to feel the Light. No matter how resistant, once they agreed to a touch of Light, there was an immediate conversion. Ego-states were responding in exactly the same way.

The clinical implications of this were profound. First, initiating contact with the higher self promised to resolve any resistance or fear an ego-state might be feeling, and at the same time, kindle its own motivation to participate in the healing process. Unlike promising a place of integration to come later, contact with the higher self was an immediate experience for an ego-state, and so an even more powerful motivator.

The second implication followed from the first. Since ego-states were a primary source of resistance, it made sense to initiate that contact with each one right from the start. Why wait for resistance or blocking to develop? If contact with the higher self led to such quick cooperation, then it could pre-empt a good deal of that resistance. It was the same logic behind making contact with the protective part in our first session: to pre-empt future blocking, and also to elicit its active cooperation. The same was true here for ego-states.

This strategy worked as promised. Each time I identified a new ego-state, I asked that it have a direct communication with the higher self. When it did, I had its cooperation from that point on. The strategy was so successful that it became a standard step in the healing process. It was a watershed moment in the development of Soul-Centered Healing. This is when the soul's Light, in the form of the higher self, came to play a direct and powerful role in the healing process.

Refusing the Light

There was a flipside to this dramatic conversion by the Light. After I began initiating this contact, I discovered many ego-states who refused to receive the Light or have contact with the higher self. The situation mirrored what I was seeing with earthbound spirits. Once they chose to see the Light or touch it, they would go to it in an instant. There were other spirits, though, who refused the Light or fled from it. I found the same thing happening with ego-states.

Ego-states refused the Light for many of the same reasons that earthbound spirits did. They felt guilty or unworthy of the Light, or it began to trigger their pain and memories, or they were afraid the Light would reject them. Some were angry at the Light. They either blamed it for what had happened, or felt betrayed because the Light had not protected them. Still others had been told to stay away from the Light because it would harm them or destroy them.

Besides those who refused the Light, there was a second complication in helping ego-states through the process of sharing and release. I had assumed that once an ego-state had contact with the higher self and I had its full cooperation that would pre-empt the need for further blocking. I thought that once an ego-state said *yes* to the healing, then it would just be able to move through its sharing and release. This didn't happen. Even with its full cooperation, there were still points in the healing process where an ego-state would become frightened or stuck and would stop the process.

I also learned during this same time that I couldn't use the higher self as a magic wand. I couldn't just send it to every ego-state and expect it to force an experience of the Light. It didn't work that way. Here was the rub. Just as guides or loved ones will not approach an earthbound spirit without permission, the higher self will not force its Light on an ego-state (or the self, or anyone else for that matter). The Light must be freely chosen. If an ego-state refuses the Light, or says no to it for any reason, the higher self will respect that boundary. It will not violate the ego-state's position or choice. So, while contact with the Light could work magic, the issue with many ego-states was first getting them to agree to the contact.

In the beginning, Gerod was instrumental in teaching me about the fears and obstacles that made ego-states refuse the Light. He also taught me about the kinds of things that could block or interrupt an ego-state's sharing even though it was trying to cooperate. These were the questions I took to Gerod each week. They dealt with the blocks I encountered in my work with specific clients. Week after week, Gerod talked to me about different clients and who or what was blocking the process, and why. Every week, I took this information back to my sessions with those clients and time after time Gerod's information bore fruit and led to a resolution of the blocking.

Over time, patterns began to emerge and I was able to identify the most common sources of blocking. I saw where ego-states would typically get stuck, what frightened them, or who might be in their way. I learned what questions to ask in order to quickly determine the source of an ego-state's blocking or refusal. Working at this level of resistance and blocking taught me a great deal about these inner beings. It meant stepping deeper into their world and the psychic reality in which they lived. The question was always the same, though. What would make it worthwhile or safe enough for this or that particular ego-state to say yes to the Light, or to take the next step in its sharing?

Solving All Resistance

Knowing where an ego-state was stuck or blocked was only half the story. The other half was in knowing how to help it get unstuck. This is where we come back to the power of the higher self. At the same time I was learning about ego-states and different sources of blocking, I was also learning more about the higher self. I learned about its capacity to intervene at any point to help an ego-state that had become stuck, or was being blocked. Through Gerod's information and my new understanding of the higher self as an inner self helper, I learned that it could bring an ego-state the Light in any form it needed. The higher self's particular presentation depended on who the ego-state was and what it needed to feel safe. Whether it was a child or an adult, angry or terrified, hiding or confused, the higher self could provide what it needed. If the ego-state were a child, for example, the higher self could send a doll, where the doll *is* the Light. The higher self could appear as an angel, a fairy godmother, or a glowing Light. The only stipulation, again, being that the ego-state had to agree to receive it. In effect, contact with the higher self could be tailor-made to almost guarantee that the ego-state would consent.

The higher self's adaptive abilities had profound implications for the healing process. It meant that my client's higher self was not only a source of Light, but that it could be an active agent in the person's healing. It was conscious, and it could do things. It could bring the Light, in whatever form was needed by a particular ego-state, even to those that carried the deepest pain and hurt, or were the most afraid.

From a clinical point of view, the higher self offered a method ideally suited for resolving any ego-state's resistance or fears. The higher self would be able to meet it on its own terms and at its own level of consciousness. In practice, this is what happened and it proved most successful. In these situations, my role as therapist became that of the negotiator, a go-between. When we ran into problems with an ego-state, it was my job to find out what the problem was, and the higher self would provide the fix. Once I learned to work this method, we were able to resolve any resistance or blocks by ego-states most of the time.

I still cannot tell you what happens in an ego-state's contact with the higher self and the Light. I can say with a certainty, though, almost without exception, that once an ego-state has contact with the higher self, it will say yes to the Light, and then to the healing process. Ninety-nine percent of the time, it is willing to take the next step of sharing its memory and experience to the conscious self. I'm quite confident that other therapists using this same method would see these same results. This method was so successful in obtaining ego-states' cooperation that initiating this contact became a standard step in Soul-Centered Healing.

Preventing and avoiding resistance is not the only reason, however, for having an ego-state make contact with the higher self. Even if an ego-state is fully cooperative and willing to share its experience to the conscious mind, I will still ask that it first have a contact with the higher self. I picture the contact as opening the ego-state's connection to the soul and to the Light. It's a way to give it further affirmation about healing and its place within the self. From my point of view, an ego-state's contact with higher self not only helps to resolve or pre-empt resistance, but also helps fortify and reinforce an ego-state in taking the steps it requires for its own healing and release.

12

Ego-States: The Inner Beings

The astral domain has certain unique properties, one of which is the principle that astrally or emotionally charged thoughts have a life of their own. At the astral energetic level, certain thoughts, either conscious or unconscious, may exist as distinct energy fields or thoughtforms with unique shapes, colors and characteristics. Some thoughts, especially those charged with emotional intensity, can have separate identity apart from their creator. Certain thoughts may actually be charged with subtle energetic substance and exist (unconsciously) as thoughtforms in the energetic fields of their creators. These thoughtforms can frequently be seen by clairvoyant individuals who are very sensitive to higher energetic phenomena. —Richard Gerber M.D. from Vibrational Medicine.

The Birth of an Ego-State

Ego-states are created for the purpose of survival and protecting the self from pain. They're a defense mechanism. An ego-state is created when a person can no longer consciously tolerate what is happening in his or her experience—physically, emotionally, or psychologically.

A painful fall, a feeling of terror, or the deep hurt of rejection—all are examples of situations where a person's consciousness, especially with children, may be overwhelmed or so frightened that it triggers the creation of an ego-state to take over and survive. (See Figure 1.)

When an event occurs that is not painful or threatening (Event Y), the self remains conscious and aware throughout the experience. If, however, an event is too painful, hurtful, or threatening (Event X), then

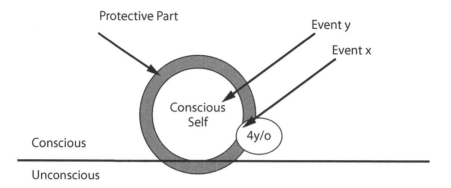

Figure 1: The Creation of an Ego-state

the protective part reacts and triggers the creation of an ego-state to separate the pain or trauma from the conscious self.

The ego-state will live the experience until it is safe again for the conscious self to resume consciousness. We might look at the ego-state as a *stand-in* for the conscious self, somewhat like a stunt-double *stands in* for the actor.

The problem, however, is that once an ego-state is created, it does not dissolve, die, or just disappear when the crisis or trauma has passed. Once it is safe for the self to resume consciousness, the ego-state, as a conscious being, moves to the unconscious, outside normal awareness, where it continues to live in its own reality separate from the conscious self.

As I talked about in Chapter 8, it is not a physical reality or dimension that the ego-state moves to. Psychologists would call it the *unconscious*. Gerber calls it the *astral* domain. I think of it as a *psychic* realm. We just don't have a language for it yet. Whatever term we use, it is a nonphysical dimension of mind, outside time and space; a realm ruled by consciousness and thought, not matter. This is the realm in which the girl in red shoes lives.

In this realm, an ego-state can be any age and take any form that is needed or will work at the time of the trauma or threat. Most ego-states are in human form, for example, but not all. I have met ego-states presenting as animals or plants, or even as cartoon figures or a vaporous form.[1] Each one, though, is conscious, intelligent, and able to communicate.

While an ego-state's reality usually reflects our three-dimensional world, it is a realm that does not obey the laws of physical reality. In this realm, a child can fit into a thimble, grow a new arm, or even fly. In this realm, monsters are real, and a child can disappear into a *never-never land* to escape what is happening in the present. It is the ego-state's consciousness and perception that matters here and largely determines the reality. It can be a different reality for each one, like different universes existing side by side.

What is consistent for these ego-states, though, is that each lives in a reality born out of trauma and threat. These inner beings are defensive creations. They don't come into existence when the self is safe or having a good time. Ego-states are created in reaction to pain and fear, when the self is in trouble and cannot handle what is happening. So when an ego-state moves to the psychic level, it is this painful or overwhelming reality that it takes with it. The ego-state's fragmentary experience and consciousness becomes its whole reality. It is separated from the ongoing flow of life. The ego-state continues to live in a world centered in its pain and trauma long after the trauma has passed for the conscious self. Most ego-states know no other world than the world that gave it birth.

Living in this psychic dimension, ego-states continue to serve the primary purpose of protection for which they were originally created. Each ego-state, conscious and alive in its own reality, continues to keep its experience of pain, fear, or distress separate from the conscious mind. The ego-state is like a bubble of consciousness whose purpose is to stay away from, and keep from breaking into, the self's conscious awareness.

Take the example of a four-year-old—I'll call her Connie—who is playing in her yard one day when the neighbor's dog is somehow incited and attacks her. In the child's shock and panic, an ego-state is created who takes over until it is safe for the ego-self to resume consciousness. Once the child is rescued from the situation, and the threat of pain and danger recedes, she begins to calm down. Somewhere in the process, she will also have begun a return to her normal awareness. When she does, there may be little conscious memory of what happened. Her instinctive defense reaction, in fact, will be to forget, if possible.

There may even be a complete dissociation of the experience where the child has no memory at all of what occurred. In the following days, she may believe that she was attacked by a dog because people tell her so, and because she sees the evidence of the bite wounds on her arm, but consciously she has no memory of it. Either way, she is safe now and any memory or thought of it is likely to fade in the following weeks and months. Years later, if asked, she may not even remember that it happened.

The Price of Protection

Every defense has its price, however, and creates its own problems. The problem with dissociation is that in keeping the pain or distress cut off from the conscious self, the ego-state is keeping the pain alive at another level. Like burying toxic waste, how deep is deep enough?

This still might not be a problem if there were no ongoing connection or interaction between the conscious self and the ego-states once they moved to the unconscious level. This is not the case, however. There is not an absolute boundary between these levels. Ego-states can, and do, affect the conscious self. How frequently, or how strongly, depends on the conscious person and the ego-state(s) involved. The effects can range, though, from negligible to overpowering.

This happens when an ego-state is triggered by events, feelings, or thoughts occurring for a person at a conscious level that resemble or match the ego-state's experience in one or more significant ways. When this confluence happens, it can trigger an ego-state and it will react. It is reacting, though, from within its own reality and perception, not to events in the person's present reality.

Take the example again of Connie who was attacked by the dog when she was four. It's thirty years later, and Connie, now an adult, is standing in her driveway talking to her neighbor when she begins to feel an over-whelming panic. She suddenly breaks into a sweat and her heart starts to race. She has no idea why she is feeling so terrified. She only knows that she wants to run into the house or get into her car as fast as possible. The only thing stopping her is that she's afraid her neighbor will think she's crazy. (She may even be questioning her own sanity at this point.)

Connie may or may not have noticed the man approaching from several houses away who is walking his dog. The four-year-old ego-state, however, has noticed. At an unconscious level, the earlier trauma has been re-activated. Four-year-old has seen the dog, and she is in a panic. To the four-year-old ego-state, in her limited consciousness, every dog is THE dog, and she responds in the only way she knows. She tries to escape.

Connie's experience of the anxiety and panic is what I call *blending*. The four-year-old ego-state has been triggered, and it's as though she begins to move toward consciousness. (See Figure 2.)

The closer she approaches present consciousness, the more her feelings and emotions begin to resonate and the more the thirty-four year-old starts to feel anxiety and a growing panic.

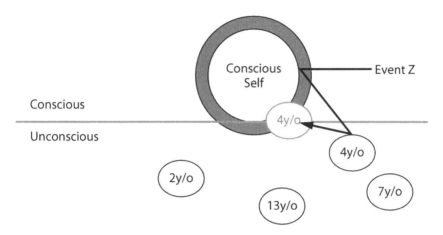

Figure 2: Ego-state Blending with the Conscious Self

I call this blending because the four-year-old does not break into consciousness. At a conscious level, Connie is not remembering the dog's attack while she stands there with her neighbor. She is not having flashbacks of her front yard nor is she thinking back thirty years. She is not even aware of the four-year-old ego-state directly and, therefore, has no way to distinguish between the four-year-old's panic and her own. A person can be affected by an ego-state's perception, emotions, and kinesthetic reactions, but not remember the ego-state's experience. So, Connie will most likely look to her external reality for what is so threatening because at a conscious level she has no internal reference by which to understand it.

I view this triggering and blending of ego-states as part of a person's psychological defenses. It serves to alert and mobilize the self to defensive action against a situation perceived by an ego-state to be painful or threatening. In this way, ego-states act as a kind of early warning system that can alert the self to dangers, and even lead the self to take action if necessary, and all of it happening at an unconscious level.

In our fictional example, Connie may find an excuse to end her conversation with the neighbor and hurry back to the house. Or, she might look around and reassure herself that everything is all right, including the man and dog that are approaching. She may not make any connection between the dog and her panic.

Either way, once the crisis is over, the four-year-old ego-state returns to her normal place within the mind and Connie's feelings of panic and fear start to subside. Before long, she is feeling normal again and able to get on with her day. In a simple case such as this, the panic reaction may not happen often enough to really warrant any serious concern. The adult Connie might look at it as "just one of those weird things," and after a day or two, she may not think about the incident again.

This triggering of ego-states and blending with consciousness happens to people every day, sometimes several times a day. When something occurs for a person that is close to an ego-state's original issue or trauma, the ego-state can be triggered and react as if the trauma is still happening, or threatening to happen. A person sees something, or hears something, or is in the middle of a situation, when he or she is suddenly reacting with feelings and thoughts that don't fit, or that threaten to overwhelm him or her emotionally.

The person may not know why he or she is feeling a certain way, or having a particular reaction, or why all of a sudden it seems like a dark cloud has closed in on them. They may know their feelings or reactions are out of proportion to what the situation calls for, or maybe they only become aware of that afterwards when the feelings and reactions have subsided. Often, at these times, there doesn't seem to be any connection between what is going on in their present conscious reality and what they are feeling or how they are reacting. The mood, thoughts, and emotions may last only a moment or two, or they could persist for hours.

How an ego-state affects a person once it has been triggered will depend on the particular ego-state involved. It will also depend on the person's conscious awareness, and whether they possess the psychological and emotional strength to tolerate and resolve what is happening without having to shut down, lash out, or flee the situation. The blending can be mild, or it can be strong enough to interfere with what a person is doing, even causing them to change their course of action altogether, like Connie running to her house in a panic, but not sure why.

Sharing

If Connie were a client and, through hypnosis, I communicated to this four-year-old ego-state, she probably would not know who I am, what the present year is or where I was talking to her from. This would not be unusual. Most ego-states, on first contact, are not aware of the present physical reality. The four-year-old, most likely, would not even be aware that the conscious personality is now an adult and living in a very different reality than her own. Four-year-old, for example, would not know about Connie's husband and children, or the house she lives in, or the place where she works.

Ego-states often are surprised and amazed when they learn of the conscious self in an adult body and see the changes that have occurred since their own creation. They begin to realize there is a bigger picture. In the healing process, this realization in itself often brings the ego-state some relief and leads to a greater willingness to communicate.

In our example, the four-year-old's lack of awareness of the present reality is not because she has been asleep. She hasn't been. She is awake and still living in the reality in which she was created. She is still four-years-old, it is still a clear and sunny day, and she is still in her front yard. If asked, she could tell me where she is in the yard, what she is wearing, and what toys are there. She could also tell me what is going on around her and, if willing, she could tell me what is happening to her.

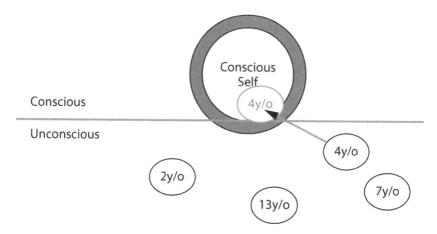

Figure 3: Ego-state Sharing to Consciousness

More importantly, four-year-old can also share her experience directly with the conscious self if she chooses. In contrast to blending, I picture *sharing* as an ego-state not only moving *close to* consciousness, but *entering* into consciousness. (See Figure 3.)

Through sharing, the conscious self will begin to remember, and to some extent, relive the ego-state's experience(s). Unlike with blending, where the conscious self and ego-state remain unconscious of each other, in sharing, the four-year-old *opens* her consciousness, so to speak, and thirty-four-year-old Connie, then, will see, feel, hear, or know the experience of the attack itself.[2] At that point, she is remembering. What was once cut off becomes a part of the whole.

While blending happens frequently with people in the course of their day-to-day experience, sharing is not as common. Normally, the boundary between these two realms of consciousness remains intact. There are occasional times for a person, though, when an ego-state is triggered and breaks through into consciousness as a complete memory, or a flashback, or even a living reality. This can be a shock to a person, but the boundary is usually, and quickly, re-established.

If that *breaking through* were to happen too frequently, though, a person would become overwhelmed by the sheer confusion and emotions running riot through his or her every day life. These are people, for example, who might be diagnosed as psychotic. For the most severe, it's as if the boundary is riddled with holes. We need the boundary between these realms for survival and to live a stable and productive life.

Opening the Boundary

In the healing process, however, the attitude toward sharing is just the opposite. We do want to open that boundary so there can be a sharing between these levels. We do want the ego-state and the conscious self to know each other, and in the knowing, resolve any need for dissociation. This sharing is a central step in the healing process because it is the point where two conflicting realities meet and are reconciled. This is the abreaction I talked about in Chapter 1 in which the conscious self reclaims the ego-state's experience, psychologically and emotionally.

Going back to our example, when Connie remembers the dog's attack, she will most likely experience some level of the four-year-old's terror and pain. She will also gain insight and understand clearly what happened that day when she was talking to her neighbor and went into a panic. She'll know that the four-year-old ego-state had been triggered and was reacting to the attack from so many years ago. Connie might also make the connection that this early trauma could be involved in the general discomfort she has always felt around dogs. She might see for the first time just how much she had actively avoided dogs in her life. These are the kinds of cognitive insights that typically result for a person once an ego-state has shared its experience.

At an emotional level, the person experiences the feelings and emotions that were blocked from consciousness and expression when the ego-state was first created. It's as if one's experience had been short-circuited and the energy of the emotion locked up at an unconscious level. The ego-state's sharing to consciousness, then, finally completes the circuit and allows the energy to become conscious and be discharged.

Once Connie remembers and has had some level of catharsis, there will no longer be a need for four-year-old to maintain the dissociation. In reclaiming the experience of the attack, the conscious self reclaims the four-year-old as herself and the experience as her own. The sharing resolves any need to keep the two separate.

Release and Integration

In the process of sharing, the ego-state herself is also transformed. By opening herself to the conscious mind, the four-year-old is able to move free of the reality where she has been caught for so long. It is important to remember that four-year-old's experience of connecting

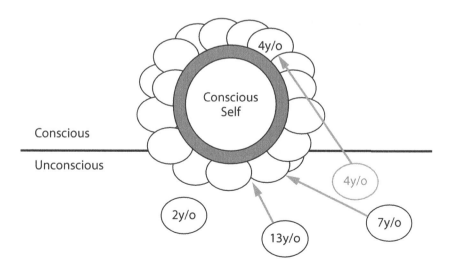

Figure 4: Integration of Ego-states

with the conscious mind and conscious reality has been an abreaction for her as well, altering her perception and therefore her reality. The old reality at that point no longer applies.

The abreaction puts four-year-old into a position to release the pain, terror, and distress that she has been carrying since she was created. This doesn't mean that she forgets what happened, but it is no longer her present reality and she is no longer in the pain and distress of that moment. The release and transformation frees her to move to a new consciousness, her own place of integration. (See Figure 4.)

Integration is a state of consciousness, and so the place of integration itself will be determined largely by the consciousness of the particular ego-state involved. If an ego-state really needs to live alone in a house on the river in order to be in harmony with the self, then that is where she will move. If the ego-state is a child who needs to be with other children, then she will be. In general, though, an ego-state's integration means that it moves into a new balance and compatibility with the self and frees the conscious person and the ego-state from an old perception and painful reality.

For Connie, the conscious personality, integration will mean that the next time she is close to a dog, her extreme *fight or flight* reaction won't be triggered, and if the situation does cause concern, she will have more freedom to determine whether the dog is a real and present threat or not. She also will not be caught between two perceptions where a little concern and anxiety cascades into confusion and a rising panic.

A large part of the healing process, then, is the accumulating effects, or synergy, created by the integration of these inner beings as each comes into alignment with the conscious self. Each one of these integrations is a healing of the fragmentation and pain that has, at some level, kept a person blocked, afraid or splintered for many years. Each integration of an ego-state frees a person from hidden conflict and backward looking protection. It is a reclaiming of the self; and each reclaiming brings the person increased clarity and understanding about him or her self, the world in which they live, and a greater feeling of safety and freedom.

13

Inner Worlds

A (psychological) complex with its given tension or energy has the tendency to form a little personality of itself. It has a sort of body, a certain amount of its own physiology. It can upset the stomach. It upsets the breathing, it disturbs the heart—in short, it behaves like a partial personality.—C. G. Jung

Keys to the Kingdom

As far as I was concerned, when it came to ego-states, the promise of integration and the immediate contact with the higher self were like being given the keys to the kingdom, to many kingdoms, in fact. Once an ego-state received information about healing and integration, and had contact with higher self, it was usually more than willing not only to share its experience and memory, but also to answer any questions about itself or the reality in which it existed. These were powerful keys, a kind of *open sesame,* and I began to use them with each client and with each ego-state I encountered.

The overall result was that more ego-states than ever before, with more clients, were sharing their memories and experiences. I also felt sure that contact with the higher self and the promise of integration also pre-empted a significant amount of blocking from ego-states that might otherwise have been frightened and resistant.

Once I began using these keys in my work with clients, it virtually eliminated a source of blocking and confusion that I always had to contend with before. When I was working with an ego-state and the communication became blocked, I could never be sure that it wasn't the ego-state itself that was stopping it. Once I began using the place of integration and contact with the higher self to gain an ego-state's cooperation, I was able to determine much more quickly whether the ego-state I was working with was blocking or whether it was coming from somewhere else.

Sometimes, it was the ego-state blocking. There were ego-states, for example, who carried more than one experience or had deeper feelings than they had been aware of. These ego-states, then, might stop the sharing as these levels of experience began to surface. There were also those who instinctively blocked the sharing as they began to experience the emotional pain. Even in these circumstances, though, the particular ego-state cooperated in letting me know that it had been the one who stopped the sharing. It was also willing to answer questions and do what it could to complete its sharing and move to release.

Gaining an ego-state's cooperation from the beginning was a major advance in the healing method. It meant more ego-states moving through the process of sharing, release, and integration. For my clients, it meant that experiences that had been dissociated for many years were now coming forward into consciousness, often for the first time. Clients were reclaiming and integrating parts of themselves that had long ago been separated from the self, creating conflict and confusion.

The Inner World Web

This greater cooperation of ego-states led directly to another major advance in the healing method. By being able to rule out the ego-state I was working with as a source of blocking, I could focus my questions more effectively on identifying who or what was blocking. In this way, I began to learn about other levels and dynamics of blocking that could interfere in the healing process.

I discovered, for example, that one of the primary sources of blocking, even after I had an ego-state's cooperation, was other ego-states. The emphasis here is on the word *primary*. The phenomenon itself was not new to me. Before I met Gerod, I knew that alter-personalities could interact and communicate with each other directly. I also knew that one alter-personality could sometimes block another. More than once I had seen one alter-personality shove another aside and take over consciousness right in the middle of a conversation. I did not know, however, just how prevalent this dynamic was and how often other ego-states were a source of blocking. I learned that interconnection and interaction between ego-states was the rule, not the exception. I also discovered that most of the ego-states I worked with were not alone. They did not exist in isolation, but were usually part of a group. There could be two, several, or many ego-states comprising a group.

It would not be unusual, for instance, to find an older ego-state acting as a protector for younger ones who were with her. An eighteen-year-old ego-state might tell me, for example, that it was her job to protect the children and so that is why she stepped in and blocked my attempts to explore certain areas of a client's pain or distress. She might tell me that my questions were triggering some of the children in her group and threatening to set off their pain. So, the eighteen-year-old had blocked all further attempts to access those children by shutting off all communication with me.

As with alter-personalities blocking one another, the existence of groups was also not a new phenomenon to me. I knew from my own practice that some alter-personalities formed groups, and I had read about them numerous times in the literature. What was new for me, however, was learning how frequently the ego-states formed groups.

The discovery that ego-states typically existed in groups, and that other members of a group could be involved in blocking, raised further questions about the nature of these groups and the interrelationships among ego-states. It became increasingly clear to me that when an ego-state I was working with was blocked from communicating or sharing, it was often another or others in their group, or close by, who were coming forward to stop the process.

My advantage now was that I possessed the keys to elicit the cooperation, not only of the one I was working with, but also of any other ego-state that came forward to block. When that happened, I could adjust the line of inquiry to easily identify the one blocking and gain its cooperation as well. Knowing how to elicit an ego-state's cooperation had a kind of cascading effect. When necessary, I could follow a thread of ego-states as one after another was triggered. This applied also to entire groups who were triggered and blocking. The higher self could bring Light and information to all of them and elicit their cooperation as a group.

Clinically the bottom line was still the same: identify and work with each presenting ego-state to share, release, and integrate. The fact that they formed groups and interacted with each other did not change the bottom line, but it made it more complex. The discovery that this kind of blocking was prevalent forced me to develop a whole new level of understanding about these inner beings, how they can affect and interact with each other, as well as how they affected the conscious personality. These groupings and the interrelationships among ego-states, therefore, began to emerge as a major issue and focus in the healing process.

This was new territory to me. These interconnections and interactions among ego-states were another development I had neither anticipated nor bargained for, but it came with the territory. It's just the way it was. If I was going to deal with ego-states, then I also had to deal with their groups and interconnections. I had to think in terms not only of the individual ego-state I was working with, but its context as well. I began to understand that when I made contact with one ego-state, it often would mean I was stepping into a matrix of already existing relationships among different ego-states and their experiences.

The Master Key

The promise of integration and contact with the higher self led to major changes in my approach to ego-states and learning about the inner world. I don't know, however, how far these two keys by themselves would have taken me in understanding the complexity and depth of the inner world. The fact was I had a third key I was using at the same time to also help me look behind the blocks and see who or what was in the way. That key, of course, was Gerod and his ability to access and share with me information about the inner world of each of my clients. In this sense, Gerod was a master key.

I was hearing Gerod's view each week, oftentimes in depth, on these same clients and their inner worlds. Whenever I encountered a block with a client that I could not resolve, or where I was confused about responses I was receiving, or I couldn't locate the source of a client's powerful reaction, then I would bring my questions to Gerod. I would ask him in our next session whether he could find that block or see the problem. He was able to view the situation in present time with the particular client and almost always was able to give some specific information about the block and how to address it.

We quickly came to a point in our dialogues where we would often discuss eight to ten clients in a session, some briefly, and others at length. Our collaboration, at this point, was moving into high gear.

Often, the information Gerod gave me about a block pointed to the same thing I was learning from ego-states, that is, that another ego-state or a group of ego-states was the source of the blocking or interference. Gerod's description, however, often revealed a complex and dynamic interrelationship among these parts of the self that I could not have imagined and probably would not have been able to decipher on my own.

Again, I believe Gerod was already aware of these interrelationships between ego-states, and I was the one who had to catch up. Early on, for example, I talked to Gerod about a client where I had just discovered three ego-states who seemed somehow connected to the one with whom I was working. I did not know, however, how they were connected. I asked Gerod for any information he could offer about the situation. He said that my work with this particular client was "stirring things up and there was a lot of activity." He went on, then, to describe an interrelationship among ego-states.

Session #49—October 15, 1988

> This is one of those situations I am not sure we have discussed before, but where certain pieces of information that need to be withheld from the conscious mind in order to protect and in order to survive are tucked away in other places, and many times these different ego-states are connected; they can be traversed with ease. And that is the way it has been for a very long time with her. But often times, as people reach that critical point in their soul's growth and development, situations are triggered and when the pain starts and the memories start, it is not unusual from my point of view to see strong reactions begin where each ego-state will close up and separate and go on its own in order to keep those memories very secure.

This was one of the first inklings I had of the inner world as a web or network of interconnected ego-states and groups of ego-states, but I was not in a position to grasp its significance.

There were many times like this in my early work with Gerod where he gave me information that one ego-state was blocking another, or that I was dealing with not just one, but with a group of ego-states. Gerod's information was so specific about so many clients that it revealed a unique and incredible inner reality for each of the clients we discussed.

The following excerpts, I hope, give at least a glimpse of the inner worlds that Gerod was describing. I hope these examples convey to the reader some *sense* and *feel* for this opening up and exploration of the psychic dimension.

In each of the following excerpts, I am talking to Gerod about a different client. In each case, I had encountered some kind of block and I was asking Gerod for any information he could offer. Often, the information he gave raised more questions and led to further discussion as I tried to be more specific. At times, this could lead to a lengthy dialogue, as you will see in the second excerpt.

Session #127—January 7, 1990

> In the circle of the nine there is a leader who could help you. It is a girl and she is stronger than the rest, and she is the leader and if you can engage her, you can probably be able to find an in-road. I don't have a name; I don't have an approximate age even. She wears yellow ribbons in her hair, she is belligerent, she is very strong, she is defiant, and if you address her in some way that she is able to identify it as her you are calling out, I believe she will talk to you.

Session #131—January 28, 1990

> G. There is a place within him that is hiding something. It is very, very strongly defended. The blocks are all hiding one place. They are very strong, and you would picture it almost as a maze, with this box at the center of it. And it is not so much that you even need to remove these blocks, as to find the way through them, because they are not so much holders of any substances, they are just there to block your way into this box where you will find what you need to work through what is going on with him. I would suggest you ask for the higher self's assistance in finding one that is almost a shadow or a ghost-type of being. It is not an earthbound spirit, it is more of an ego-state, but it is not one created out of an experience, as much as it is one created to be a keeper.
>
> T. Of the box?
>
> G. Of the maze. Almost like a guard. Now this one has no great fears, because it does not know what is in the box. It does not know that it necessarily is something to be feared, but only that it is the only one that knows the way through the maze.
>
> T. Gerod, my communication with the higher self has also been consistently blocked each time. Do you think if just by asking for that

assistance without requiring a response from the higher self, the higher self will receive that communication and look for this one?

G. It will. It is unable to respond. The maze is strong, and those blocks that create the maze are very strong. It is as if anything behind or around or being protected, so to say, by the maze, it is very hard for it to do anything. But the higher self is fairly capable of receiving a message and doing internal work. You may not be able to communicate directly with it. Now this keeper is one that I believe will communicate with you, because as I say, it has no fear and it has no instructions not to communicate. It just has the instruction not to allow anyone in.

T. Are you able to know, Gerod, whether the blocking I've encountered so far is blocking by just one, or several, or everybody together?

G. Several.

T. And they will, in a sense, give way to the keeper?

G. No, it's not that they will give way, it is as if to say that the blocks are not necessarily ego-states in the typical sense of what we understand by those that have personality and history, as much as they are strong walls.

T. Can you say how they were created?

G. They were created by the ego, and they were created, to some degree, by the one in the box.

T. So in the box is an ego-state?

G. It is.

T. Can you say whether this is present life?

G. It is present life. And these blocks that create the maze, you are aware of the perimeter wall, it is as if they become interior walls. And I do not see these blocks as connected. It is as if they are a maze, but they do not have connecting walls. So, you can get in and around all of them, and there appears to be at least twelve of them. So you need some guidance through.

T. And if the keeper helps with that, would that mean basically not having to deal with the blocks but just be able to move to the box in the center?

G. That is right. The box is small, but the box is deep. It is layered.

T. And only one ego state? Or could there be more?

G. The top layer.

T. Is the ego afraid of the higher self at this point?

G. I don't think it is necessarily as afraid as it is unwilling. Not so much fear as uncertainty as to why there is any need to communicate or pay any attention to the higher self. There is not great awareness on the part of the ego as to what the higher self is, and therefore views it as something that it does not understand and does not see the value of it. And so there is quite a high disregard for it, pretending it's not there.

T. Well, every time I've moved to communicate with the higher self, things shut down.

G. That is right. Because to allow you access is to allow . . . It's like stopping up your ears. If they are to allow you to communicate and hear the higher self, then it's almost as if they have to unstop their ears to allow that to occur, and they don't want to. They'd just as soon not hear it, because then they don't have to deal with it and try to decide what it is.

Session #147—May 26, 1990

G. There is a jackknife that the 7yo has. Ask him to put it in his pocket and to leave it there. Tell him it is okay; not to feel dismayed with the thoughts he has had about what he would wish to do with this jackknife; that there is nothing that he will do with it that is harmful, not even to himself. Help him to feel more comfortable about it, about what he has thought that he would do with it. That will perhaps instill a sense of safety for him to be able to go ahead with the work.

Every time Gerod talked about a client's ego-states like this, I had to bend and stretch my thinking in order to picture or conceptualize the inner world he was describing. Where exactly were these nine little girls who were in a circle, and what was it about the girl with yellow ribbons that made her the one to talk to? Who was this *Keeper,* and what were these sentries that created a maze of energy to guard the box? What was it 7yo was afraid he would do with the jackknife he was holding . . . and who was he afraid he would do it to?

You can see already from these examples the depth and complexity of the inner world. It makes absolutely clear that every person's inner world is unique. Week after week, Gerod was describing these worlds in a way that brought them alive for me and revealed the complex and dynamic relationships that existed among the ego-states. As I tried to communicate with ego-states I couldn't see, Gerod's descriptions were like turning on a flashlight in a dark room for me to see with whom I was working, and what was happening to them, or around them. Gerod's information gave them a face, and placed them in a context. His descriptions revealed a reality and depth to the inner world that I could not have imagined.

Going back to the above examples, I did find the different ego-states—the girl with the yellow ribbons, the box at the center of the maze (which turned out to be a cage with a little boy inside), and the 7yo who was able to do his sharing once he put the jackknife in his pocket. I used Gerod's information and suggestions and they almost always worked. I was able to establish communication with each of these ego-states and help them move through their sharing and release. At the same time, Gerod's information also forced me to begin thinking in terms of the dynamic reality that existed within each person.

It was one month after telling me about the boy with the jackknife, that I talked to Gerod about Martha K. and the girl in red shoes. (See Chapter 8.) This was where my own breakthrough came. It's where I began to realize that ego-states were real beings existing in what I could only call a "psychic realm." I came to a point clinically where I began to think in terms of psychic realities and the interrelationships that existed among these inner beings.

Once I awakened to the psychic reality of ego-states and started using the keys I now possessed, I began to learn a great deal more not only about the ego-states themselves, but also about the interrelationships among them. Who was alone, and who wasn't? Who blocked whom, and why? What brought some together into a group, and kept others apart? This kind of thinking and these kinds of questions became a part of my work with each client.

I think it is accurate to say that this was another period of quickening like the one that followed my discovery of earthbound spirits. This quickening, however, went on for a much longer time and at a level far deeper and beyond anything I had known before. It was a journey of exploration and discovery leading to new understandings about the inner world, how it is structured, and how it operates within the self.

Part 3
Soul Dimensions

Part 3
Soul Dimensions

Introduction

Soul-Centered Healing began as psychology. Ego-states were viewed as psychological phenomena, complex states of mind. They were created out of the client's own experience, and so were grounded in the physical, historical self. Part 2 focused on the individual and the inner world of ego-states. In Part 3, the focus shifts from the psychological to the *psychic* (taken from the Greek term for *soul).* These are realms and phenomena beyond the ego and its sense perception. They cannot be understood from a strictly ego-psychology point of view. They include past lives, attachment or intrusion by spirits, and the primal forces of darkness and Light.

In my communication with Gerod, it was clear from the beginning that he viewed all persons as more than their physical body and ego-personality. He viewed all persons as souls incarnate, most with a history of many lifetimes. He also talked from the beginning about darkness and Light, the existence of evil spirits, and reincarnation. For Gerod, these were all a matter-of-fact. For me, it took a long time, personally and professionally, to explore and understand these phenomena, form some kind of classification and framework, and learn how to deal with them clinically. The process involved thousands of client sessions, several hundred sessions with Gerod, and many phenomena always being investigated at once.

Part 3 takes us into these psychic realms from a clinical point of view. It focuses on those phenomena that consistently presented with clients over the course of many years. This also meant that the phenomena could be tested and verified over those many months and years as well. Each chapter in Part 3 focuses on particular phenomena, but taken together, they reveal interwoven dimensions of the self best described as *soul dimensions.* They also reveal a far greater reality of which we are all a part.

14

Past Lives: The Weave of Soul Stories

For from the moment the soul assumes a physical form, the memory of the celestial spheres from which it has descended is obscured; we remain conscious only of the things that have occurred to us since our birth. But the lost knowledge of the Universe still resides within our unconscious. Like an archeologist who picks and tunnels through layers of stone, we can retrieve that knowledge by deepening and expanding our consciousness through meditation, prayer, and glorification.—Pir Vilayat Inayat Khan, from *Awakening*

The equilibrating law of karma, as expounded in the Hindu scriptures, is that of action and reaction, cause and effect, sowing and reaping. In the course of natural righteousness, each man, by his thoughts and actions, becomes the molder of his destiny. Whatever universal energies he himself, wisely or unwisely, has set in motion must return to him as their starting point, like a circle inexorably completing itself. An understanding of karma as the law of justice serves to free the human mind from resentment against man and God. A man's karma follows him from incarnation to incarnation until fulfilled or spiritually transcended.—Paramahansa Yogananda, from *Autobiography of a Yogi*

Considering Past Lives

Before I met Gerod, I *believed* in reincarnation, but I didn't *think* in terms of reincarnation. I came to the belief in reincarnation primarily through my readings and an intellectual acceptance. From my point of view, the evidence—not proof—for reincarnation was overwhelming.

As with the near-death-experiences, there were too many reports from too many sources, and too many reputable studies, to be just flukes or fantasies. We are talking, for example, about many children who possessed very specific past-life memories, and details of people, places, and events from previous lifetimes that were investigated and corroborated in ways that left no room for doubt.[1]

Although I believed in reincarnation, however, I had no idea why, if we were souls, we should live many lifetimes; and if we did, why so many of us had no memory of them. Other than vague notions about soul and theories of karma, I also had no explanations for how such a vast system of cause and effect over lifetimes might work. I could not tell you how events in a person's present life were connected to his or her previous lives, or vice-versa. I believed those connections were there, but what it all meant in practical terms, as it applied to real people, was far beyond me. Without active past-life memories myself, there was little I could do but think about it through second hand sources, and compare the different theories and traditions among cultures.

Clinically, I did not address reincarnation in my treatment of clients. I was aware of therapists around the country who were practicing what is called *past life regression therapy*. I had read a good deal of the literature on it as well, but I had no training in past-life regression therapy myself. I had no clinical model to guide me, nor at the time was I convinced about the effectiveness or benefits of this approach.

After I started using hypnosis, there were clients who spontaneously brought forward what some would call past life memories. This did not happen often, but when it did, I tried to follow a client wherever they needed to go with their experience. I just didn't know enough to do anything more. While considering the possibility that a client's present complaints and difficulties might be rooted in a past life, I would talk with a client about reincarnation if they wished to, but that's about as far as I could go.

This changed when I started working with Gerod. He referred to past lives from the beginning. It was one of those things he talked about so matter-of-factly that you knew for Gerod there was no question that souls reincarnate. Early in our collaboration, he also began to identify past lives as the source of problems for particular clients. It worked the other way around too. When a memory did come forward in someone's therapy that appeared to be from a past life, I could now ask Gerod about it directly.

The following excerpts are from the first few sessions after I met Gerod. He was already bringing up past lives as an issue for some clients.

November 20, 1987—(Written Sessions)

Celia needs to know that this life is not her pain; her past life is her pain, and she must heal herself now or go on forever so long unfulfilled in not knowing love or peace . . .

December 8, 1987—(Written Sessions)

Jennifer will continue to surprise you with her information. Michael is a past life name. Developing souls carry their unfinished business with them to the present. Michael is the past life and his history holds the roots of her unhappiness. Therapy based upon this present life cannot be completely successful for it is not these events that hold the roots of her misalignment in life.

Session #2—January 16, 1988

I don't see a spirit involved but I do see that this is a person who was born into this life with an unresolved past life issue. If you were to do a regression with her, you would discover this depression coming from a past life where she was a woman who was beset with many, many problems and she died of a suicide. If you would wish to pursue that area, you may find for her some resolution through forgiveness.

Once we started our verbal sessions, it wasn't long before past lives were a frequent topic weaving in and out of our dialogues. Gerod's information was always intriguing in terms of what it might mean for a particular client and interesting in what it implied about the relationship between the soul and the present personality.

There were many cases like these over the months where Gerod discussed a person's past lives as affecting or influencing their present life. At a clinical level, however, past lives remained on the backburner. I thought about it, and I thought about past life regression, but I didn't know how to implement Gerod's suggestions yet or how to use his information. It took time to put the pieces together. So, while Gerod and I talked of past lives, my primary clinical focus was still on working with earthbound spirits and ego-states.

Also, for many of my clients at the time, reincarnation was not part of their worldview and I had to decide on a case-by-case basis whether this information would be more disturbing than helpful to someone. Some clients were just not ready to deal with these possibilities. If a past life memory spontaneously came forward, then I would talk to the person afterwards to see if it was something he or she wanted to address.

This situation began to change as new clients came who already believed in, or were open to, the concept of reincarnation. These clients were also open to past life regression if that's where things led.

The Clinical Question

Gerod's information about past lives confronted me with a question that, as a therapist, I was compelled to address. Was it true that past lives could be the source of a person's present pain, conflict, or confusion? The compelling issue was the same one as with ego-states and earthbound spirits. If a person's past lives were a source of his or her conflict, pain, or distress, then it would be important to know that, take it into account, and help those clients address it who were being affected in this way.

For many months, I talked to Gerod at a general and theoretical level about reincarnation and about specific clients for whom he said past lives were significantly involved in their present life issues. Clinically, I did not try to work at these levels unless a past life memory presented on its own. When it did, I treated it as I did present life memories, that is, I tried to help move the memory complex through to some sharing and release. This was my basic understanding of past life regression therapy. I might not have understood what was being shared, or why, or why it was appearing at this point in the therapy, but my role was to assist the process and help bring it to resolution and release.

The move from theory to practice occurred in stages over two to three years. As I look back now, I see that my exploration of past lives was on a parallel, and ultimately converging course with my learning about ego-states. I viewed them originally as memories breaking through into present awareness; then I recognized them as past life ego-states; and finally grasped their reality as psychic beings.

As with ego-states, Gerod played a central role in that process. He talked about these past life memories as though they were distinct personalities or beings, just as he talked about ego-states. In that first year of working with Gerod, past lives was becoming a clinical topic, emerging simultaneously along with the phenomena of earthbound spirits, higher self, and ego-states. In my dialogues with Gerod and in my work with clients, questions about past lives became more pressing.

By the end of that first year, past lives had become enough of a focus in my clinical work that I began looking for ways to address this phenomenon with particular clients. Gerod's suggestion, which I could not grasp at the time, was to "talk to them." To me they were memories, video replays, if you will, of a static past rising from an ocean of experience. Gerod's suggestion, however, just like with ego-states, was to communicate with them directly as beings.

Talking to the Past

In the next year, I began to identify and communicate with some of these past-life personalities. This was not a remembering or a reliving by a client of some static past, but communication with an intelligent and dynamic part of the person that engaged with me directly. In terms of my clinical experience to that point, these parts resembled alter-personalities in their ability to take over a client's consciousness and communicate with me as an autonomous part of the self/soul.

Two cases in particular stand out in my mind. The first involved my client, Candace J., and two different personalities that presented within several weeks of each other. One was a priestess who overtly blocked our work several times before finally coming forward. She would not give her name and refused to do what I was asking, i.e., share her experience with Candace at a conscious level. She said it involved "women's mysteries," and since I was a man, she would not share them with me unless she received the okay from higher-level guides. I had to assure her that she could share the information with Candace and that it did not have to be shared out loud. She eventually decided, however, to share her experience with both of us.

The experience she shared took place in a temple. She said that one day soldiers invaded the temple in order to take it over and destroy the sacred objects. In the process, the soldiers also beat and raped the women, both priestesses and attendants. She couldn't make sense of it at the time. She said they (the women) had not hurt anyone. She found out later that the high priest, a male, had betrayed them and had conspired to let the soldiers into the temple. Later, reflecting on the experience, she said it was part of a larger "changing from the goddesses to the war gods." It was a shift in their society from a matriarchal to a patriarchal power structure. Anthropologists have studied a number of societies in which this kind of change occurred.

Several weeks later, while working with Candace, another female came forward. She was from a different lifetime than the priestess. She said her name was Marasena, and that she was locked in combat with a man and was at a standoff with him. She said he always tried to control her and every time he does, she spits in his face and despises him. She said he controls her through sex, that he overpowers her in that way. She said, "It's a contest of wills."

I talked to Gerod at length about Marasena. During that dialogue is when Gerod suggested I have her come forward and help her have a conscious experience in the present.

Session #103—August 11, 1989

T. Gerod, I talked also with Candace J. We had a very interesting session with Marasena. She apparently is locked in combat here with a male. She seems to have little or no awareness of the Light; is very intent on keeping her power for survival; and she lives, in a sense, in this constant state of combat. I asked whether she would like to resolve this. It doesn't seem like a very comfortable place to live, and yet, she sees no solution, no way to get out of this. So my question is: is there a way to help her resolve this and still have what she feels she needs, all the power and security we can offer her?

G. Certainly. Part of the importance is to have her come forward for an introduction, so to say, to this present life. And that is very possible to bring together this past life one to see where the soul is living in the present, and to see also the degree of understanding that is present, to see what is and what can be and what is possible for her. It is almost like finding a past and taking it into the future so that the past may then recreate itself into a place of peace, which then most certainly does affect the future.

T. So what you're suggesting, with the help of the higher self, is that she can come forward into the present. Would that also mean a sharing?

G. It will somewhat, and also what it will mean is for her to have a certain absorption of the present, to see that this person that she is part of in this present day is a very capable person who has power but whose own power is being somewhat immobilized because of the conflicts existing in the past, and that power is not just for survival but it is for creation.

. . . It will be an interesting process. It is very much the same procedure as conversing with ego-states and conversing with all the many personalities that you have met throughout the years that exist within one body. It is almost like bringing her forward into the present and putting her close to this consciousness. She may even be allowed to stay for a while, for a period of minutes or a period of hours or even a period of days, to enhance her awareness. It will depend upon the level of comfort that is felt by this person and also by the perception of the higher self in the advisability of doing this.

T. And would Candace remain conscious and aware at that time also?

G. Certainly she would. There would be a certain degree of discomfort perhaps, a certain degree of disorientation, but if she is prepared and aware of it, it can certainly be worked through without any great distress.

The suggestion that Marasena could come forward and be conscious of my client's present reality, as separate from her own, and that this new perspective might lead to her cooperation with the healing process was one of those insights and techniques that would apply to other cases. I labeled it as *having a conscious experience* and discovered that it could be very helpful for present life ego-states as well as past-life personalities. Since these parts of the self were so often caught in the timeframe of their own experience, bringing them to the conscious mind was a very quick way to give them a present day perspective and reassure them that whatever the trauma was that they were caught in, it was no longer happening in the present.

My direct communication with Marasena also emphasized to me the autonomous nature of these kinds of personalities. The description of her ongoing conflict with this male and the priestess's concern about revealing the women's mysteries to a male gave me the very strong impression that they were operating in a present reality, only it wasn't the reality that Candace and I lived in. This impression only grew stronger as I gained more experience with these past-life personalities.

The second example, taken from this same period, involved a military general who came forward with my client, Theresa P. He was trying to take over the body so that he could get back to his troops and deliver a warning. As we communicated, it came out that he had betrayed them for what he thought at the time were good reasons, only to learn that he had been deceived. He was trying now to return to his troops and undo the massacre that had resulted from his actions. I had to explain to him that he was no longer in that reality, and that even if he took over Theresa's body, he would not find his troops in this present time.

One week after meeting the general, I talked to Gerod at length about these past life personalities (I had encountered several by now), and he described how he viewed them.

Session #109—September 6, 1989

It is almost as if they have created their own world there. The problem with that is that they do not move on. They stay within that same framework, that same place that they were when they left. It is as if what they were creating at that time—what problems they might be with, whatever is happening at that time—they take with them into that reality that they have created, they just continue that. And it is as if they never get out of it.

Gerod's comments and perspective raised the question of whether I was dealing with a whole past life personality or a fragment from a past life.

The implication was that a past-life personality I encountered in the therapy was not necessarily the core self or personality from that lifetime, but rather a fragment from that life still being lived out at some level within the vast territory of the self/soul. The further implication was that these fragments of other lives were, in effect, like the ego-states I already worked with, only they were created in different lifetimes.

Gerod's description suggested the logical possibility that ego-states somehow survived from one lifetime to another. I had to ask myself whether this is what was happening here with the past life personalities that I encountered. Were they fragments?

I raised this question with Gerod a few weeks later from the point of view of present life ego-states.

Session #113—September 30, 1989

T. Gerod, after death, when there are these ego states that have been unresolved, what is their reality in terms of the soul at that point? What happens? Do these ego-states continue to exist? And if they do, do they all still have influence?

G. They are with the memory of the soul, just as the memory of the personality is there also. And this is where the difficulty for the soul comes in, often times having to work through issues in the spirit realm or to have to work through issues in the present life by doing past life therapy. When you go back to do past life regression and you are doing therapy in past life, you are dealing with ego-states, so to say, that have influenced the soul. A soul that has a memory of a life with an ego-state that was very dominant and unresolved will bring that forward because it is the memory, it is the history, and it is recorded in the soul.

This equivalence between present life ego-states and past life personalities pointed to a parallel process. The implication was that they were all the same phenomena. The creation of ego-states in one's present life was a process that had occurred in other lifetimes of the soul as well.

This insight forced my thinking to a different level. It lifted my understanding about self and ego-states from a psychological point of view focused on the present personality and pushed it into a far larger context—what I would call now the *soul perspective*. It was like studying a city map, and then stepping back and seeing a map of the whole country. The city map doesn't change, but it is now viewed as one city interrelated to many others that all make up a larger whole. For me as a clinician, extending my work from present life ego-states to past life ego-states was like starting out to explore this larger territory.

The recognition of past life ego-states as part of the healing process shifted my thinking from a psychological to a soul perspective. It also suggested the possibility that these past-life parts could be worked with and healed using the same methods and techniques that worked for present life ego-states. From this point of view, what regression therapists were calling past life personalities, I viewed now as past-life ego-states. This brought them within the clinical framework of ego-state therapy where similar therapeutic methods might apply. This was familiar territory. It was also something I could put to the test and know whether it worked or not.

The major difference in working with past-life ego-states is for the therapist who has to adapt his or her thinking and language, and be ready to communicate with someone from any time, any culture, carrying any experience. We cannot assume that an ego-state will know about the conscious personality or this 21st century reality. We have to talk to them in a way that does not frighten them, or violate their own beliefs and framework of reference, at least until they've had contact with the higher self and the Light. It is not going to work very well, for example, if I use an analogy involving automobiles with an ego-state from Roman times, or talk to a Celtic druid in terms of Jesus or Gandhi.

The Interweave of Self and Soul

This was where my exploration and work with past life personalities and present life ego-states began to converge. I learned that the higher self, for example, could make contact and communicate with the past-life personalities just as it did with ego-states. I began to get glimpses of how the present life ego-states were alive within their own timeframe in the same way past-life personalities were.

When I finally grasped that ego-states were real beings, I came to understand that the same was true about these past-life personalities. They also were beings living within a psychic reality, fragments of a past self, with a limited perception and consciousness. I discovered too that the same keys I used to elicit a present life ego-state's cooperation also worked with these personalities from past lives. Through the process of receiving Light and having contact with the higher self, these past-life parts of different clients were now sharing their experience with the conscious self more often than before, just as was happening with present-life ego-states.

Ultimately, I found that these past life ego-states were also part of that inner structure I described in the last chapter. When I learned to identify groups of ego-states, I found that past life ego-states were just as often part of a group along with ego-states from the present life. I also found, at times, that just as some groups were entirely composed of present life ego-states, there were also groups composed entirely of past life ego-states.

The same principles, though, applied for both. All the ego-states in one group, whether from present or past-life, all shared some common element or bond. In a group of six ego-states, for example, they might all share an experience of feeling shame. Three of those might be experiences from a client's present life, and the others coming from different lifetimes. In this example, I would think of the group as comprising a *shame energy*. That shame energy, however, as I saw it now, could reach deeper than this present life and extend into previous lives as well. From this more inclusive perspective, I would look at this complex of shame energy as being a soul issue.

This interplay and interweaving of past and present lives around specific themes added a new dimension to my understanding of self and soul. Clinically, this understanding also opened a new dimension in the healing process. I could never know ahead of time whom I might find and what configuration of groups was present for a client, but I was in a position to identify these groups, their interconnections, and follow the inner trail whether it led through one lifetime or through many.

I did not have the big picture on all this. I could only learn about these inner pathways and groups as they presented and unfolded within each of my clients. Healing was still always the focus and my role as a clinician was to help resolve whoever or whatever presented and to facilitate the unfolding. My general understanding of these inner structures and dynamics and the interweaving of lifetimes only emerged slowly after following hundreds of trails and mapping thousands of groups.

The interweaving of the past and present through ego-states and their groupings also expanded my concept of *fields*. Initially, I thought of these defined groupings as energy fields. In time, however, I began to view these fields as psychic manifestations, not only of the self, but also at a deeper level as manifestations of the soul. It was clear from what these past life ego-states were sharing that a person's soul had experienced the same and similar difficulties and conflicts in other lifetimes that my client was experiencing in his or her present life. It also became clear that resolving an issue for a person in this present life could mean having to follow the trail and resolve it, to some extent, at a soul level as well.

The Karmic Layer

The shift from a *psychological* to a *soul* perspective was actually much easier to make clinically than it was theoretically. Once I understood that these past-life ego-states were also inner beings, I could work with them using the same methods I had learned for working with present life ego-states. The goal was also the same: to help these past-life ego-states share what they needed to in order to move free of their pain and distress. Contact with the higher self, receiving Light, and the promise of integration worked just as effectively with past-life ego-states as it did with those from present life.

Theoretically, however, I had no explanation for how these past-life ego-states continued to exist within the soul as distinct beings and were able to manifest in a person's present life, specifically, my clients. Even given the understanding that they were conscious beings and could survive the death of the body, that still didn't explain how they could travel with the soul into the Light and not be healed. This contradicted everything I had learned so far about the healing power of the Light. I knew from clinical experience that these past-life ego-states could receive the Light and release their pain and confusion, just as with present-life ego-states. So why wasn't this happening, at the end of each life, when ego-states went into the Light with the soul? Why were they still living in their painful realities as though they never went into the Light?

These questions led to others. If an ego-state did not integrate when the soul moved into the Light, then what happened to it? And what about the past-life ego-states I worked with every day? Where were they coming from? Where did they exist, and what was the nature of their existence? How strongly or not could they affect a person in present life?

It took several years of work with many clients to be able to answer these questions The piece that finally brought it all together is when Gerod told me about the *karmic layer*. He said there is a layer within the soul where unresolved ego-states move to when the body dies and the soul returns to the Light. What happens, he says, is that these inner beings recoil from the Light because it begins to trigger their pain and distress, just as happens in the therapy process when an ego-state isn't prepared for it. Their natural reaction is to stop the Light or escape it. As conscious beings, Gerod said, they have the capacity to refuse the Light. Because they are parts of the soul, the Light will honor these choices.

So, instead of being infused with Light, these parts of the soul, Gerod said, are folded up into what he called a layer within the soul where they will be shielded from Light. He said, "it's as though they are folded up into a pocket." He also gave the impression that they become dormant there and remain so while the soul is in spirit.

Gerod described this layer, then, as a reservoir of the soul's unresolved experiences and distorted perceptions that accumulate and blend over lifetimes. He also said it is this reservoir of unresolved experience, with its particular themes and issues, that a soul attempts to address in subsequent lifetimes. He said the soul makes choices and creates a blueprint for each life with specific goals for healing this reservoir:

> The karmic layer becomes the soul's resource for choosing experience. It's like looking into that level, isolating particular trails of energy, and choosing to follow it to resolve it.

Gerod went on to say that in reincarnating, as the soul enters into the physical reality, it will trigger the opening up of this layer. He said these parts of the soul can reawaken and be reactivated once again as they resonate to the physical reality, the reality in which they were originally created.

> It's a layer that when one goes into the spirit realm it's almost as if you would say it folds up and encapsulates all, and that when the soul moves back into the physical, it unfolds.
> . . . They (the unresolved ego-states) are the pinions of the experience, so when they come forward from a past life into the present, that energy, so to say, puts it all back into play. They don't make choices but they are activated and they begin reacting from their point of experience, reacting to the present environment and stimulus. And the present environment and stimulus is what starts it all.

Gerod's information about the karmic layer answered my questions of how these past-life ego-states could go with the soul into the Light at death, remain unhealed, and manifest again in subsequent lifetimes. It also helped explain why, during the healing process, ego-states from different lifetimes presented in groups or in series where they all shared a common issue or conflict. It's as though they formed fields, or as Gerod called them, "trails of energy" within the soul that called for healing. Finally, the existence of the karmic layer reinforced the idea that the soul was actively involved in its own process of learning and using past experiences and future lifetimes to expand and evolve in its own consciousness.

From a clinical point of view, knowledge of the karmic layer did not change how I worked with past-life ego-states, except in one significant way. Unlike present-life ego-states, once a past-life ego-state had completed its sharing and release, it did not move into integration with the conscious self in the present. Instead, Gerod said, it would be integrated within the soul with that past lifetime in which it had been created. He said the client's higher self is still the one who can escort the past-life ego-state to its place of integration.

Imagining the Inner World

In 1995, I did a series of drawings trying to visualize the model of self and soul that was emerging in my work. While keeping in mind

Korzybski's axiom that "the map is not the territory," models can be helpful in articulating and expressing complex ideas. The illustration at the beginning of the book is based on that series of drawings. The image is essentially an expansion of the limited diagrams I presented earlier around dissociation and the creation of ego-states. (See Chapter 12.)

This image depicts the incarnated soul where the conscious self, buffered by the protective part, looks out into the physical reality. The higher self acts as a conduit between the self and soul, and is also able to function in many ways throughout the self at both the conscious and unconscious levels.

At the unconscious level, then, are the ego-states that exist alone or in groups. The lighter spheres indicate present life ego-states, and the darker spheres represent past-life ego-states. Groups can be comprised of any combination of past- and present-life ego-states depending upon each soul's unique history, those parts from the karmic layer that have been activated, and the ego-states created in the person's present-life.

The image also shows the presence of earthbound spirits represented by cones and dark souls represented by black cubes. Spirits, when present, are often found with an ego-state or within a group of ego-states. This may be an ego-state from the person's present life or from a past life.

Based on this model, when a person dies, the conscious personality would assume its place within the soul consciousness, and the constellations of unresolved ego-states would fold up within the karmic layer of the soul, remaining dormant between incarnations. When the soul again incarnates, the karmic layer would reopen and the past-life ego-states would again re-constellate where, as Gerod said, they once more "come into play" to continue their part in the soul's evolving consciousness.

15

Darkness and Evil

*As many teachers before have proclaimed, there is an ongoing battle
in the Universe—between the pure light of selfless dedication to the
highest ideal, and Luciferian light that is clouded with the shadows
of selfish egotism. What exactly is Luciferian light? It is light that has
become disconnected from its Divine source. When we lose our sense of
belonging to the totality, our experience of light can become misleading,
deceptive, and ultimately counterproductive, as in the case of Lucifer,
the fallen angel.*—Pir Vilayat Inayat Khan, from *Awakening*

*Among the fallen dark angels, expelled from other worlds, friction and
war take place with lifetronic bombs or mental mantric vibratory rays.
These beings dwell in the gloom-drenched regions of the lower astral
cosmos, working out their evil karma.*—Yogananda Paramahansa,
from *Autobiography of a Yogi*

Making the Distinction

Of all the things I learned in my work with Gerod, the distinction
between darkness and evil was one of the most significant. Before we
met, I confused the terms and made no clear distinction between them.
I think in my own mind, they were nearly synonymous. I associated
darkness with evil, and when I thought of evil, it was cloaked in darkness and shadow. Other than the darkness of night, *darkness* had no
reality for me except as a metaphor or a description for what was evil,
menacing, and frightening.

Talking to Gerod about darkness and evil was another of those cases, as with the terms ego and ego-states, where Gerod and I used the same terms, but we were not meaning the same thing. We both, for example, used the terms *dark* or *evil* to describe those harassing and intruding spirits that I found with certain clients. Gerod, however, also used the term *darkness* as something in itself, a reality or dimension separate from the existence of spirits. Evil spirits dwell in darkness, but spirits are not the darkness itself. Darkness was not a soul, but a primal energy and force operating, like the Light, at every level of reality. Souls could exist in that energy and consciousness, but it was a very different existence from souls in the Light.

Personally and clinically, the idea of darkness as an existing reality or force was outside my framework of thinking. When it came to evil, my focus from a clinical point of view was on evil spirits, not darkness. It was only gradually that I came to hear the distinction Gerod was making between darkness and evil and began to address it in my work with clients and in talks with Gerod. There were three clinical phenomena in particular that I was encountering with clients where darkness was a central issue.

Souls in Darkness

Intruding and harassing spirits were the first phenomena that opened up this whole question of darkness and evil. These spirits were the kind I talked about in Chapter Six. Gerod was the first one to name them. He called them "evil spirits." He pointed to the distinction between *earthbound spirits* and *evil spirits* early in our dialogues when the whole issue of spirit involvement was still new to me. According to Gerod, these were not just earthbound spirits—lost, confused, or mischievous—trying to hang on to the physical reality. They were spirits who were intentionally intruding upon or threatening the client with whom I was working, and they seemed to know very clearly what they were doing. The more I learned about them, the more I came to understand that although they existed in darkness, the darkness itself was something different.

Unlike with the earthbound, these spirits wanted nothing to do with the Light or receiving help from spirit guides, no matter how safe it could be. When they were identified, they refused to cooperate and, on the contrary, would often deliberately try to block or interfere with the healing process, especially through blocking the communication signals. They also consistently refused to voluntarily leave a client or cease their harassment. Their attitude was, "make me." They weren't leaving unless forced to, and most believed that neither my client nor I had the power to do that.

In that first year and half of working with Gerod, I had a number of cases that involved these kinds of hostile and aggressive spirits. As I became more proficient at recognizing and working with earthbound spirits, I also became more adept at distinguishing them from these dark spirits. Dealing with them, however, as opposed to earthbound spirits, required a shift in tactics. Unlike with earthbound spirits, I was not communicating with entities who would welcome our assistance and were looking for a way out of their predicament.

In the beginning, my encounters with evil spirits were more like skirmishes, because I didn't know exactly who or what I was dealing with. I would engage these spirits directly—or try to—but I did not know enough about them to ask the right questions. These exchanges could quickly deteriorate into saber rattling and threats being hurled back and forth. When it came down to it, I did not know what leverage, if any, my clients had, and that I could use, to force these spirits to leave. With those clients where I found these dark spirits present, the question of how to address them, and remove them, was the immediate concern and became a focus in my discussions with Gerod.

His suggestion in these situations was to call on the Light. According to Gerod, when a person calls on the Light for assistance, the Light will respond.

Session #6—February 4, 1988

> These spirits are evil but not that powerful. They are working their way, so to speak, to the higher, (or lower perhaps I should say) levels of capability. Command that those spirits leave by the will of the Creator, Who created all, Who is the Light and Who created them . . . They will be conniving and protesting but they will go, for ultimately the will does have the choice and the choice for God's love and freedom will prevail.

When I encountered a spirit like this, and push came to shove, I used this approach and called on the Light and the higher self to remove the spirits. The image in my mind was of flooding the spirit with Light and, essentially, flushing them out. It was not a very sophisticated technique, more like a shotgun approach. It seemed to work in some cases, and with some spirits, but others left only to return later, and still for others, calling in the Light did not even seem to faze them.

When this did not work, the original question remained: how to remove them? If calling in the Light had worked in all cases, it probably would have been the end of my investigation into these dark souls. Any time I encountered one I would have just had them removed. The fact that many of these spirits were able to resist the attempts to force them out raised questions about who they were, what they were after, and how they were able to maintain their presence. These were the questions I kept in mind when I encountered a dark spirit and tried to communicate with it.

These were also the questions I took to Gerod, both theoretically and regarding specific cases. I asked him for any information he could give about these different situations and the specific spirits that were present. As with other phenomena I was investigating with Gerod, the increased focus on evil spirits and the more frequent discussions sharpened our language and our definition of terms.

With those clients where these dark spirits were an issue, my aim was to find some kind of leverage that could be used to evict them. Each time Gerod and I discussed a case or an issue having to do with these dark spirits, I learned something new or thought of something in a new way. The same principle I have mentioned before was operating here: the better I understood who or what these entities were, the better I would know what might motivate them to leave or, if necessary, force them out. Negotiation was always preferable to combat.

It was in discussing these spirits more specifically that Gerod began to make a distinction between darkness and evil spirits. In one session, for example, he made the point that these spirits were souls, and that many of them had lived a human existence. He went on to say that they had been "dragged down into the darkness."

Session #7—February 6, 1988

These evil spirits that you met with were souls, but at one time they also became tinged with the evil that slowly dragged them down into the darkness. It is their choice. When you read of the cases of very severe examples of possession, those evil spirits are souls. They were at one time a human person that lived on earth, or a being from some other reality, but they are a soul that has crossed that line because it is what for some reason appeals to their sense of being.

As Gerod talked about evil spirits, I continued to hear the distinction between the darkness and the souls in darkness. According to Gerod, the souls in darkness cannot reincarnate. They exist in some state or dimension of consciousness outside time and space. Also, according to Gerod, these souls in darkness—some of them at least—could maintain a constant presence with someone, or they could make periodic contact at different times in a person's life. Even more troubling, he was saying that these souls, from their vantage point in the darkness, could have access to a soul once it incarnates, and that it could even have access to a soul over lifetimes.

Rhonda

The implications of all this started to become clear to me when I talked to Gerod about a new client, Rhonda P. Rhonda was referred by her uncle, a former client of mine, who saw her spinning psychologically and emotionally out of control. He knew she needed help.

When I met with her, Rhonda reported that in the last two weeks she had been having intense feelings of anxiety and she described a number of dissociative symptoms. Talking about herself, she said it was "like an insane part talking to a nice part." She said things were coming out of her mouth that didn't feel like her own, and sometimes she was saying things out loud but didn't know whom she was talking to.

What had precipitated this crisis, according to Rhonda, was a meeting she attended the week before in which she and others had met with Marty, the new regional manager for the company where she worked. Marty was relatively new in this office, having transferred from another city. He had only been in the job for six months. Rhonda felt that there was some attraction between them even before this particular meeting, but said that after the meeting she felt very strange and began to experience brief panic attacks. Since that time, she said she had been obsessed with Marty and actively wanted to pursue an affair with him.

Given some of her descriptions of these voices, I knew enough by this time to consider the possibility that spirits might be involved. I asked Gerod for his reading of the situation and he concurred that spirits were present.

Session #55—November 7, 1988

T. Gerod, the sense that I got is that Rhonda may have some strong spirit involvement, and there's even kind of an uneasy feeling that they may not be very nice spirits. Also, as part of this, she's been getting involved with this supervisor at work, Marty T., and whatever is going on seems to be growing stronger and becoming more and more distressing. So I wanted to ask whether you see spirit involvement or evil involved and/or maybe past life issues that are happening for these two people.

G. There is some past life involvement that influences this situation but not to as great an extreme as the dark influence that is present in this unfolding. This woman is strongly influenced by spirits from the dark side and they come from her past to find her again, and what is happening is collusion between the spirits with this woman and the one with this man. They are being drawn together for purposes not altogether healthy, not altogether within the realm of the Light, it is rather involved.

You are able to be effective in this situation. However, it cannot be completely alleviated unless she severs her relationship with this person unless he himself will take the opportunity to break away from his tie to these spirits. If he is not in a position to do that, then it would be quite strongly recommended that she avoid him. And I realize often times that is not an easy step to take under certain circumstances, but when one is fooling around with darkness, one is opening oneself up to trouble.

T. And these spirits from her past, you're talking about previous life?

G. They have attempted to be part of her life before. There is a strong attraction to this soul. A past life experience shared with one of the spirits that is with her continues to follow her and plague her somewhat from life to life, and this is what is happening again.

T. Are we talking, Gerod, about these spirits being around her or, like an earthbound spirit, inhabiting her?

G. They are, at this point, inhabiting. They have not previously. They have been around her, following her, and that relationship from the past life seems to be involved in this, but there is inhabitation at this point. And it has not been long that there has been this state, but these spirits have been around her off and on for many, many years, but only more recently have they taken that close step of sharing space with her and this partly has come about more with the involvement with this other person.

T. If this develops, would we be talking more about like an exorcism?

G. That would be necessary, and it would be similar to that in the description of the stronger, perhaps more violent, reaction. I am not so certain that it will be extremely violent, but let us just say that these spirits are not the kind that are going to cooperate so willingly and they are certainly going to give you a very tough time before they would depart, but you do know that they will go.

T. Yes. Is the relationship between them—the spirits with this man, and the spirits with Rhonda—is there a kind of plan or scheme that is being done with intention? I'm just wondering if that would make this all the more difficult to have these spirits leave.

G. There is a plan. There is a scheme. It gives the spirits a way of communicating through a physical body, of establishing a base, and that is why it is important for this woman to avoid this man as long as he is also inhabited by these spirits because they will always be an influence, they will always attempt to influence, and they will always attempt to draw the spirits back to her. It will be an on-going battle somewhat. So, I would highly recommend severing as many ties as possible if this man is not also free of spirits.

This dialogue and others concerning different clients brought home to me the complexity and depth of entanglement that might exist when there is spirit involvement. These interrelationships could be occurring on one, or even all of these planes at the same time—in the present moment, from ongoing contacts in a person's present life, and from contacts made in other lifetimes, and between spirits who are attached to different people. These interrelationships and interactions, furthermore, were being carried on outside the three-dimensional world of time and space.

I continued talking to Gerod about souls aligned with darkness and as the questions became more specific, so too did the questions about darkness. In one of those dialogues, Gerod became more explicit about the distinction between darkness and the dark souls. I asked him again about those souls, as humans, who had lived an evil life. I was still trying to understand this idea of souls who, at the time of death, do not go to the Light, but continue to exist. Gerod said these souls "become very aligned with that darkness."

Session #61—December 2, 1988

G. There are people that are aligned with this darkness, but they are in error; there is misunderstanding primarily because these souls have become involved in physical form in the dark side, in certain practices of evil and negative polarity and in turn, when they pass from a physical life, they become very aligned with that darkness, just as people in physical reality become very aligned with it.

T. Is there more that you can say about this darkness, any of its parameters or principles?

G. This energy collectively is very aware in some respects of what it is. It knows that it is not of the Light. It is aware of the Light, because there is always an opposite. As it knows it is darkness, it knows there is Light, but it also has that awareness that it is not based in the Light and that were it to believe in the Light it would no longer exist. That energy would dissipate because there would be no power to keep it generated. It has limits that it works within. It knows it is not of the Light and it knows the Light has more power than it does. It also knows that there are certain truths; that there are certain universal laws and rules that it cannot cross because if it does it will destroy itself. Therefore, it is cautious and it works within its own limits and anyone working with darkness, with evil, must be drawn in to work within its limits, for once darkness or evil is drawn out to work within the Light, then it loses its power and destroys itself. That is why the will is extremely valuable. It keeps one from crossing the line completely. Once the will completely crosses over into darkness, it is extremely important to extract that soul from that side, but as long as the will keeps Light involved, it can never be completely drawn in and the will has the power to drive out the darkness. It is somewhat simple, but yet extremely complex. . . very definitely opposites of intelligence, very aware, and each one knows who is the most powerful.

I didn't understand all the metaphysical implications of what Gerod was saying, but I knew he was talking about something beyond words. He was describing darkness as a force and consciousness in itself, separate from souls. He was talking about darkness in the same kind of terms he used to talk about the Light—not as a soul, but a primal energy operating at every level of reality.

The difference between *darkness* and *evil souls existing in darkness* became one of those major threads in my dialogues with Gerod. From a clinical point of view, the focus was still on the eviction of intruding and harassing spirits. Learning how to do that, however, was going to require a deeper understanding of the reality of darkness itself.

The Dark Spot

The second phenomenon that led me to distinguish more clearly between darkness and evil was what Gerod called "the dark side." We later called it the "dark spot." This was one of those pieces of information that came at me from out of the blue. I was talking to him about how difficult it was at times to discern between when a person is acting or reacting out of human hurt, need, or fear and when there was evil involved. When do actions and feelings stop being *man's inhumanity to man,* or passions out of control, and become something more, something evil?

I was asking the question generally, but I was also thinking of situations with certain clients. I was not always sure when their problems and inner struggles were the result of their own emotional pain and confusion, and when those problems and struggles involved evil spirits or influences. I was groping for words just to be able to talk about it.

Session #74—February 24, 1989

T. It still is not always clear to me, nor does it always feel reliable, to make a judgment about whether darkness is involved with someone or whether it's more this kind of human struggle. This darkness can seem so difficult to locate or identify.

G. And it is difficult, because you see within each person there is a dark side and it is not necessarily that that darkness is evil, because what appears evil, quite often, is just an absence of knowledge and an absence of understanding, and each person can have that within them. It is almost as if to say that the darkness within each person is part of the impetus for growing, for moving into the Light. So the darkness that is aligned with evil can often times be mistaken. Usually though, if a person is strongly involved with the evil forces of darkness, it is quite often discernible.

Gerod made this statement about twenty minutes into our session and it immediately changed the focus of our discussion. I wanted to know what he meant by the *dark side* within each person. I also wanted to understand the distinction he was making between darkness and evil. I spent the rest of that session questioning him about it, trying to pin it down. My only concepts for inner darkness were psychological—Jung's concept of the shadow, the story of Jekyll and Hyde, Freud's unconscious *id* with all its primitive instincts, etc. Gerod, however, was talking about it as a kind of psychic region or zone.

He went on to say that, during his or her life, a person periodically passes through this dark spot, that there is a cycle.

T. . . . this dark spot, this darkness within each of us. It makes me think of Jung's talking about the shadow. And I find it very interesting to talk about this dark side within each of us without necessarily saying that it is aligned with evil, or headed for evil.

G. That darkness and the shadow are a very good parallel. It's like when the planets are orbiting and an eclipse will occur and the day will become dark. It's almost as if to say there is an eclipse within each person that from time to time the personality will pass through. And the crux of the matter is: is the person going to pass through that shadow, through that darkness, and come into the Light again, or are they going to get stuck there and stay there? And quite often those people who stay too long in that shadow, in that darkness, are those who will attract spirits. They will attract the spirits of darkness because in that dark place there is despair, there is sadness, there is depression, and there is a weakening of the will to move into the Light and that is where the forces of evil can move into that darkness.

But it is most definitely a purposeful place because it is that impetus for growth. When, in the shadow, those feelings are the feelings that propel one forward oftentimes to finding the opposite.

The experience of this darkness, he said, is unique for each person. In general, though, he said it is characterized by such feelings as depression and sadness, mistrust, loneliness, and a lack of love. He also continued to emphasize that this darkness itself was not evil.

Most people in describing from this point of view would talk about a feeling of darkness, of suffocation almost at certain times. And when those types of descriptions are entering in, then the perspective is often times from that deep void that is there. Persons who finally come to suicide are usually quite locked into that dark side, and they are not moving well enough to keep glimpsing what it is they need to glimpse, which is the Light, to keep them moving, to keep them struggling, and often times they have stopped so much in that dark place, and it does not mean they are evil; it does not mean that they are bad. It often times means they have abandoned hope, they have let go of the idea that they are purposeful, that they have meaning, that they are here for some reason. Once you lose sight of that fact, that you are here to grow, that you have purpose, that you have meaning, that you are here for some reason, then hope is gone and the soul may choose to leave.

What Gerod was describing in this session was plausible. It was also clear that the *dark spot* could have significant clinical implications for some people, especially if one were stuck there. It raised obvious questions about whether a person's feelings such as depression, hopelessness, or despair might involve this dark spot.

There's no question that I would have pursued this issue of the dark spot in future dialogues. Before this session ended, however, Gerod offered a way for me to address these clinical questions directly. He said that a person's higher self could locate this dark spot and see into it.

Session #74—February 24, 1989

T. So if I ask the higher self to move into that dark spot, become more aware of it, to learn what that experience is and come back out, the higher self could do that.

G. Most definitely. And it can let you know what is in there that is stuck, that needs to move forward.

If true, it meant I would be able to verify Gerod's information through my own work with clients.

Caught in the Dark

Over the next several years, I carried on an active investigation into this phenomenon, first with select clients, and then more generally. The clinical results confirmed to me that this dark spot does exist and that a person does cycle through it periodically. It's difficult, however, to say much in general about it because of the extreme variations in frequency, duration, and effect from one individual to the next. Gerod said that every person's experience and passage through the dark spot is unique. I found this to be true. One person, for example, might go through his or her dark spot once every two years and each time it may last only a couple weeks. Another person might have a nine-month cycle where they are in the dark spot for three months and then out again for six. While in the dark spot, one person might describe it as feeling "low" or "out of sorts" and then it's gone. For another, it might trigger deep feelings of despair and hopelessness even though everything in the person's outer world is just fine.

From a clinical point of view, the dark spot is a significant issue when a person has become stuck in this darkness, or when his or her passage through it has become prolonged and painful. I have worked with some clients who had been stuck in the dark spot for several years, or who have been in it most of their lives.

What I discovered when I first began to address these situations with clients was that ego-states were often a significant factor involved in the blocking. I learned that some of the ego-states I was communicating with lived in the dark spot. As Gerod explained it, when a person enters the dark spot in their normal cycle, the experience of darkness can trigger ego-states that exist there. If it was one that was already active, the direct experience of darkness seemed to energize it, as though it were operating once more in its own element. Instead of seeking the Light, however, that ego-state's response would be to actively avoid it, or oppose it. If strong enough, such an ego-state, or more than one acting together, can block forward movement and entangle the self in the darkness.

These ego-states, as it turned out, were the ones who so often refused to receive any Light or contact from the higher self. They were the ones so often involved in blocking. From their point of view, the Light was a threat. Some were afraid that the Light would hurt, or even destroy, them. Some felt they didn't deserve God's Love, or that they would be rejected once the Light saw who they were. Still others were angry at the Light, and felt that the Light had betrayed them, either didn't warn them, or didn't rescue them, or allowed a loved one to die.

I was aware of these kinds of resistive ego-states and alter-personalities, but I had not thought of them as cut off from the Light. They were like the earthbound spirits I encountered whose ignorance, feelings, or beliefs kept them cut off from the spirit realm of Light. This insight gave an added depth of understanding about these ego-states and the intensity of fear and resistance I encountered with them. It also suggested a different approach in their treatment. It was the same approach that I took with the earthbound spirits, i.e., help them resolve any fears or conflicts first and make it safe for them to receive the Light.

As with the spirits, this approach was very effective. Once an ego-state felt safe enough and agreed to receive the Light, it responded just like other ego-states. It gained new understanding, opened itself further to the Light, and began to cooperate in the sharing and release.

Passing Through

There are some clients with whom the dark spot never has to be addressed directly. Their passage through it, while maybe uncomfortable or unpleasant, does not last long, or knock them off balance. For others, it is a critical issue. It's usually because the person's cycle involves prolonged periods in the dark spot or they have become stuck there. Long periods in this darkness have colored his or her entire outlook and feelings about life. When this is the case, the dark spot will usually become a primary focus. The goal then is to address those factors keeping the person in darkness, so they can once again start moving toward the Light.

Helping a person resolve this situation is fairly straightforward. A client's higher self can determine whether he or she has entered the dark spot. It can also determine whether the person is moving through it all right, having significant difficulty, or is stuck. If there is difficulty, the higher self can look into the dark spot and find the source of the problem or block. It might be powerful ego-states, for example, that have been triggered. If so, the higher self can identify those involved and bring them forward to communicate. It might also be that a person has experienced a severe trauma. The death of a child or a life altering accident, for example, might cause such overwhelming pain and grief, that it triggers a move into the dark spot where a person becomes lost in depression, rage, or despair. It's also quite possible that one or more ego-states were created during the trauma who are in deep enough pain and strong enough to block the self from moving toward the Light. The goal then is to resolve these blocks so the person can begin moving again.

While the method is straightforward, thanks to the higher self, it doesn't mean dealing with the dark spot is easy. The process itself can be very painful depending on who or what one finds in this darkness. It would not be a surprise, for instance, for a client to find his or her deepest pain or fear in this area. When the dark spot is a significant issue for someone, it's not unusual that in addressing it, the person's cycle itself will change. Their movement into the dark spot may become less frequent and/or less intense. For some people, this is a major positive change in their life.

Darkness in Itself

When Gerod first identified the dark spot and described it as a potential source of pain and distress for a person, it immediately became a clinical issue. His statements raised questions of whether this dark spot, and one's passage through it, could be a significant factor in cases where a person experienced prolonged feelings of depression, anxiety, or hopelessness, even to the point of clinical depression and suicidal thinking. On the face of it, these were questions worth investigating, and the dark spot was added to the list of those phenomena that I would explore with Gerod and clients.

There was a second issue, however, bound up with this phenomenon of the dark spot. Gerod's description implied a correlation between this inner darkness and the cosmic darkness he alluded to when he talked of souls who "go into darkness" after death. The implication was that he was talking about the same darkness, only at different levels. In effect, dealing with darkness at one level was to be dealing with it potentially at all levels. When the inner darkness became a clinical issue, so too did the cosmic darkness. By focusing on the issue of the dark spot in my work with clients, I was opening up the entire issue of darkness itself.

Up until this point, even though Gerod made a distinction between darkness and the evil souls in darkness, I still did not think of them as separate phenomena. I was not focused on darkness but on the dark spirits who were intruding or interfering with my clients. After learning about the dark spot, though, and gaining some clinical experience with it, that began to change. I began to think of darkness as an energy, separate from the souls who dwell in it.

Eight months after Gerod first talked about the dark spot, I engaged him in a long and wide-ranging discussion about darkness, evil, dark souls, and the dark spot. It was one of those culminating sessions where enough questions, thoughts, and clinical experiences had accumulated to the point where I needed to take stock and try to get clear in my thinking.

During that session, Gerod talked more directly about the darkness as a cosmic energy and force.

Session #120—November 19, 1989

> True darkness, darkness that would want to be the balance or the op- posite of the Light, does not even necessarily wish to work within the physical reality. It is as if it would wish to absorb the Light, to draw it in, so that it no longer exists. It is almost as if that darkness is that energy and that force that would very knowingly destroy the Light and would very knowingly almost destroy itself. It is willing to sacri- fice itself in order to absorb the Light. Not a completely understood concept, but it is there nonetheless. So in many ways, the darkness and the evil that is present in the physical form are those variations of that original darkness that have gone awry, so to say.
>
> . . . Where this deepest and densest form of energy works is within the universe, within its own realm, and it in many ways has no regard for what takes place in any particular physical reality; its only concern is to destroy the Light as it exists in the whole. And the emanations of that energy into these physical realities is not its main intent and purpose, but it becomes the byproduct of its main purpose which is to obliterate the Light and its source.

Gerod described the darkness as a primordial and impersonal force opposing the Light at every level. He talked about it as a force of nature that will eat everything away and grind everything into dust if it can. It is not good or bad. It just is what it is.

Session #120—November 19, 1989

> T. So in some ways, this darkness, this power, is neutral, . . . like going down a river, if you were to know of a dangerous whirlpool, you can avoid it. The whirlpool is neither good nor bad, it just is.
>
> G. Yes. That is correct. This darkness is like the snake that consumes itself; that is what this void tends to do to some degree. It has a certain energy about it, but it goes around and around and so there is no final consumption and it just is as it is.

Darkness no longer had a face. This wasn't a devil, or Satan with horns, but some primal energy and force directly opposing the Light. As I thought about the darkness, I was looking, in my mind's eye, into a vast and faceless void, an infinite darkness in which a soul could become lost, preyed upon, and swallowed up. A darkness also where a soul could be caught up in the promise of power, and so itself becomes the predator.

When we first talked of the dark spot, I had asked Gerod why this darkness had to be a part of the human experience in the first place. This is when he shifted the discussion from the personal to a soul-level perspective. He said souls incarnate in physical reality without conscious memory of the Light, in order to learn and awaken to their own true nature. He said it was through the encounter with darkness—what the soul is not—that a soul can learn what it is.

Gerod then talked about the dark spot in the context of this greater darkness.

Session #120—November 19, 1989

> And it is almost as if when that dark spot was created, it was not a place of evilness; it was not a place of badness; but it was that place where every soul may have the choice to go should it wish to. And I will tell you that many souls have explored that dark spot, for the dark place within each being is in connection with that darkness and when you go through your own dark spot you go through that core dark place and you find what it is that you are. You can only know what you are when you have the experience of what you may not be; or what else you may be. And it is as if through that sojourn in that void, in that void where the Light is absent, only then can you become aware of what the Light truly is. And it is in that journey through that void of Light that you become aware of the choices that you do have. But in that void, there is power, there is a feeling that would attract some, because it will align that void with the darkness that they do have within each soul and if it, so to say, attracts one another, then it may become easier to stay there and to explore that experience for awhile.

Two weeks later, another long discussion followed, and Gerod talked again about this connection between darkness and the dark spot within each person.

Session #122—December 1, 1989

That darkness has energy, and when that energy is manifested in the physical, then it is as if the interpretation of it becomes more greatly elaborated upon. That energy exists in the universe. The parallel energy is the dark spot within each person. As each person journeys through their own darkness, their own dark spot, what happens there depends upon their life experience, the choices that they have made as they have entered into this life experience and the ability of the soul to cope with or to understand and view the choices that this being is making, and when the soul is obscured and not aware, then this being can spend a greater amount of time in this darkness, and as I say, the longer you stay there then you start drawing this like energy to you. And when this 'like energy' comes, it carries a wallop, so to say. It carries the message that the Light is not good and then that energy and that thought entering into physical form into the dark place begins to grow.

Gerod's linkage between this primordial darkness and its potential connection with a person's dark spot is where darkness itself became a clinical question, as well as a theoretical one. Gerod's statements about this darkness also implied that these questions, at a clinical level, would ultimately have to be answered from a soul-level perspective.

I continued to explore and work with the dark spot when it appeared to be an issue for a client, or when a client's reports indicated that they might have begun their cycle into the dark spot. The difference was that these dialogues with Gerod opened me to the possibility that a person's struggles with darkness could involve a far deeper and more profound level of entanglement than I had previously recognized. Looking back now, I think these dialogues marked yet another shift in my work with clients from an ego-centered to a soul-centered perspective.

Evil

The dialogues with Gerod brought into focus the idea of darkness as an energy and force, separate from souls. Making this distinction, I also began to focus more clearly on those souls who existed and operated in darkness. Specifically, I was concerned about those spirits whom I described as intentionally harassing, intruding on, or acting toward a client in threatening or destructive ways. These kinds of spirits had been an issue all along and they were very much a part of these long discussions with Gerod about darkness.

Gerod's attitude toward these spirits was always one of deep compassion. He viewed them as souls, as beings of Light who had become cut off from the Divine and the Light of their own souls, some to a greater extent than others. He saw them as souls who through fear or rage or pain or confusion had become entangled in the consciousness of darkness. Gerod saw their disconnection from the Light as these souls' deepest pain. No matter how hateful, ruthless, or conniving these spirits might be, Gerod saw their feelings and actions as born out of their pain and confusion.

Gerod talked about these discarnate souls caught in darkness, but he also talked about souls incarnated here on earth that can be ensnared or caught up in darkness. Unlike with darkness itself, these incarnate souls "do not seek to obliterate Light in a universal way, but they seek to gain power and control in their physical reality."

This also is where Gerod made the distinction between souls in darkness who were evil, and those souls who were lost in it, or hiding in it, or had become prey to the evil souls and demonic powers that exist in darkness.

Session #122—December 1, 1989

G. There are people whom we would refer to as evil but they are not evil people. They are people who are confused, they are in pain, they are looking for avenues to take them out of their darkness, and yet they are making choices that run them around in darkness more and more. And as they keep running around in that darkness more and more, they do draw in that energy from the universe and it is as if they are in a maze and it can go one way or the other. As long as they are not interfering with free will, taking away the opportunity of another soul to make choices, then it is not truly evil. It is experience. It may be dark, but that is because the person is in the darkness and then their actions are not well understood themselves.

Darkness is not necessarily evil and I know that we are speaking of words here. How do we define what darkness is? I would tell you that darkness itself is not evil. Darkness is just an absence of light and knowledge. Evil only manifests when there is interference and I would say that that will usually be when someone would end the life of another so as to take away their free will, or force them into an act or a situation where they have absolutely no ability to extricate themselves from it. Then you are interfering with free will—when someone is not able to make a choice to be in some different place and to be able to go there freely.

T. Mentally and spiritually, as well as physically?

G. Yes. True evil is when you would wish to interfere with the free will and the choices of another soul. This is what evil is, and then it is something that can become expressed in very many different ways but those are the basic tenets of it because that is the promise that God gave all, that you have free will, the ability to create your life in any way that is appropriate for you. When you take away that right from any individual or any soul, then you have created the opposite of what has been promised; you have taken that away from them and interfered with their basic right as an existing being. That is where evil, then, can now begin to come in because it is a controlling and manipulative act and it is tending to interfere with what should be.

This is what it came down to for Gerod: evil is when one soul intentionally violates the free will of another soul, whether that is occurring between souls at a physical level, spirit level, or across dimensions. He was talking about the will not only on the level of the physical personality, but also at a soul level. Many agreements, according to Gerod, are made between souls before they incarnate. And each soul that incarnates also agrees to the laws and rules that govern the physical reality. So where the conscious personality may believe his or her will is being violated, there may be other levels of soul agreement and choice that are in play between people.

Gerod had always talked about the soul's free choice as an absolute, and in this session he defined the violation of a soul's free choice by another soul as the root of evil. Darkness at times can be brutal, frightening, and draining, but it wasn't evil. After this session, I began to think a great deal about these distinctions between darkness, souls in darkness, and evil souls. I also had to think a great deal about the difference between conscious level choices versus soul level choices.

At a clinical level, however, my questions centered on the intruding spirits that I encountered with some of my clients. I was still looking for the leverage by which to force them out, since with these particular spirits that's what it usually came down to. After making the distinction

between darkness and evil, I began to focus more clearly on the violation of my client as the critical issue. According to Gerod, dark souls
affecting my clients were in violation of the soul. From a therapeutic
perspective, therefore, resolve the violation and we resolve the intrusion or attachment.

So who were they? What did they want? How did they get in?
How do we stop them? The answers to these questions, I hoped, would
lead to answers about what to do to help a client be cleared of such
intrusions and interference.

16

The Agreement

One day the Sons of God came to attend on Yahweh, and among them was Satan. So Yahweh said to Satan, "Where have you been?" "Round the earth," he answered, "roaming about." So Yahweh asked him, "Did you notice my servant Job? There is no one like him on earth: a sound and honest man who fears God and shuns evil." "Yes," Satan said, "but Job is not God-fearing for nothing, is he? Have you not put a wall around him and his house and all his domain? You have blessed all he undertakes, and his flocks throng the countryside. But stretch out your hand and lay a finger on his possessions: I warrant you, he will curse you to your face." "Very well," Yahweh said to Satan, all he has is in your power. But keep your hands off his person." So Satan left the presence of Yahweh. —Book of Job

Devils and Demons

I have encountered many different "devils" and "demons" in my work with clients over the last twenty years, at least that's what many people would call them. These entities take many different shapes and forms, some human, some not. Different ones use different tactics and techniques to achieve their aims. They are conscious and intelligent beings, and they range from those highly aware to those who are ignorant and compliant. Most keep their activities with humans shrouded, operating at unconscious levels. Others, though, can be in your face, taking pleasure in tormenting or demonstrating their control. Some are acting individually, others in concert with a group. Most of them appear to be part of a larger network or hierarchy of souls, whether highly or loosely organized.

What I know about these souls in darkness comes primarily from my clinical work. As I've said before, I am not clairvoyant. I don't see or hear these beings except through my clients, and I do not seek contact with them outside of my healing work. I studied them much as an exterminator studies a destructive pest, observing its movements and habits, finding out what it is after or what attracts it, and discovering how it has been entering the building. The exterminator's goals are to remove the pest and take measures to close the access or take away what is attracting it. These were my goals as well in dealing with intruding and destructive spirits: remove them and close off their point of entry. Unlike the exterminator, however, I could not and did not want to follow these entities back into the regions of darkness. It was not a matter of trying to wipe them out at their source or reasoning with them, but only of removing them and preventing their further access to my client.

Two questions, therefore, dominated my communications and dealings with evil spirits who were present with a client. First, I wanted to know what these dark souls were after? What were they trying to achieve by their intrusions and activities? And second, how were they able to violate my client's boundaries, seemingly at will? How did they gain access to a person in order to do what they were doing? There were many other questions about these beings, of course, and more arose in the course of my investigation of these dark souls. From a clinical point of view, though, these two questions—motive and means—were, in my mind, key to understanding how to deal with them. The answers to both these questions came on the same day during a session with Gerod.

It had been two years since my talk with Gerod about the distinction between darkness and evil, and a lot had happened in that time. I had more than thirty clients whose inner work revealed some kind of involvement by these dark souls, either in the past or ongoing in the present. I had talked to Gerod about them often, both in general terms and those specifically involved with my clients at inner levels. In this particular session, I had prepared my list of questions about clients, and I asked Gerod if we might talk about a group of dark souls that I was encountering in my work.

Making Deals

My first question to Gerod was about a pattern that I had observed with a number of clients that involved these intruding spirits. In each case, a present or past life ego-state had shared a memory indicating that it had made a deal with the spirit that was now accosting the client. The pattern made me think that the different spirits, these discarnate souls, all belonged to one group and that *making a deal* was their signature, their *modus operandi*.

Session #209—December 11, 1991

T. I'm running into this group with Ben D., Jenny W., Linda T., and they've been there with Shelley too. I have a couple of new people I'm not ready to ask about yet, but based on their description, it seems like this group is involved. The one theme that keeps coming up is that this group appears to approach these people at very, very vulnerable times and offer some kind of deal—to either relieve their pain, or help them avoid their pain, or give them something they want, and in the deal, in a sense, get a lock on the soul or get rights to the soul. Would you agree that this is a strategy they use?

G. Yes, I do.

T. With Ben we have talked about this group of two-year-olds, severely traumatized, and in my work with them, we've got to the point where they seem to have been contacted themselves by these dark beings, and again a deal made to help them deny or get away from their pain. Would you agree with that?

G. Yes.

T. Part of my struggle about this group is that there often seems to be past life involved as well so that there's almost like a black thread kind of entangling the soul. So with Ben there was a past-life ego-state—at least one—but now I've come to the present life with this two-year-old group. They are very afraid to come forward; I think the fear is that they've made a deal and don't want to tell. Their experience is quite painful on the one hand, but deeper than that, it's like they won't come forward because they are afraid of what happens if they break the deal. So, kind of a compounded dilemma for them. Is there any comment you would make about this?

G. It is a dilemma for them because if they are to come forward and acknowledge themselves, so to say, it's like they must then recall or remember what it is they have agreed to do and so they are somewhat reluctant or somewhat unsure of the advisability of doing that. There needs to be some reassurance that they can share all that they know, and understand that there are no bargains with anyone that stand stronger than the original bargain with God.

T. Is there a way for them to get some clear understanding about this?

G. They need to be told that. And the higher self can tell them. The higher self needs to continue to communicate with them that—how do I say—it is a false bill of sale, a bargain that has no validity.

This insight about deals as an access could only have come after I recognized the ego-states as real beings. The ego-states' capacity to understand and respond to other beings extended not only to interaction with other ego-states within the self, but also to spirit beings attempting to make contact directly. The ego-states' capacity to respond to other beings meant that they were vulnerable to access by spirits who had the right approach or made the right offer. Ego-states' limited experience and perspectives made them an easy target if a spirit were wishing to manipulate them.

What I discovered in the ensuing months was that making deals was not just a strategy of one group of dark souls, but appeared to be a rule governing these intrusions. I learned that a spirit, whether earthbound, low-lying, or evil, had to have the self/soul's consent to enter into one's mind or psyche. These did not have to be explicit agreements, however, or even made at a conscious level. Most, in fact, were not. Most of these deals were made with ego-states at an unconscious level.

With earthbound spirits, that consent appeared to be more opportunistic or mutual, meaning that the ego-state's emotions or issues fit with the earthbound spirit's feelings, perceptions, or needs. The contact with ego-states by dark souls was not accidental. I began to understand that the dark souls pursued these contacts intentionally. I realized they were, to some extent, doing the very same thing therapists do in ego-state therapy: that is, making direct contact with ego-states and engaging them in some ongoing interaction. Unlike in therapy, however, these contacts by dark souls were not for the purpose of healing. They were made in order to gain access and to establish some level of power and control within a person. A spirit might offer succor to a child who is frightened and alone; or threaten a young boy with more punishment if he doesn't do what he's told; or it might hit upon an ego-state's secret guilt and repeat the message until it reverberates throughout the mind.

The ego-states were, in effect, being used as doorways into the self/soul. Gerod described it as a kind of "backdoor" permission. Technically, he said, as part of the soul, an ego-state shares in the soul's freedom, and so its choices, as limited as they are, are valid. If an ego-state says *yes* to a dark soul—whether by accepting something that is offered or submitting to a threat—then the dark soul counts that as the soul's consent. The deal for access, then, is made whether the ego-state recognizes it as such or not. With its limited perspective, an ego-state usually will never discover its power to end any deal or contract it has made with a dark soul.

It's About Energy

After talking to Gerod about deals, I switched the focus from specific clients to the dark souls in general. These kinds of discussions were like fishing expeditions. I would throw out a number of questions until I hit on one I thought Gerod and I could pursue. It was like a lawyer or detective poking and probing a witness with questions until he finds a way in. The question I came to that day was whether these dark souls that are involved with humans could not only interfere with someone psychically, but whether they could actually manifest a physical presence?

Session #209—December 11, 1991

 T. Are they able to manifest physically?
 G. Yes!
 T. Without reincarnating?
 G. Yes.
 T. That's a pretty high level ability.
 G. Yes, it is.

Gerod went on then to talk about how dark souls with high level awareness and ability are able to approach the Light directly for the purpose of becoming energized and then returning to the dark. Enough of these energized souls acting in concert, then, could generate the energy needed for a dark soul to cross the boundary and manifest a body.

They're able to do it because they go as close to the Light as they can in order to clear themselves and gain awareness of their ability. But they take that ability back into that space where they are not within the Light and they generate, so to say, a great deal of energy by their congregation. This is the reason for gathering more souls to them because as they gain more souls, it's as if they live parasitically and expand their abilities. They cannot exist in a singular fashion, so to say. One soul who may wish to take shape or form and come into the physical reality needs the amplification of souls to help it do it.

It was an astonishing claim: that under certain conditions, a discarnate soul could cross the boundary from spirit to matter and manifest in a physical body. From our point of view, it would be like seeing someone materialize out of thin air. Gerod described such a feat as a function of Light energy that dark souls were able to subvert and use. He went on, then, to talk in general about the dark souls' need for Light energy, and the use of incarnate souls as a convenient source.

G. And, I would add, that it needs the amplification of those souls that are in the Light. So when one is in the physical form on earth and is a soul of the Light, it will bring very fine amplification to one of these beings but once it is absorbed and used up, so to say, then that soul of darkness has nothing more to offer to those higher up, so it must then feed upon the Light again.

T. The vampire.

G. Yes.

T. This would appear, Gerod, to be the most developed form of darkness that we've discussed.

G. Yes, it is.

T. What the churches maybe refer to as the devil or Satan.

G. That is correct.

T. And you're saying one of the basic issues about them is that they must gain their energy from the Light?

G. Yes, and you see that is where one of the misconceptions lies, that they are trying to gather souls into the darkness to make the darkness stronger. And it is true, the more that are there it does give it a certain power but that is the illusion. What they are doing is absorbing the Light to keep themselves strengthened, so to say. The power of the

Light amplifies their energy but it is like when one eats food or fruit. You take it in your mouth and you chew it, and eat it, and it nurtures the body and gives it energy for just so long and then it's gone. So you keep eating. And that's what they are doing.

I could believe what Gerod was saying about a soul manifesting physically, though I did not understand or have a language for this level of energy and consciousness. It was a topic we would come back to a number of times in the coming years. The idea, however, that humans could be an energy source for these dark souls was the glimmer of an answer to my question about *what* these intruding souls were after. They were after energy.

According to Gerod, souls in darkness are still beings of Light and so still need Light energy to survive. He said that each of these souls could return to the Light any time they chose, that "redemption is always, always available for everyone." Since these souls were not willing to go to the Light themselves, however, they had to obtain the Light energy from other souls, specifically, souls incarnate. Gerod said that dark souls could not access souls in the spirit realm of Light—that would be too close—but once a soul incarnates, he said, that soul might be vulnerable then to access by these dark ones.

Session #213—January 31, 1992

T. Gerod, I wanted to come back to this question of how these dark beings live off of or feed off of our energy. I don't understand that process or the mechanism. There have been many clients now where we have encountered these beings. I assume in some way the access they have is that they are using these peoples' energy. Can you say more about what the process is of using this energy or draining this energy, what is happening there?

G. Well, I'm not sure how to say it other than simply one must be rejuvenated constantly to survive. A soul of the Light has steady access to the Light so it keeps itself going, but when a soul exists in the darkness, Light is not readily available and it will not take the chance of moving fully into the Light because that might be dangerous, it might be too confrontive, so the Light is siphoned off from those who exist within the Light.

T. And this would be a process that might never reach the conscious level for a person?

G. It is very possible it would never reach the conscious level, yes.

T. Is it like when we talk about getting energy from a car battery—it just flows once the contact is there?

G. Yes.

T. So it would be pretty much the same for them. They may have their tools and their devices and they can't necessarily see the energy but they know they are receiving the energy?

G. That is correct. It's the thought process that creates the access.

T. Do we do that same thing when we pray or meditate on the Light?

G. Yes, you draw that energy to yourself, you tap into it.

T. They, of course, would not do that. They would only go through another soul for that energy?

G. That is correct, because the energy is stepped down, so to say. It's like as it comes through the physical form, through a soul in the physical form, it is stepped down to a different level so that it's like receiving stolen goods. You don't go and steal it yourself; you take it from the middleman. So you cannot be discovered as the thief. It is one thing to pray and it is another thing to steal.

T. This looks like an awful big picture with these beings. I mean it's kind of like they must be working all the time to create access and keep access open.

G. They have to work very hard.

T. And to create an opening, say, at an unconscious, past-life level, is that enough of an opening then for them just to get what they need or might they need to make more access in order to get more energy, a bigger charge?

G. They are safest if they are undetected so it is more that they will have a small access to many people rather than large access to a few. Therefore, they can remain quite obscure.

According to Gerod, the dark souls' involvement with humans was primarily about their need for Light energy, and their focus on incarnated souls as a primary source for that energy.

Energy Exchange

This view of dark souls and the primary motivation behind their activities answered the question of what they were after. This understanding, though, also revealed a deeper significance to those situations where I found that deals had been made between ego-states and spirits. The dark souls' need for energy made me look at these situations in a different way. While the specific ego-states and spirits differed from one client to the next, I came to view the deal (contract, or agreement) essentially as a means of energy exchange or transfer. The goal in the healing process was still the same, i.e. remove the spirits, but removing the spirits also meant ending the siphoning off of my client's energy.

Understanding the contact between spirits and ego-states as an energy exchange also offered an explanation for a number of situations where an ego-state, a person's higher self, or Gerod gave me information that a piece or pieces of soul energy were missing, or had been encapsulated within the soul. Once I understood that it was about energy, I began to pay more attention to the way energy was moved about in the inner reality—it may be in the form of a book, in suitcases, in trucks, or pipelines. Pieces of soul energy, for example, might be hidden in an old steamer trunk, or carried in the pockets of an ego-state, or may have been handed over to a spirit who subsequently took it out of the soul. Once I recognized the principle of energy transfer, I knew what trigger words to listen for and when to ask questions.

Taken together, these two insights—the dark souls' need for Light energy, and the deals they made to acquire it—added another dimension to my already expanding perspective on the psychic and spiritual realms of the mind and soul. Regardless of what strategies, techniques, or deceptions the dark souls might use, the ultimate aim of contact with humans, as I came to see, was access to energy.

I also began to grasp that the psychic intrusion and entanglement of someone by spirits was not primarily about the conscious personality (although in certain cases that was important), but about gaining access to the soul. If enough contacts and deals could be made with parts of the soul, including present- and past-life ego-states, these dark ones could weave a web of connections extending over lifetimes. It was a frightening picture. They could, so to speak, set up camp within a person's soul and, if secure enough, it will be waiting for them to move back into when the soul returns to the physical in a subsequent lifetime.

The dark souls appear to use two primary methods to set up this ongoing access to a soul. The first are the deals that I discussed earlier. These deals appear to be made with an ego-state—from the person's present life or a past life—in which a dark soul offers the ego-state something it wants or needs: relief from pain, immortality, revenge, protection, etc. The ego-state often doesn't seem to know there's a price to pay until after it has said yes. Later in the person's life, or in a subsequent lifetime, the particular ego-state can be approached by a dark soul or dark energy. The ego-state reacts when it feels the proximity or probing energy of the dark souls. The ego-state recognizes and responds to the energy. Depending on the original contact, an ego-state may perceive these dark souls as friends or benefactors, or may be frightened and respond only because of the deal they made. Whatever the reaction, it's what the dark souls look for and then focus in on.

Another way in which dark souls establish a connection with a soul that can be used as a point of access later on is by placing what I've called a *psychic device* within the soul. You might think of these devices as an *energy marker* or *anchor,* and they are placed within a soul through the ego-states. A dark soul might, for example, give an ego-state a new hat, a piece of jewelry, or a weapon. It might give the ego-state a special box and tell it to hide it, or hangs a painting on the wall that is really a window. The dark soul will use whatever works for the particular ego-state involved. At a future time, when the dark soul returns, the device then would act as an energy connection and access.

The ego-states, with their limited understanding, usually have no idea that these objects are devices or how they are being used to exploit the soul. I have had a number of ego-states, for example, who were given a device and refused to have the higher self remove it because they believed the device was keeping them alive, or it was a favorite toy, or even a pet. Conversely, there are ego-states where a device is present that causes pain if the ego-state goes near the Light. These ego-states have no idea that it's the device that is affecting them and causing their pain. Rather, they believe it is the Light causing their pain and so in the healing process they refuse the Light or block contact with the higher self.

This use of devices by dark souls is extremely common. They are employed not only to set up future connections with a soul, but they can be placed within a person in their present life, usually through an ego-state, in order to cause pain, distress, fear, or confusion for a person. The higher self has the ability to scan ego-states—present life or past—to determine if there are any devices present, and if so, can remove them. However, since it is the ego-state that has *accepted* the device, it usually must give permission to have it removed.

According to Gerod, these dark souls do not have the ability to track souls into the Light and know when and where a soul will next incarnate. When a soul does incarnate, however, it's as though its energy signature shows up on their radar screen, and the dark souls can make an approach. They can send out energy looking for vulnerable areas or trying to trigger reactions, like pressing doorbells at random until someone buzzes you in.

The Agreement

As our work progressed, I continued to press Gerod on the issue of darkness and dark souls, and especially on the issue of justice. Why would a soul knowingly subject itself to the human experience in the first place, especially when it could involve becoming prey to such dark and evil forces? And why would an all-loving God demand or permit that to happen?

Gerod's answer came during another of those periodic sessions where I was trying to integrate my clinical observations and my theoretical understanding. I started the session by laying some groundwork. I reviewed with Gerod several points he had made over the months, including the view that a soul's incarnation is, at different levels, an encounter with darkness (not necessarily evil).

I reiterated that there were souls who could be drawn into or become lost in the darkness and asked Gerod if there was anything he would add at that point. He responded by talking again about darkness as a primordial energy.

Session #271—February 6, 1993

I would make the point that the darkness is—how would I put it—the underpinning. The darkness is the void that supports the universe. It is not separate but very much a part of it. It is the mirror, so to say, of the creator.

. . . Darkness is an energy, but it is the void in which the universe grows. It is the fertile ground, so to say, where the seeds are sown, so that the Light may grow. And that it is always, in essence, larger than the Light. But it is without purpose, except for that purpose it may create in its response to the Light as it feels itself being drawn into knowledge and understanding and warmth and love. It may react in its ignorance in many ways.

He went further, though. He said that darkness existed before the Light.

Session #271—February 6, 1993

G. Darkness was here first. Its energy, its awareness, such as it is. It was here first.

T. You mean here in terms of the universe?

G. Yes.

T. That's a big statement, Gerod.

G. I know.

T. The question obviously is: where did the Light come from then?

G. The darkness created it.

T. The darkness created the Light?

G. Yes. I am not sure how well I can describe this. I will work my way around it until I feel we can find it. Darkness existed first and it created the Light because there was no purpose. There was no focus. There was no reason for being. The darkness had consciousness but there was no purpose for that consciousness so, in essence, it took its awareness and turned it in on itself. It's as if to say, it created something that was bigger than itself. And that which it created began to consume it. And it was much more powerful than the darkness and in reaction to the consumption, so to say, of the voracious appetite of its creation and its superior ability to conceptualize and to conceive and create, the darkness, in reaction, began to defend and to protect itself from that which it created. Very simply put, it is like the parent who has a child that is far more intelligent than itself and therefore becomes, not the creator, but the subordinate to that which it has created.

T. It's as if you're saying that once the darkness created Light, if the darkness would have allowed it, the Light would have spread throughout.

G. Yes.

T. But instead, the darkness stopped and opposed itself.

G. Yes. The compromise is the physical incarnation. That is the only way the Light can expand. It is as if it was put to a test—a way to limit the rapid expansion; a way for the Light to go through a testing; to go through obstacles; to go through—I don't know the word but—to go through a process by which it gained the right to expand, and having to do that with challenges being thrown at it. The soul being encapsulated within a physical body that caused limitations, that limited its understanding and made it almost as limited as the darkness is in comparison to the Light. And thus, it gave the darkness a chance to be able to curtail the growth of the Light and to also have the opportunity to transform the Light back into darkness through the absorption process.

In essence, Gerod was saying that human incarnation was a way to give souls the freedom to choose between darkness and Light. To go back to Gerod's earlier metaphor, the physical incarnation is where the game would be played out. A soul's limited human consciousness gave darkness a level playing field to entice a soul with its promises of power and control, or relief from pain, or the oblivion of dreamless sleep. Day in, day out, in so many ways, each soul is choosing.

This scenario raised more questions. Some would take weeks to get to. My immediate question for Gerod, though, was why, if the Light were so powerful, would it acquiesce to such a demand? And second, why would so many souls *freely* choose to incarnate into a life of pain, suffering, and hurt rather than remain with other souls in the spirit realm, in the Oneness and Love of the Light.

Gerod said the Light agreed to this in order that souls have the same choice that the Light itself possessed.

Session #271—February 6, 1993

G. It's as if to say the Creator is aware of its own creation from darkness and therefore knows from whence it came and chooses to allow that which it has created to have a choice.

. . . The Light knew that it came from the darkness, and in that realization it believed that it did not have the right to deny that source to anyone.

T. Or else it would get into somewhat the same position of controlling and darkness . . .

G. Yes. So, it's as if the compromise, then, was created.

T. (Pause) It's a tough compromise.

G. It is. It is very difficult. And this is why the Light has never abandoned anyone, even when they are in the darkness.

T. Well, this makes me think of the story of Job and it certainly could shed a different light on that.

According to Gerod, what the Light created were souls, seeds of itself, so to speak, whose nature also, then, was to grow, create, and expand. This is the unbridled expansion against which, Gerod said, the darkness reacted and opposed the Light.

Session #272—February 13, 1993

T. When the Light was created, was that also the moment that all souls were created?

G. No.

T. When the darkness realized what was happening and attempted to stop it, was that the time when all souls were created?

G. Yes.

T. Can you say why it occurred at that time?

G. Because that was the moment at which the darkness realized that the Light had the ability to reproduce, re-create itself, and to expand itself.

T. That's when the darkness reacted?

G. That is when the darkness discovered the ability of that which it created, the Light, and realized that that which it had created could do exactly what it had done, only its power was far greater. Once the Light re-created itself, it was doing it in a more concentrated way.

T. So was there a limit, then, put on the creation of any more souls, once the reaction by darkness happened? You've said that all souls were created at one time. I'm not sure what there was to prevent the Light from creating more souls.

G. The agreement.

T. The agreement. The compromise. No more souls to be created.

G. No more souls would be created until that moment, as we have talked previously, of the next expansion. In that next expansion, then more souls could be, and may be, created.

This Agreement did not sit easy with me. I could see where a person—a soul—might feel he or she had been sold down the river, or that the Light was ultimately weaker than darkness. I pressed Gerod on this point.

T. I just don't understand, Gerod, when you say no more souls can be created . . . and a negotiation or compromise had to be reached. I'm not sure I understand the power that is able to demand the Light to make this compromise.

G. I would respond to that by saying it is the compassionate, loving response of the Creator. It is the child who has the ability to recognize the fear, the concern of the parent and rather than overriding it, overruling it, it compassionately recognizes and negotiates so that there can be born an understanding, an awareness. So, it's as if the response is a response that hopefully will engender an expansion of consciousness within the dark, so to say. It's as if the Light does not necessarily have an agenda that must be met. It's purpose is only to exist, to be, and therefore does not have any—I'm not sure of the word—does not have any goal for which it must push and override everything else.

I knew that was true. This was how Gerod always talked about the Light, and it's how the Light worked with ego-states and earthbound spirits. It would never force or violate a soul's free choice. To do that would be for the Light to violate itself. It would only make sense, then, that the Light would not violate the darkness either.

I came back to Gerod about this agreement a number of times in the following months. It was another of those ideas that challenged my thinking in a fundamental way and triggered feelings of resistance. I didn't know which was more difficult: understanding this agreement and what it implied for souls, or accepting it emotionally as somehow necessary or good in spite of the human suffering it involves.

Session #300—September 6, 1993

T. It's still difficult to grasp this issue of the agreement.

G. Yes.

T. It seems like in some way, to have this agreement made would mean that the agreement, in a sense, had to be made; that there is something essential about the agreement. Do you think the agreement had to be made?

G. No. But it was the way the Light honored its creator. It's the way the Light offers into that dark void the opportunity to make a choice also. In darkness is always the seeds for new understanding. To not negotiate and come to agreement with it would be to cast aside something that could be of great value. In the darkness, evil exists, yes. But in the darkness are also all of the unanswered questions that can be the vistas for new horizons. All that the darkness is, is unexamined consciousness.

T. So the issue of evil and the dark souls really is more what happens when one enters into that horizon and may in some way get scared, or lost, or entrenched and then react in ways that we have talked about before—may try to have power over others or control over others, use it for selfish purposes only. Is that right?

G. That can occur. But, the darkness can also be the tunnel to someplace new.

T. Yes. That's where you are saying the potential for greater consciousness, greater Light—all of that is there?

G. Yes.

The agreement, in Gerod's view was not a standoff or an impasse between darkness and Light. Rather, it was the Light's natural response to opposition—advancement through love, not violation and force.

In Gerod's story, the creation of souls—Light creating Light—was an exponential step in the Light's expansion. It was a flashpoint. It was also the point at which darkness reacted. The darkness knew, that if left unchecked, the power of the Light to recreate itself would overwhelm it. Souls were, so to speak, the leading edge of the Light's expansion, and as the means of that expansion, souls became a focus of contention. Darkness opposed them and would extinguish them as it would extinguish all Light if it could.

According to Gerod, incarnation was the compromise, the meeting ground. The soul assumes a limited consciousness and enters the world of duality and choice. This was a very different story than the one I had grown up with, i.e., souls expelled from the garden because of their sins, and banished to a life of suffering and toil, with no guarantee or promise of redemption.

In Gerod's story, it was not God expelling His children from Eden because they were sinful and bad or because they now knew too much. On the contrary, God was sending souls on a journey of awakening. Given the limitations of physical reality and ego-consciousness, it is a journey the soul makes usually over lifetimes.

Gerod's view of human incarnation as a soul's journey to awakening was not completely new. He had always talked about each person's life as an opportunity for the soul to evolve and become conscious. He also had always insisted that what was happening in a person's life was not random or accidental but was the result of soul choices—those made by the soul before incarnation, as well as the person's own choices in the present life. Gerod's story of creation, the birth of souls, and the agreement between darkness and Light was consistent with these views. His story offered an explanation and larger context for understanding the meaning and purpose of human incarnation as the soul's means to awakening. This was, to me, a clearer answer to the question of why a soul would choose to enter a limited consciousness and reality.

Gerod's story also emphasized and reaffirmed the soul's freedom as part of its essential nature and a source of its power. The agreement did not make souls free, but recognized their freedom as an absolute condition of human incarnation. While the soul's consciousness became veiled, it did not surrender or lose its freedom when it incarnated. This was the Light's demand, according to Gerod, in the agreement with darkness. A soul's freedom could not be taken away or suspended. Even if a soul were to enter the darkness, it had to be by its own agreement. And if a soul became entangled in the darkness, or willingly pursued the power of darkness, that soul was still free at all times (if it could find its way clear) to make a new choice and return to the Light.

True Evil

Gerod's story of the agreement was told in mythic terms. It's the only way we have of talking about such ultimate forces and realities. Like all cosmic myths, it was a story of beginnings and of man's relationship to the Creator and each other. They are not the kind of stories one tries to prove in empirical terms. Talking at these levels can so easily become anthropomorphic and egocentric, casting God in our own image and likeness, rather than the other way around. They are, rather, stories of spiritual truths.

It took me a while to come to terms with the idea of the agreement and the spiritual truths it implied. It called for a radical shift in my own point of view about souls and human incarnation, about ego-centered and soul-centered consciousness and choice, and about the relationship between darkness and the Light. The agreement also recast the problem of evil within this larger perspective and drew the distinction between darkness and evil even more clearly. Darkness was about a devouring chaos, a force that would consume all souls, and the Creator itself, if it could. Evil, on the other hand, was about souls, living in darkness, who violate the agreement by taking another soul's energy and gaining control through deception and manipulation.

Satan has been called the *father of lies*. The agreement, with its guarantee of every soul's free choice, would explain what earned him the name. Since a soul cannot be forced to submit, the devil must have a way to persuade a soul to say yes to its interference. Dark souls can promise a person immortality, freedom from pain, power over his enemies, or protection from harm. These are not all lies. There is some truth in each promise, but they are half-truths. The soul is already immortal, so in the promise of immortality, the person is being "given" something that, as a soul, he or she already possesses. A soul can find relief from pain in the darkness, but only by sacrificing its consciousness. Dark souls do exercise power, but it's a power taken from incarnate souls that has been twisted and distorted in darkness. The central lie, though, at the heart of every deceit and deal is that once a soul agrees, it is no longer free.

This connection between evil and the violation of a soul's freedom echoed what Gerod had said at different times about dark spirits and the true nature of evil.

Session #5—January 29, 1988

A truly evil spirit will wish to possess because they do not want to allow you any freedom of will.

Going back to an earlier quoted passage:

Session #122—December 1, 1989

True evil is when you would wish to interfere with the free will and the choices of another. This is what evil is, and then it is something that can become expressed in very many different ways, but those are the basic tenets of it . . . because that is the promise that God gave all—that you have free will, the ability to create your life in any way that is appropriate for you. When you take away that right from any individual or any soul, then you have created the opposite of what has been promised. You have taken that away from them and interfered with their basic right as an existing being. That is where evil then can now begin to come into the picture because it is a controlling and manipulative act and it is tending to interfere with what should be.

Over the months, it was clear that in Gerod's view the violation of another soul's free choice was a defining issue of evil. A soul who violates another soul is violating its own nature, and it can only do that by stepping into the dark, creating a separation from its own light. This understanding also revealed a more complex and symbiotic relationship between darkness and the evil done by souls in darkness.

Session #321—November 19, 1993

T. Gerod, I've thought a lot about the distinction or difference between darkness itself and the souls aligned with darkness. It seems that you're saying both are active agents.

G. Yes. As we have spoken before, darkness itself is not evil. It is not the activator of events per se. It is acquiescing to some degree to the actions of those who dwell within it. Quite often when I use the term "darkness," it is a general term, a generic term, to include and to suggest the activities that are taking place there at all its various levels.

T. Is it the darkness itself that puts out the message or call for pieces of the soul? Or are the souls aligned with darkness the ones who are focused on taking pieces of soul energy?

G. Darkness is much like a human who does not wish to take responsibility. It wants to achieve a result but it does not wish to have responsibility for how that result is achieved. Darkness, of course, its goal is to consume the Light, to eradicate it, for its supposed self-preservation. Those who dwell in the darkness are aware of this of course. They feed on the Light. They go about their business of self-preservation without the consciousness of darkness interfering with their methods because their methods, though done for their own reasons, in essence, achieve the goal of the darkness.

T. Besides the ultimate ensnaring of a soul into the darkness, is there some benefit that the dark souls derive from having possession of pieces of the soul? Can it use its energy or live off its energy or . . .

G. Yes. It's a very direct source of primal energy, a very direct source of Light. It does not consume at the rapid rate—how would I say it—when a being in darkness is draining light from someone existing in the light, in a physical body, it has only limited energy. A piece of the soul is like a glowing coal. It burns much longer, much more intensely. And the more pieces you put together, the longer it will burn. And should it choose to develop its own consciousness within the dark, it can keep itself generated for a very long time. If a piece is too small, without the ability for awareness, it may, in essence, go dormant after a period of time. The energy is only successfully perpetuated when it is restructured with its own energy. This is why one piece is desirable but two pieces are more; three pieces are better, four even greater. So the more that can be accumulated . . . it's almost being done with the idea of taking the whole soul, piece by piece, until it is rebuilt in the darkness.

The dark souls' capacity to gain access to a person at a psychic level was a disturbing thought, but their ability to manipulate ego-states into dealing away pieces of soul energy was more disturbing still.

17

The Power of Light

The soul in its manifestation on the earth is not at all disconnected to the higher spheres. It lives in all the spheres, although it generally is only conscious of one level. Only a veil separates us. The seer's own soul becomes a torch in his hand. It is his own light that illuminates his path. It is just like directing a searchlight into dark corners which one could not see before.—Hazrat Inayat Khan

No Deal

Intellectually and theoretically, I worked with the idea of the *Agreement*. It was a very different way of thinking. What helped most, I think, in coming to terms with it were its clinical implications. There were three kinds of situations I encountered with clients where Gerod's claim of an Agreement between darkness and Light was put to the test.

The first were those situations I talked about earlier where an ego-state had made a deal with a threatening or intruding spirit. As Gerod described it, the Agreement offered a new perspective on these deals. They were not simply one strategy among many but a necessary part of any strategy dark souls used to gain access to another soul. They had to have that soul's permission to enter or attach to the soul. The clinical question was whether deals, once made, could be un-made.

Gerod's response to this question was an unequivocal yes. He looked at the deals made between spirits and ego-states as a dark soul's backdoor permission. By targeting a vulnerable and fragmented part of the soul, a dark soul gets a foothold and then claims the deal was on the up and up. They seem to follow very closely the letter of the law.

Session #313—October 24, 1993

G. Primarily the same limitations apply to darkness as applies to me. As we discussed, I cannot drag anyone into the Light nor can darkness drag anyone into the dark. I cannot interfere with an unfolding if it is essential. There are times when I may offer information but there are times when to offer information would be very very intrusive on my part. Darkness, essentially, has that same limitation. However, it is not as respectful of that. Darkness, so to say, must move individuals into choosing it because it cannot necessarily force. But it does have its ways. It does not choose to work with consciousness necessarily and it may choose to ensnare the soul by working with all of those many levels internally, with ego-states or energies that are present, whereas the Light will choose to work primarily with the soul and with consciousness.

T. It's like you're saying the darkness would obey the letter of the law very precisely.

G. Yes. And as your experience has shown you, there are many individuals who work in concert with darkness not because of a conscious choice and not necessarily because of a soul choice but because an ego-state may be aligned with darkness and opening the door to allow it. Darkness perceives that as a valid contact. However, the Light perceives ego-states as not the whole self but a fragment of the self and therefore not the one to make necessarily such important choices. But darkness does not make that discrimination. It's like darkness will knock on a door and whoever answers is good enough.

Gerod said these deals were invalid. They violated the original Agreement that guaranteed every soul its absolute freedom to choose. He said an ego-state, as part of the soul, shares in the soul's freedom of choice. So it has the power to end any deal or contract with darkness anytime it chooses. The problem is that ego-states, with their limited perspective, don't know they have this power. From their point of view, once a deal is made, they believe they have no choice but to abide by it. Not so, Gerod said.

What is needed in these situations is for the ego-state to become aware of its connection to the soul and its freedom and power to end any deal or agreement it has made. Once an ego-state does that, the spirits lose their permission, and if they don't leave on their own, they can be removed. Gerod also said that in these situations where spirits refuse to leave, the higher self should be able to identify the ego-state(s) being used for access.

This understanding suggested a very different strategy in dealing with spirits who refused to leave or disengage from a client. It shifted the focus of treatment from forcing the spirits out to finding their point of access. So instead of fighting, Gerod was suggesting we find out whom they were using for access and help that one(s) undo any deal or agreement. No deal, no access. In essence, instead of trying to get the keys back, we were going to be changing the locks.

I started testing this strategy with those clients where spirits were refusing to leave, and the higher self was unable to remove them. In some cases, this new approach showed immediate and dramatic results. Even the most menacing and resistive of spirits were summarily removed or their connections with the person severed once the ego-state(s) involved ended its deal. This is also why a higher self, acting on its own, cannot remove some spirits. It will not violate the ego-state's free choice agreement. Once an ego-state chooses to end its agreement, the higher self is free to remove them.

These deals, as you would expect, were contrary to the Light and in one way or another prohibited the ego-state(s) from receiving much Light, if any. A good example is the seven-year-old ego-state in Chapter 13 who had the jackknife. The jackknife was a dark device. An external spirit had given him the knife and as long as 7yo held onto it, the opening for the dark soul was in force. Once higher self communicated to him about his ability to heal, he gave the knife to the higher self, and at that point the agreement was ended. 7yo was free to move, and higher self could sever the spirit's connection to the soul.

It took several years to learn the deals, tricks, and deceptions these dark souls use to engage an ego-state and gain access. I don't want to make it sound easier than it is. Many times these spirit intrusions are complex. They can involve more than one ego-state. There can be deep entanglements as with Rhonda whose panic attacks began after meeting her new boss. The entanglements can extend over multiple lifetimes. What has been consistent, though, from then until now, is 1) that intruding spirits need permission to access a person, and 2) when that permission is found and withdrawn, the higher self can remove the spirits forcibly, if they don't leave of their own volition.

I saw this strategy work so many times that it seemed to provide strong confirmation of the Agreement. How else to explain it? No matter what kind of fight or resistance these dark spirits put up, once an ego-state agreed to have them expelled, that was it. They were expelled. The main point being, the spirits *had* to leave. They didn't have a choice. It was the ego-state's choice that unleashed a power that forced them out. I thought of it as the soul's power. It had been there all along, but it also apparently respected the ego-state's choice and would not override it. So once an ego-state came into accord with the soul's Light, then its choices were fully supported and acted on by the Light.

This is what the Agreement would predict, and it's what I saw happen again and again. It said to me very clearly that the ultimate power over whether intruding spirits stay or go resides with the person, not the spirits.

Soul Retrieval

The second confirmation I had of the Agreement involved clients where pieces of soul energy or ego-states were missing. In the early years, I did not appreciate the full significance of the missing pieces of soul. I simply operated on the general principle that all parts of a soul's energy belonged with the soul and that any missing part should be returned. As I learned about the dark souls' need for Light energy, and the predatory nature of their involvement with incarnate souls, I began to see missing soul pieces as a more critical issue in the healing process. With clients where dark souls were involved, I began to pay closer attention to whether any part of the soul was missing and became more discerning about any deals that had been made.

Session #321—November 19, 1993

G. Pieces of the soul are relinquished to the darkness for many reasons by many different parts of the soul. Each soul, each body, may have an ego-state; may have some part of themselves that has taken authority to negotiate with the devil, so to say, and they have created a bargain or a contract that darkness expects to be fully honored and that particular part of the whole self may be very willing to honor it.

Of course, it is not an honorable agreement because it is not made on behalf of the whole self but is made on behalf of the self-serving interest of one or maybe more parts of the whole self. So, it is a contract that is on shaky grounds. That is the leverage that one has to renegotiate.

Darkness knows it is a shaky contract, so to say, that it is not dealing with the whole self. It is dealing with bits and pieces of the whole self and that is why it is getting only bits and pieces of the soul.

The missing pieces and deals with ego-states answered the question of *how* dark souls obtained another soul's energy. I began to view the activity of dark souls and their interactions with ego-states more clearly as predatory, and within that context, began to see soul energy as a commodity to the souls in darkness.

With those clients where dark spirits were involved, I began to pay closer attention to whether any part of the soul—anyone or anything— was missing. I became more discerning about any deals that had been made. It became clear that the deals with ego-states were not only about gaining access *into* the soul, but about bringing energy out as well.

The Agreement Gerod described explained the importance and necessity of the deals I heard about from ego-states. A soul's energy could not just be taken; it had to be given over. Ending these deals and closing the access was a primary aim in these situations. The next question was: could the soul energy that had been taken be retrieved? With its absolute freedom to choose, did a soul possess the power to reclaim and retrieve whatever part of its energy had been bargained away? Gerod said yes, that in accord with the Agreement, the soul may choose at any time to retrieve any part of its own energy. But there's a hitch: the higher self or spirit guides cannot go into the darkness to retrieve those parts of the soul; they must be handed over by the souls that hold them.

What needs to happen, Gerod said, is a renegotiation of the original deal that gave up the soul energy. He talked as though darkness and dark souls really had no choice about it. It was more like he was saying the exchange had to be done in a formal way. Once it was, he said, the dark souls involved *must* relinquish the soul energy. Not to do so, at that point, would be a violation of the Agreement.

Session #321—November 19, 1993

Renegotiation can be carried out by the higher self or it can be carried out by, for example, the ego-state that created the original contract. If it withdraws its support for it, that is the clear signal to darkness that it was and is an invalid contract and was invalid in the sense that it wasn't the whole self.

I put this procedure to the test with several clients where we found ego-states or pieces of soul energy missing. In each case, I followed the same basic steps suggested by Gerod.

- Find the one(s) who made the original deal.
- Help them to experience the Light and make their choice.
- Begin a renegotiation.
- Receive the soul energy as it is returned.

Over the next several years, I saw this retrieval process work over and over again. Once an ego-state ended any contract or deal with these outside spirits, I asked the higher self and guides to use the soul's Light vibration to retrieve any ego-states or soul energy that was missing. It was quite clear that these dark spirits returned a soul's energy not because they wanted to, but because they *had* to. I didn't know how this renegotiation took place. I only knew that in each case, once it was done, the soul's energy was retrieved. Some gave it up more easily than others, but in every case I remember, the soul energy was returned. Even those spirits who refused and tried to fight it or claim ownership of a soul were, in the end, forced to surrender it. It was as though the dispute was taken to a higher court and then a ruling made.

Redemption

The third situation where Gerod's information about the Agreement was put to the test involved the dark souls themselves. Before I learned about the Agreement, my approach to intruding or attached spirits was to have them look inside and reconnect with their own light. Then I asked them to allow a teacher from the Light to come forward and give them information about their own place in the spirit realm. This approach worked extremely well with spirits who were willing to take these two steps. The promise of redemption, along with the guarantee that they could say no at any time, were strong inducements for many of these spirits to allow an initial contact with the Light. Once they did, almost all chose to return to the Light.

But then there were the spirits who refused to take either step. They would not look inside for their own Light, as Gerod suggested. They would not allow a spirit teacher from the Light to approach them or even send a communication. There was an absolute boundary here, and these spirits in darkness couldn't, or wouldn't, cross it. Despite all reassurances and inducements, they still would not allow even a sliver of Light. Most gave the impression that something terrible would happen to them if they did. Some were afraid of the Light—afraid it would hurt them or destroy them. Some were angry at the Light and blamed it for what had happened to them. Many were enslaved by other souls through deceit and their own ignorance, and still others were evil and would rip out your throat if they could. What they all shared in common, though, was this sharp boundary between themselves and the Light. These were the ones I called *dark souls*. Not surprisingly, these were also the spirits who adamantly refused to leave a client, or sever their connection to the soul. They were also the ones usually involved in taking soul energy.

Before I knew about the Agreement, my encounters with these dark souls usually ended in a shoving match trying to push them out. Sometimes it worked, sometimes it didn't, or it took several sessions. I didn't consider this optimal. Optimal is when a spirit agrees to leave on its own and withdraws all its hooks.

When I learned about the Agreement, it changed my understanding about the deals that the dark souls made with ego-states. Helping ego-states end these deals was far more effective both in severing ties to intruding spirits and moving through their own healing and integration. At some point, I realized that the same thing had happened with these dark souls. They were in darkness because at some level, knowingly or not, parts of the soul had made their own deals or agreements. The reason for their absolute refusal of the Light was because they, too, had made an agreement(s) and now believed there was no way out. They too didn't know about their absolute freedom to end those deals. Many had been in darkness for so long that they had forgotten the Light.

This insight changed my approach to these dark souls. When I encountered this absolute refusal, I began to ask the spirit involved whether it could not receive any Light because there was an agreement? A significant number of them said yes. It was some confirmation in itself that agreements were important. It was another case of finally asking the right question. For those who said yes, I told them the agreement was invalid, and as souls, they were free to end any agreement any time they chose. This was new information to them, and most of them said yes to having more information sent to them. Once they took this step, they followed the same course as other spirits with whom I had worked. They chose to move to the Light immediately or soon after receiving the information.

I watched this switch happen over and over again. A spirit refuses all Light, receives information about the Agreement, and then chooses to move into the Light. Knowledge of the Agreement appeared to be the critical factor. Once they knew they had a choice, they made a choice. This happened so consistently that it was further confirmation to me of the Agreement. It worked. It still does. Given a clear choice, a soul will choose the Light, its own source. I saw this happen with spirits who were deeply entangled in darkness, and with evil souls as well. Once a soul made the decision for the Light, it was done. I knew some power must be enforcing this because souls in darkness fought the return of soul energy. They didn't give it up willingly. They also stepped into block other souls in darkness who began to break ranks and accept information. In the end, though, they could not override a soul's free choice.

18

The Soul

The steps a man takes from the day of his birth until that of his death trace in time an inconceivable figure. The Divine Mind intuitively grasps that form immediately, as men do a triangle. —Jorge Luis Borges, from *The Mirror of Enigmas*

There is no general rule of method applicable to all who aspire to realize God. Every man must work out his own salvation, and must choose his own method, although his choice is mostly determined by the total effect of the mind impressions (sanskaras) acquired in previous lives. He should be guided by the creed of his conscience, and follow the method that best suits his spiritual tendency, his physical aptitude and his external circumstances. Truth is One, but the approach to it is essentially individual. The Sufis say, "There are as many ways to God as there are souls of men." —Meher Baba, from *God Speaks*

Gerod's View

According to Gerod, every person is a soul, created of Light, who chose to incarnate and most of whom have had other incarnations. Somewhere in our dialogues he said that every soul is still anchored in the Light when incarnate. It's as though the soul always has a piece of itself anchored in the Divine to guide it in life and to call it home at death. As humans, most of us cannot directly perceive or know this level of our soul's consciousness. As a condition of incarnation, Gerod said the soul agrees to enter a limited consciousness in which direct knowledge of itself as the Light is veiled from its human consciousness. As some cultures have put it, on entering the body, the soul forgets.

This boundary of consciousness, according to Gerod, this *forgetting,* is deliberate. It is not a punishment, or an exile from Eden, or a severing from the Light. Instead, this boundary is one of the necessary conditions for the soul to experience freedom of choice. By assuming a limited consciousness, the soul enters the world of duality, Light and dark, and begins a unique lifetime of experience and choice. It is in the person's choosing, Gerod said, that the soul learns and grows in its consciousness of the Light. Ultimately, he said every soul's aim is to awaken consciously to its Oneness with God.

Without this boundary of consciousness, there would be no challenge for the soul, no point of resistance, no mirror. There would be no choosing. A person living in full knowledge of the soul's Light would never experience a problem, or need to choose. Like a babe in its mother's arms, the soul's consciousness would remain in its oneness with God. This knowledge, Gerod said, would defeat the soul's purpose for taking on the challenge of incarnation in the first place. It would be like always knowing the answers to the test ahead of time. There would be no test. Yet, it is in the testing, Gerod said, that the soul grows in consciousness and awareness of itself as the Light; it's in the testing "that it comes to know what it is."

For most souls, Gerod implied that this journey of awakening takes place over many incarnations. As a soul, every person carries within them not only knowledge of the Light but also the soul's experience and memory accumulated over many lifetimes. As with the Light, however, direct knowledge and consciousness of these lives is veiled from the conscious self or it too would defeat the soul's purpose for incarnating.

Gerod does not see a person's present life, or the soul's past lives, as random or accidental. He said the soul chooses each lifetime for specific purposes and aims. He said that each soul carries within it a plan of lifetimes designed, like a sequence of code, to orchestrate the soul's awakening. These lifetimes build on one another and the blueprint for each life keeps the soul—if not always on the straight and narrow—at least on its true trajectory. It's as though in each lifetime the soul sends its champion into the world of experience and choice to achieve a significant advance in its process of awakening. Though we may often feel like Don Quixote fighting windmills, we are doing the work of our soul.

Our soul grows and expands through our experience. Through a life of trial and tribulation, joy and sorrow, success and failure, a person's experience opens the eyes of the soul to a greater consciousness. In one of our dialogues, Gerod called the soul "a sleeping giant." I came to think of the soul as a sleeping, thousand-eyed giant in the process of awakening. Each lifetime, opening another eye, and at some point, all eyes will be open.

According to Gerod, each soul incarnates with a blueprint for that particular lifetime. Each soul, usually with the help of high level guides, chooses its parents, along with knowledge of the genetic body it will ensoul. In collaboration with the souls of the parents, a soul chooses the time, place, and circumstances of its birth. The blueprint also includes the soul's choices of significant relationships, events, and challenges that the person will experience during his or her lifetime.

Gerod said that once these choices are made and the fetus conceived, the soul may enter the body at any point in time between conception and moments after birth. (He said a human body can survive only moments without a soul present.) The incarnating soul may stay close to the mother during the pregnancy until it enters the body, or a soul may remain focused in the spirit realm until the moment of birth. There seems to be no strict rules.

It can also happen that a pregnancy is terminated through illness, accident, or abortion. Gerod gave the impression that most souls incarnating into these situations are aware of these probabilities in advance. A soul may agree to participate in such an unfolding knowing that the brief experience of a physical body could be a significant step in its own learning and evolution. It may, for example, offer a lesson that the soul needs to address about oneness and separation. The soul's choice is also to participate in the lessons unfolding for the other souls involved—the parents, extended family, and friends of the family, all of whom will be impacted by the loss of the child.

While a soul makes choices and creates a blueprint for its next incarnation, that doesn't mean the lifetime will unfold exactly as planned. Once incarnate, the soul retains its freedom to choose. He describes the conscious person as "the soul's point of consciousness" during that lifetime, and so is exercising that free choice. We may be unconscious about our choosing, or claim ignorance and deny it, or put it on someone else, but that doesn't change it. We choose.

The life we live also depends on agreements we made with other souls before incarnating. Because every soul is free, those agreements can change and new choices have to be made. Because of free will, there can be no absolute prediction of what a person will choose and what effect those choices will then have on others, and on the soul itself. Once incarnated, the soul can have a tremendous influence on the conscious self, but it does not control the self. While the soul may set the stage, it is the person who chooses what happens once the curtain goes up.

In some ways, it is no different than presenting a child with a problem, so that in the experience of solving the problem, the child learns and grows. The soul sets itself a number of problems and challenges that it knows it will have to choose its way through when incarnated. The soul is using incarnations, so to speak, as a way to grow its consciousness.

Earlier, I likened the process to a game in which the soul enters a lifetime with a plan, knowing certain things and having certain strategies and goals. Once the game begins, however, the conscious personality makes the choices and plays it out. The game may very well go according to plan in its most significant particulars, but there can also be significant deviations, tangents, and detours.

According to Gerod, this is not a problem. A soul's blueprints and plans of future lifetimes are not set in stone. It is more like a living tapestry. When there is a significant deviation from the blueprint due to a person's choices, the choices of others, or unexpected events, the soul will alter its blueprints for future lifetimes to accommodate it. The soul makes new choices and creates new paths that will be woven into those lifetimes in order for the soul to still achieve its aim of awakening. Gerod said more than once that there are no wrong choices. The soul is learning through every experience and is always, so to speak, a work in progress.

From Gerod's point of view, each person's life is part of his or her soul's evolving consciousness. He sees each of us as living our own soul story right now and that it matters how we live it, what we choose, and what we desire to manifest. He said every choice is a personal choice, but it is also a soul choice. Many of the greatest challenges and most difficult ordeals a person faces in his or her life, or may be facing now, very likely involve experiences and lessons the soul has chosen for itself in this lifetime. My impression from Gerod was that most of a person's significant relationships in life are based on agreements made between souls before incarnating.

The implications of Gerod's view are dizzying and, from an ego-centered perspective, can be overwhelming. The ego can't imagine the levels of consciousness and knowledge that must exist for this scenario to be true—that souls choose lifetimes, address karma, create challenges, and make agreements with other souls to participate in each other's lives. The only name we have for that consciousness is the name we have for God. It takes Borge's analogy, quoted at the start of this chapter, to another level. Instead of a man's footsteps in just one lifetime, it is the soul's footsteps over many lifetimes that are tracing an inconceivable figure. For the ego, to grasp this figure would be like trying to grasp the mind of God.

Shifting Paradigms

This book hasn't tried to give an exhaustive theoretical overview of the psychic and spirit realities. It does make a case, though, for the existence of these nonphysical dimensions of the self and reality. There are many phenomena I encountered in my work with clients that could not be included in one book. I have not talked, for example, about the power of prayer and conscious intention; the soul's travels in the dream realms; or the psychic communication and interaction that goes on unconsciously between people all the time. These are all important phenomena to recognize, both in general and in terms of healing. What needs to happen, though, for us to be able to talk about these realities is to first acknowledge them.

In the Introduction, I talked about our Western paradigm and its limitations in addressing psychic and spirit realities. It is a paradigm dominated by empirical science and its root assumption that matter is the ground of all reality. We do not officially acknowledge or recognize the existence of spirits, psychic realities, or supernatural forces. We treat these realities in our public discourse as though they don't exist and don't matter. People's experiences of these dimensions—a vision, a dream, an encounter, a sense of the sacred—are treated officially as though they aren't real or significant. Hallucinations, chemical imbalance, or overactive imagination are a few of the explanations thrown out to explain away these phenomena as *only* mental phantoms.

Science has no empirical basis or methods by which to recognize, study, or even think about these invisible realities. Empirical science, by its own rules of evidence, has drawn a boundary at the threshold to these nonphysical realms and ruled them off-limits. In the empirical paradigm, something is real only if it can be reduced ultimately to physical components that can be observed, measured, and tested experimentally. Conversely, if something has no mass, no physical measure, then it is not real (or must be treated as unreal). From a strictly empirical point of view, taken to its logical extreme, the psychic and spirit realities do not exist.

Just by raising the question, empirical science would be calling into question the validity of its own assumptions, i.e., that matter is the ground and final measure of reality. The idea of nonphysical realities is a contradiction in terms for empirical science and would ultimately bring it to the edge of its own horizons. Science must resolve this apparent contradiction before it can address the question of what—if anything—lies beyond this horizon. To answer the question, I believe science will have to sacrifice (at least theoretically) the ground on which it stands, and establish a new ground, one centered beyond the physical. We are not there yet. This is the paradox.

Because of these limitations, I asked the reader at the start of this book to temporarily step outside our Western paradigm and its assumptions about what is real. I knew that the phenomena and realities I would be writing about in *Soul-Centered Healing* would not fit this paradigm. To the contrary, they would challenge and contradict what that empirical paradigm says is real and true. I did not want us to get caught at the outset in arguments about what was real and what was not. If judged from a strictly empirical point of view, this book would make no sense at all. I knew that I could never *prove* the psychic and spirit realities based on empirical standards alone. From my point of view, it would be like comparing apples and oranges. So, for those who had difficulty believing these dimensions could be real, I asked, for the purposes of this book, that you treat the psychic and spiritual dimensions "as if" they were real.

We come back to this point now. What I have written in this book about the psychic and spirit realities does not constitute empirical proof of their existence. I would argue, though, that it provides strong clinical evidence of these realities. I would also argue that there is a wealth of such clinical and anecdotal evidence coming from many different sources.

What we lack is not evidence, but a way of understanding what the evidence implies, what it means. We need a new paradigm, a new vision of ourselves that recognizes the psychic and spiritual dimensions of reality as well as physical reality. Without this recognition, we will keep these dimensions of reality closed-off and continue to speak about them as only metaphor and imagination. As long as this is the case, we won't truly grasp who we are as souls and spiritual beings. It is living in ignorance of our true nature. The words of Teilhard de Chardin capture it exactly: "We are not human beings having a spiritual experience. We are spiritual beings having a human experience."

I think that when we shift to the new paradigm this view will be accepted as fact, that we are all spiritual beings, souls incarnate. There are no Muslim souls, Jewish souls, or Christian souls. There are no American souls or French souls or Democratic or Republican souls. There are only souls. The new paradigm, I believe, will recognize that our human nature *is* a spiritual nature. This recognition at a cultural level will mark a turning point, I think, in our shift to a new point of view. At that point, we will also accept at some level that we are all brothers and sisters in the Light, and that what we do to one another or for one another, we do to and for ourselves. This step will include a collective recognition that we are part of an all encompassing, transcendent reality.

I believe we are undergoing this shift as a culture right now. We are changing the way we think about reality and about who we are as individuals, and as a race. I don't know whether we are on the verge of this shift or still approaching its threshold. A shift of this magnitude takes place over decades or generations. It could be three years from now; it could be twenty. The shift itself, though, will include a public recognition of the psychic and spiritual dimensions of reality. I also believe it will recognize all humans as souls incarnate. We are all souls living among souls.

I know I am talking of grand concepts in broad and sweeping terms. There is, however, a great deal of support for this idea from many quarters, including science itself. A full discussion of this paradigm shift is far beyond the scope of this book. My purpose here is to acknowledge these cultural and collective forces rather than focus on them specifically. There are many excellent books whose authors write in depth about the shift in paradigm they see happening today in our Western culture and around the world. Examples include *Global Mind Change* by Willis Harmon, *The Great Turning* by David C. Korten, *The Passion of the Western Mind* by Richard Tarnas, *The Hidden Connections* by Fritjof Capra, and *Science and the Akashic Field: An Integral Theory of Everything* by Ervin Laszlo.

The central point here is that we cannot talk about, study, or test our knowledge of these realities from within the empirical paradigm alone. We don't have the scientific concepts or language for it. At the same time, from a clinical point of view, this book argues not only that the psychic and spiritual phenomena are real, but that they also can be a primary source of a person's illness, emotional pain, or mental confusion. The cause of one's difficulties may be due to spirit intrusion, or past life conflicts, or sub-personalities who are still living in trauma. When any of these are the case, a person needs a way to identify what is happening at these levels and what he or she can do to resolve it.

In writing this book, I remained focused on the clinical story—the experience of my clients and the consistent phenomena that I encountered in our sessions together. These have included sub-personalities, higher selves, spirit involvement, past-life trauma, and spiritual forces. These are phenomena that I repeatedly observed and verified in my clinical practice over many years.

This focus on the clinical rather than the theoretical reflects the traditional tension between practice and theory, working in the trenches or the ivory tower, but it goes deeper than this. The implications of Soul-Centered Healing lead into the larger issue of paradigms and what vision of reality we will hold about the universe in which we live. We are not going to be able to heal the problems that are rooted in these deeper levels of consciousness and reality until we acknowledge that they exist.

There are other cultures in the world in which many of the phenomena I am writing about (and many more phenomena besides) are familiar and accepted. While they may have varying beliefs and teachings about these realms, these cultures have recognized the existence of psychic and spiritual realities for centuries. Forces of Light and dark, contact with spirits, or the idea of reincarnation, for example, are not strange to them, but are seen as just part of "the way it is."

In our culture, we do not have a common language or framework yet in which to think and talk about these realities. I believe, though, that in our sciences, we will continue to push at the boundaries of matter until we are forced to step beyond them. Such is humanity's drive to know the truth.

It is not necessary that we continually focus our conscious attention on these levels in order to live our day-to-day life well. It is important, though, to be aware that these dimensions are immediate and real and that they do affect us in different ways and to different degrees. Every person may become more directly aware of or involved in these dimensions at different times during the day, in different activities, or during particular periods in their life. Whether it is in prayer or meditation, in thought or dreams, or in crisis or fear, everyone focuses attention in these other levels from time to time. Just as with our bodies, however, we do not have to be focused on the psychic and spiritual realities in order to be in harmony with them. In fact, the opposite is more likely to be true: the more in harmony we are with those levels of our self—body, mind, and spirit—the freer we are to live in the present.

Soul-Centered Healing

Soul-Centered Healing recognizes every person as a soul, a being of Light, who has incarnated in this life with a unique soul history and soul aims. It's an approach that recognizes that there are dimensions of consciousness and reality beyond the physical and beyond the grasp of ego-consciousness. Soul-Centered Healing accepts that, as souls, we exist in these dimensions just as really as we do the physical. They are called *subtle* dimensions, and they certainly are more subtle than the physical, but they are real nonetheless.

Soul-Centered Healing recognizes that there are phenomena, conditions, entities, and forces operating at these subtle levels that can cause a person pain, conflict, and confusion. Soul-Centered Healing is a method for helping a person gain access to and work therapeutically at these levels when they are a source of the pain and distress. The question with each client is whether there are things happening at these levels that are causing or contributing to his or her pain and distress—physical, emotional, or mental.

This can include, for example, the strong or frequent triggering of ego-states, whether from past lives or present, whose pain and perceptions can still affect a person very deeply. The problem can be the intrusion, often a deep intrusion, by spirit entities into a person's mind and soul through psychic vulnerabilities. The problem could also be a psychic attack by another person, or an entanglement in darkness that the soul has been trying to resolve through many lifetimes.

There is no "typical" case in this healing process. Each person's history, inner world, and soul story are unique, and each person's healing journey follows its own distinct course. To quote the Sufis again, "There are as many ways to God as there are souls of men." It is not the purpose of the healing process to know a person's unfolding soul story ahead of time, or to predict the course of treatment. The purpose is to help a person enter into a conscious dialogue with normally unconscious levels of the self in order to resolve the conflicts and blocks that are a source of one's pain, fear, or anger.

While each person's healing journey is unique, they share these common aims: to bring fragmented parts of the self/soul into accord with the conscious self and the soul's Light; to secure the self and soul from psychic intrusion and violation; and to know one's self and others as spiritual beings. This last is not so much a direct aim as it is a natural result of the healing process itself. When a person experiences the higher self, past life memories, or contact with a spirit entity, these experiences carry with them their own confirmation of the psychic and spirit dimensions. They also carry with them a conviction of one's own spiritual nature.

When a person resolves the competing voices, emotional triggers, and misperceptions, they also become more centered in themselves as spiritual beings. This shift from an ego-centered to a soul-centered perspective is different for everyone. For some, it's a radical change in thinking, while for others it may feel like their center of gravity has shifted. Still others come into treatment having already experienced this shift in consciousness. In general, the aim of healing is to help a person become more clear, centered, and confident about who they are in the present and who they choose to be.

It's not that all the voices and emotions have to be resolved before that clarity and confidence can begin. Clarity can come just from knowing whose voice is whose, and where it is coming from—from within the self/soul or from outside; from this present life or from the past; from Light and Love or from darkness.

Clarity comes also in knowing that what is true of us is true of others. Our family, our friends, neighbors, and strangers are all incarnated souls who also live with competing voices, emotional storms, misperceptions, and inner guidance. Knowing this can help keep us open to others, even while recognizing the protections, defenses and limitations that keep all of us tangled and bound by fear and confusion. We do not have to understand all of a person's inner realities and struggles to know that their feelings and behaviors, like our own, are often driven by the ego's fears and protective instincts. This clarity makes it easier in our everyday life to respond to others *soul to soul* and be conscious of our choosing between darkness and Light.

Soul-Centered Healing is based on the healing power of the Light. Its techniques and methods are more often for identifying and removing blocks, so the Light can expand and operate more freely within the self. The process is like going through an old house, room-by-room, throwing open all the shutters to the morning sun. I cannot explain the Light's healing properties but I observe its effects. The Light acts as a self-organizing principle and transcendent force that brings all it touches into a consciousness of Oneness and right relations. The central aim of the healing process is to help a person connect with and open more fully to the Light, so the Light then can do what it does—expand!

By bringing Light to parts of the self that hold pain and bringing Light into areas of the soul that have become clouded or dark, Soul-Centered Healing helps a person to know his or her own Light. This is not merely a cognitive recognition. It's an experience. It's a knowing, and the healing itself occurs through the person's experience of the Light. This is the part that cannot be passed on through a book.

In its deepest sense, Soul-Centered Healing is about helping a person open and expand their connection to his or her soul. It's about deepening the channels of Light that flow between self and soul. And in opening to one's own Light, a person opens to the Divine and to the Light of all souls. It is at this level, as Gerod would say, that we know the Oneness of All That Is.

Epilogue

It has been nearly ten years since my collaboration with Gerod ended. I still talk with him occasionally about specific clients, but we no longer carry on the active dialogue and exploration of the psychic and spirit dimensions.

My fourteen-year collaboration with Gerod ended in 2001, and it did so for many reasons. To continue would have required taking our dialogues to a new level, drawing me away from my work as a healer. For Katharine, it would have meant further demands on her energy. Primarily, however, it ended because I had to digest and integrate everything that I had learned and put into practice from this collaboration. This book is a result of that reflection and consolidation.

During this period, I've continued my work with clients, and I find the principles and methods I learned from Gerod hold up well in clinical practice. The protocols and techniques for working with ego-states, past lives, and intruding spirits work consistently, and every client's soul story and journey of healing remains absolutely unique.

I've emphasized throughout this book that it is a clinical work. The focus has been on healing and the individual. There is so much more, though, that has been implied and stated here that cannot be pursued without shifting our focus from healing to metaphysics. Questions about the existence of spirits and spirit realms, for example. Or about the dream dimensions, or the chakras, or the implications of reincarnation for our Western culture. While this book did not address all these phenomena directly, I do believe that we need to pursue these larger questions.

Changing beliefs, giving up long held traditions, and changing life-styles are not easy to do. I've come to realize the radical transformation in consciousness that would occur in our society by acknowledging these nonphysical realities and beings. It involves an entirely different way of thinking. Acknowledging the psychic and spirit realities would, in effect, confirm that we ourselves are part of a much larger picture than the egocentric paradigm we have today. Whether consciously or unconsciously, it would shift people's psychological center of gravity from the body as the basis of identity to the soul/essence that survives death. I hope this book can act as a bridge to that new paradigm and the awakening to soul.

Glossary

Alter-Personality—See *Ego-state.*

Astral Plane—A generic term for those nonphysical dimensions or planes of existence in which discarnate souls and entities exist outside the spirit realm of light. Since Western culture does not recognize these realities, it has no clear definition or delineation of these dimensions. This is something we can learn from the eastern traditions.

Dark Spot (Dark Side)—An interior region of the mind where there is no Light. Everyone periodically passes through his or her dark spot. Depending on the person, that sojourn through the dark can be relatively easy, to extremely painful. The conscious self can even become stuck in this dark spot.

Dark Soul—These are souls that have become separated, or in some way have cut themselves off from the Light—their own Light as a soul, as well as the Creator's. They exist in darkness, but as beings of Light, each still needs Light to exist and will siphon off the Light of incarnate souls. There are many different ways they have developed to do this.

Device—Energy/objects created by souls that can be attached or inserted into the psychic or spiritual levels of a person. Again, from a healing perspective, the emphasis here is on devices created by souls in darkness. These are the devices that can cause distress and pain for a person. Devices can come in any form—a hair barrette, a box with something inside it, a toy, or audio speakers. The form doesn't matter, only that the device be accepted. A device is like an energy marker giving an outside soul access or certain controls within a person.

Dissociation—A psychological defense in which the mind creates a split in order to separate a traumatic experience from a person's conscious awareness.

Dissociative Disorders—Dissociative disorders are so-called because they are marked by a dissociation from or interruption of a person's fundamental aspects of waking consciousness (such as one's personal identity, one's personal history, etc.). Dissociative disorders come in many forms, the most famous of which is dissociative identity disorder (formerly known as multiple personality disorder). All of the dissociative disorders are thought to stem from trauma experienced by the individual with this disorder. The dissociative aspect is thought to be a coping mechanism—the person literally dissociates himself from a situation or experience too traumatic to integrate with his conscious self. Symptoms of these disorders, or even one or more of the disorders themselves, are also seen in a number of other mental illnesses, including post-traumatic stress disorder, panic disorder, and obsessive compulsive disorder. (From PSYweb.com)

Earthbound Spirit—When the body dies, the soul is naturally drawn to the Light. A person/soul can become earthbound, though, if something interferes with that natural movement. Accidental death, for example, that comes so quickly the person's consciousness remains focused on the physical. Intense feelings of guilt or fear also can lead a person, at the time of death, to turn away from the Light. Earthbound spirits are usually benign and not aware that they can go to the Light.

Ego-state—A part of the self, a sub-personality, created for the purpose of self-protection during an experience in which a person can no longer consciously tolerate what is happening. An ego-state results from this dissociation, and it's the ego-state that lives the trauma. Once it is safe for the self to be conscious aware again, the ego-state moves to the unconscious. It continues to exist *as a conscious entity in its own reality*. Ego-states are best understood as psychic beings, though with limited consciousness.

Energy Point—That point in the body, usually in the heart center, where the soul first joins the body and becomes incarnate. It is the soul that energizes the body, and the energy point is its primary reference. When joined, Gerod said the soul and energy point form a diamond. Once joined, however, they can be separated for the purpose of protection. When this happens, it appears to cause some level of disruption or diminution in the self/soul connection.

Entity—a being created by thought energy but which does not possess a soul. Entities have a limited consciousness and intelligence, and do not act on their own initiative. In healing, the focus is most often on entities created by souls in darkness and used against incarnate souls in different ways. Most entities created in darkness cannot receive Light, and will not leave a person on their own. Usually, they must be forced to leave.

Etheric—In esoteric literature, it refers to levels of subtle energy, those closest to the physical body. The chakras, the aura, the meridians, for example, exist and operate at etheric levels. The etheric is also described as an intermediate level between the physical and psychic realms. In this book, ego-states are viewed as existing at an etheric/psychic level. They interface with the physical and etheric levels of the body, and, as conscious beings, they also operate at a psychic level.

Fragment Soul—A technique used by souls in darkness to create an entity out of pieces of a soul's energy. The resulting entity would believe itself then to be a creation of darkness, and not be aware of the soul's light as its true source. As still part of the soul, it is free to choose the Light and return to its own soul once it discovers its true nature.

Higher Self—A part of the self created by the soul and projected into a person's present life. The higher self is conscious of itself as part of the soul, and is aware also of the person's present reality. It knows about the person's present life and soul history. It knows what is of the Light and what is not. And it knows what is part of the soul and what or who isn't. It is a primary ally in the process of Soul-Centered Healing.

Ideomotor Signaling—A hypnotic technique using non-verbal signals—usually finger or head movements—to communicate with a person's unconscious mind. Milton Erickson, M.D. developed the technique and it was further defined by David Cheek, M.D. and Leslie LeCron.

Karma—The Law of Cause and Effect. We reap what we sow. Karma is the coming back to us the results of our own actions, whether in this present life or from the soul's other lifetimes.

Karmic Layer—Those unresolved parts of the soul that are closed up and rendered dormant when the soul becomes discarnate and returns to the Light. When the soul reincarnates, this pocket will open back up and at least part of it may become active in the person's present life.

Paradigm—A culture's worldview in which members share basic assumptions, truths, and beliefs about what is real. Every culture lives within a paradigm, and as a culture grows and becomes more complex, a new paradigm will replace and go beyond the old.

Past Life Ego-State—The same kind of psychic being as a present life ego-state. Only this is one created in a past or different lifetime and then carried unresolved within the soul. It is worked with in the same way as a present life ego-state, only its integration takes place at a soul level and not in the present consciousness.

Spirit Helpers—(also called *spirit guides, teachers,* and *healers*): A general term for souls existing in the Light whose focus is on the human realm and assisting souls that are incarnate. In Soul-Centered Healing, spirit helpers are called on to help in many different ways from dealing with attached spirits to communicating directly to the higher self.

Sub-personality—See *Ego-state.*

Notes

Chapter 1: Worlds Within Worlds

1. Singer and Pope, eds., *The Power of Human Imagination*, 127.
2. Today it is called The International Society for the Study of Trauma and Dissociation.

Chapter 2: Ego-State Therapy

1. John G. Watkins, *Hypnotherapeutic Techniques*, vol. 1, 50.
2. Ibid.
3. John G. Watkins and Helen H. Watkins, *The Management of Malevolent Ego States in Multiple Personality Disorder*, 67.
4. John G. Watkins, *Hypnotherapeutic Techniques*, vol. 1, 51.
5. Carl G. Jung, *Two Essays on Analytical Psychology*, 80.
6. John Rowan, *Subpersonalities: The People Inside Us*, 8.
7. Ernest Rossi and David Cheek, *Mind-Body Therapy*, xxf.
8. Milton H. Erickson, Ernest Rossi, and Sheila Rossi, *Hypnotic Realities*, 80.
9. Ernest Rossi and David Cheek, *Mind–Body Therapy*, 16–18.
10. Charles Cooke and A. E. Van Vogt, *The Hypnotism Handbook*, 122.
11. Ernest Rossi and David Cheek, *Mind–Body Therapy*, 12.
12. Ibid.
13. Ibid., 14.

Chapter 3: At an Impasse

1. John G. Watkins and Helen H. Watkins, *Ego-States: Theory and Therapy*, 49.

Chapter 4: At the Borderline of Spirit

1. Malachi Martin, *Hostage to the Devil*, 24.
2. Robert Monroe, *Far Journeys*, 3.

Chapter 6: Earthbound Spirits

1. Robert Monroe, *Far Journeys*, 153.
2. Raymond Moody, *Reflections on Life After Life*, 18–21.
3. Scott Rogo, *Infinite Boundary*, 298.
4. Melvin Morse, *Closer to the Light*, 120.
5. Wilson, *Afterlife*, 215–16.
6. Ibid., 225.

Chapter 7: The Quickening

1. Edit Fiore, *The Unquiet Dead*, 14.
2. Ibid., 134–39.
3. Ibid., 132.

Chapter 8: Through the Looking Glass

1. This is a verbatim copy of my notes from the session with Martha. In this case and in the subsequent cases that I present, I will use my notes to give the reader a sense of the client's sharing.

Chapter 10: The Higher Self

1. Ralph B. Allison, *A New Treatment Approach for Multiple Personalities*, 15–32.
2. Ralph B. Allison, *Spiritual Helpers I Have Met*, 4–5.

Chapter 11: Soul-Centered Healing

1. It may turn out that the likelihood of different forms of ego-states may depend on the culture a person is part of. For Native Americans, for example, animal forms may be more commonly seen than in our Western culture.
2. Many people think of memory as visual. I have to tell my clients when we start inner work that memory can be encoded in different ways—visual, auditory, kinesthetic, emotional, or any combination of these. I have clients whose memory is shared like a video-replay in Technicolor. The memory is so clear that the client can report the tiniest details as the scene unfolds. The remembering, though, can be limited to clients who receive only a snapshot image, or a wave of emotion, or experiences a physical pain with no images.

Chapter 14: Past Lives—The Weave of Soul Stories

1. There are countless books and articles in which to find these examples and studies. The work of Ian Stevenson, and the book, *Lifecycles*, by Christopher Bache, are two good places to start.

Bibliography

Allison, Ralph B. "A New Treatment Approach for Multiple Personalities." *American Journal of Clinical Hypnosis* 17 (1974): 15–32.

———. "Spiritual Helpers I Have Met." *Association for the Anthropological Study of Consciousness Newsletter* 6 (1985): 4–5.

Assagioli, Roberto. *Psychosynthesis.* New York: Penguin Books, 1965.

Bache, Christopher. *Lifecycles: Reincarnation and the Web of Life.* New York: Paragon House, 1994.

Barnett, E. A. *Analytical Hypnotherapy.* Kingston, Ontario: Junica, 1981.

Brennan, Barbara. *Hands of Light.* New York: Bantam Books, 1987

Berne, Eric. *Transactional Analysis in Psychotherapy: A Systematic Individual and Social Psychiatry.* New York: Grove Press, 1961.

Braude, Stephen. *First Person Plural: Multiple Personality and the Philosophy of Mind.* Lanham, Maryland: Rowman & Littlefield, 1995.

Capra, Fritjof. *The Hidden Connections.* New York: Doubleday, 2002.

Castle, Kit, and Stefan Bechtel. *Katherine, It's Time.* New York: Harper & Row, 1989.

Cheek, David. *Hypnosis: The Application of Ideomotor Techniques.* Boston: Allyn & Bacon, 1993.

Cooke, Charles Edward, and A. E. Van Vogt. *The Hypnotism Handbook.* Alahambra, CA: Borden, 1965.

Denning, Melita, and Osborne Phillips. *Astral Projection.* St. Paul: Llewellyn, 1979.

Ellenberger, Henri. *The Discovery of the Unconscious: The History and Evolution of Dynamic Psychiatry.* New York: Basic Books, 1970.

Erickson, Milton H. *The Nature of Hypnosis and Suggestion.* The Collected Papers of Milton H. Erickson on Hypnosis, vol. 1. New York: Irvington, 1980.

Erickson, Milton H., Ernest Rossi, and Sheila Rossi. *Hypnotic Realities: The Induction of Clinical Hypnosis and Forms of Indirect Suggestion*. New York: Irvington, 1976.

Evans-Wentz, W. Y, trans. *The Tibetan Book of the Dead*. New York: Oxford University Press, 1960.

Fiore, Edith. *The Unquiet Dead: A Psychologist Treats Spirit Possession*. New York: Doubleday, 1987.

Fuller, John G. *Ghost of the 29 Megacycles*. New York: New American Library, 1986.

———. *The Interrupted Journey: Two Lost Hours Aboard a Flying Saucer*. New York: The Dial Press, 1966.

———. *Incident at Exeter: The Story of Unidentified Flying Objects over America Today*. New York: G. P. Putnam & Sons, 1966.

Gerber, Richard. *Vibrational Medicine*. Rochester, VT: Bear & Company, 1988.

Grof, Stanislav. *The Holotropic Mind*. San Francisco: Harper, 1993.

Harmon, Willis. *Global Mind Change: The Promise of the 21st Century*. 2nd ed. San Francisco: Berret-Koehler, 1998.

Harner, Michael. *The Way of the Shaman: A Guide to Power and Healing*. New York: Bantam Books, 1980.

Hopkins, Budd. *Intruders: The Incredible Visitations at Copley Woods*. New York: Random House, 1987.

Jacobi, Jolanda. *Complex, Archetype, Symbol in the Psychology of C. G. Jung*. Princeton, NJ: Princeton University Press, 1959.

Jung, Carl G. *Two Essays on Analytical Psychology*. New York: World Publishing Company, 1953.

———. *Analytical Psychology: Its Theory and Practice*. New York: Vintage Books, 1970.

———. *The Structure and Dynamics of the Psyche*. R.F.C. Hall, trans. Princeton, NJ: Princeton University Press, 1960.

Kardec, Allan. *The Spirits' Book*. Revised edition. São Paulo, Brazil, 1857.

Kaye, Maribeth, and Lawrence Klein. "Clinical Indicators of Satanic Cult Victimization." Paper presented at the Fourth International Conference on Multiple Personality/Dissociation, Chicago, 1987.

Keyes, Daniel. *The Minds of Billy Milligan*. New York: Random House, 1987.

Laszlo, Ervin. *Science and the Akashic Field: An Integral Theory of Everything*. Rochester, VT: Inner Traditions, 2004.

Korten, David C. *The Great Turning: From Empire to Earth Community*. San Francisco: Berritt-Koehler, 2006.

Leadbetter, C. W. *The Chakras*. Wheaton, IL: Theosophical Publishing House, 1927.

Lenz, Frederick. *Lifetimes: True Accounts of Reincarnation*. New York: Bobbs-Merrill, 1979.

Martin, Malachi. *Hostage to the Devil*. New York: Harper & Row, 1976.

McClain, Florence Wagner. *A Practical Guide to Past Life Regression*. St. Paul, MN: Llewellyn, 1997.

Monroe, Robert. *Far Journeys*. New York: Doubleday, 1985.

Moody, Raymond. *Life after Life: The Investigation of a Phenomenon—Survival of Bodily Death*. Atlanta: Mockingbird Books, 1975.

———. *Reflections on Life After Life*. New York: Bantam Books, 1977.

Morse, Melvin. *Closer to the Light*. Boston: G. K. Hall, 1991.

Oschman, James. *Energy Medicine: The Scientific Basis*. New York: Churchill, Livingstone, 2000.

Richelieu, Peter. *A Soul's Journey*. Garden City, NY: Doubleday, 1973.

Ring, Kenneth. *Life at Death: A Scientific Investigation of the Near-Death Experience*. New York: Quill, 1982.

Roberts, Jane. *Seth Speaks*. New York: Bantam Books, 1972.

Rogo, Scott. *Infinite Boundary*. New York: Dodd, Mead, & Co., 1987.

———. *Leaving the Body: A Complete Guide to Astral Projection*. New York: Prentice Hall, 1983.

———. *The Search for Yesterday: A Critical Examination of the Evidence for Reincarnation*. Englewood Cliffs, NJ: Prentice-Hall, 1985.

Roll, William G. *The Poltergeist*. New York: Nelson Doubleday, 1972.

Rossi, Ernest, and David Cheek. *Mind–Body Therapy: Methods of Ideodynamic Healing in Hypnosis*. New York: W. W. Norton, 1988.

Rowan, John. *Subpersonalities: The People Inside Us*. London: Routledge, 1990.

———. *Discover Your Subpersonalities: Our Inner World and the People in It*. London: Routledge, 1993.

Singer, Jerome L., and Kenneth S. Pope, eds. *The Power of Human Imagination: New Methods in Psychotherapy*. New York: Plenum Press, 1978.

Tigunait, Pandit Rajmani. *The Eleventh Hour*. Honesdale, PA: Himalayan Institute, 2004.

Watkins, John G. *Hypnotherapeutic Techniques*. New York: Irvington, 1986.

Watkins, John G., and Helen H. Watkins. "The Management of Malevolent Ego States in Multiple Personality Disorder." *Dissociation* 1 (March 1988): 67–72.

———. *Ego States: Theory and Therapy*. New York: W.W. Norton, 1997.

Wilson, Colin. *Afterlife*. Garden City, NY: Doubleday, 1987.

Lightning Source UK Ltd.
Milton Keynes UK
UKOW07f1805020115

243906UK00007B/128/P